CW01360206

STUDIES ON VOLTAIRE AND THE EIGHTEENTH CENTURY

SVEC
67

VOLTAIRE
FOUNDATION
LIBRARY

General editor
GREGORY S. BROWN, University of Nevada, Las Vegas

Editorial board
WILDA ANDERSON, Johns Hopkins University
MATTHEW BELL, King's College London
MARC ANDRÉ BERNIER, Université du Québec à Trois-Rivières
NICHOLAS CRONK, Voltaire Foundation, University of Oxford
DAN EDELSTEIN, Stanford University
REBECCA HAIDT, Ohio State University
COLIN JONES, Queen Mary, University of London
MARK LEDBURY, University of Sydney
FRANCESCA SAVOIA, University of Pittsburgh
J. B. SHANK, University of Minnesota
CÉLINE SPECTOR, Université Bordeaux 3
JOANNA STALNAKER, Columbia University
KAREN STOLLEY, Emory University
W. DEAN SUTCLIFFE, University of Auckland
ALEXIS TADIÉ, Université de Paris-Sorbonne
STÉPHANE VAN DAMME, European University Institute

Senior publishing manager
LYN ROBERTS

Manuscripts should be prepared in accordance with the *SVEC* style sheet, available on request and at the Voltaire Foundation website (www.voltaire.ox.ac.uk). One paper copy should be submitted to the *SVEC* general editor at the Voltaire Foundation, 99 Banbury Road, Oxford OX2 6JX, UK; an electronic version, with a summary of about 750 words, should be sent to gregory.brown@voltaire.ox.ac.uk.

Correspondence

•

Literature

•

Voltaire

SVEC
67

VOLTAIRE FOUNDATION
OXFORD

© 2016 Voltaire Foundation, University of Oxford

ISBN 978-0-7294-0160-9
ISSN 0435-2866

Voltaire Foundation
99 Banbury Road
Oxford OX2 6JX, UK

First printing 1969

A catalogue record for this book
is available from the British Library

The correct reference for this volume is
SVEC 67

This series is available on annual subscription

For further information about this series
and other Voltaire Foundation publications see
www.voltaire.ox.ac.uk, or email svec@voltaire.ox.ac.uk

Printed and bound by Lightning Source UK Ltd

CONTENTS

	page
THEODORE BESTERMAN, Voltaire's dedication of *Oreste*	7
ENRICO STRAUB, A propos d'une lettre inconnue de Voltaire écrite en 1774	21
STEPHEN WERNER, Voltaire and Seneca	29
DONALD SCHIER, Aaron Hill's translation of Voltaire's *Alzire*	45
E. T. HELMICK, Voltaire and *Humphry Clinker*	59
J. VERCRUYSSE, Turgot et Vergennes contre la lettre de Voltaire à Boncerf	65
J. VERCRUYSSE, Madame Denis et Ximenès ou la nièce aristarque	73
ROBERT F. O'REILLY, The Structure and meaning of the *Lettres persanes*	91
M. L. PERKINS, Destiny, sentiment and time in the *Confessions* of Jean Jacques Rousseau	133
R. A. LEIGH, Jean Jacques Rousseau and madame de Warens: some recently recovered documents	165
EMITA B. HILL, Virtue on trial: a defense of Prévost's Théophé	191
ALEXANDER JOVICEVICH, Thirteen additional unpublished letters of La Harpe	211
PIERRE CHEVALLIER, Les Idées religieuses de Davy de La Fautrière	229

Voltaire's dedication of Oreste

edited by Theodore Besterman

Voltaire's literary manuscripts are exceedingly rare, so even a scrap is important, let alone a more or less substantial work. One such manuscript has recently come into my personal possession, and must immediately be made available. It is the twenty-page text, the pages numbered 1 to 20, the folded leaves still attached by the original green silk ribbons, of the dedication of *Oreste* to the duchesse Du Maine. The manuscript has this additional importance: it is the actual text, in Collini's hand, submitted to the duchess, and signed by her 'Lu / quoy que ie ne merite point ces Louanges / j'aprouue L'epistre / Louise Benedicte de Bourbon /'.

When she returned the manuscript to him Voltaire inevitably revised it, as shown below. The fact that these changes were made at this stage is not an ascertained fact, but it is an inference of a high degree of probability. Otherwise it would have to be assumed that Voltaire submitted to the duchesse Du Maine an 'official' text scored over with amendments of all kinds: nothing less likely in a man of Voltaire's punctilio can be imagined.

As an edition of *Oreste* is in hand for the recently launched *Complete works of Voltaire*, I have limited myself to purely textual annotation. Even in that respect, this does not purport to be a truly critical edition, since I have made no close bibliographical analysis of the transmission of Voltaire's discourse. My text sets out the manuscript described above, with all its internal modifications, to which I have added only the variations of the first edition (ED1), that is, the Paris *Oreste* of 1750 in

[vi].xxi.[i].212 pages[1]; and a few trifling and undifferentiated variants found in modern editions but not in ED1. The very numerous differences in spelling, punctuation and the like have been ignored. The general editorial methods are those described in Voltaire 85, pp.xv-xvii.

[1] the Paris edition of 1750 in 68 pages is an uncritical reprint of the first, without any editorial supervision, and in which only some misprints have been introduced; it has therefore been ignored.

VOLTAIRE'S DEDICATION OF ORESTE

Madame

Vous avez vû passer ce siècle admirable à La gloire du quel vous avez tant contribué par vôtre goust et par vos Exemples, ce siècle qui sert de modèle au nôtre en tant de Choses, et peut être de reproche, Comme il en servira à tous les âges. C'est dans ces temps Illustres que les Condez vos ayeux Couverts de Tant de lauriers cultivoient et Encourageoient les arts, où un Bossuet Immortalisoit les héros et instruisoit les Rois, où un Fenelon le second des hommes dans l'éloquence et le premier dans l'art de rendre la vertu aimable enseignoit avec tant de Charmes la Justice et l'humanité, où les Racines, les Depreaux, présidoient aux belles lettres, Lulli à La musique, le Brun à la peinture. Tous ces arts madame furent accueillis sur tout dans votre palais. Je me souviendray toujours que presque au sortir de l'enfance J'eus le Bonheur d'y entendre quelques fois [a]un homme dans qui L'érudition la plus profonde n'avoit point éteint le génie, et qui Cultiva l'Esprit de monseign[r] le Duc de Bourgogne, ainsi que le vôtre et celuy de M[r] le duc du Maine, travaux heureux dans les quels il fut si puissamment[a] secondé par la nature. Il prenoit quelque fois devant V. a. S. un Sophocle, un Euripide, Il traduisoit sur le Champ en françois une de leurs tragédies. L'admiration, l'entousiasme dont il étoit saisi lui Inspiroit des Expressions qui répondoient à la mâle et harmonieuse Energie des vers grecs autant qu'il est possible d'en aprocher dans la prose d'une langue àpeine tirée de la barbarie, Et qui polie par tant de grands autheurs, manque encor pourtant d'abondance[b]. [c]M[r] de Malesieu mettoit dans son récit toutte l'âme des grands hommes de la Grece.[c] Permettez moy madame de rapeller icy ce qu'il pensoit de ce peuple

---

[a] MS first reading modified by Voltaire *cet homme d'une Erudition Universelle qui Cultiva l'Esprit de monseig[r] le Duc de Bourgogne et le vôtre et qui avoit été dans ce travail heureux si singulièrement*

[b] EDI *de précision, de force & d'abondance*

[c] EDI replaced by *On sçait qu'il est impossible de faire passer dans aucune langue moderne la valeur des expressions grecques; elles peignent d'un trait ce qui éxige trop de paroles chez tous les autres peuples. Un seul terme y suffit pour représenter ou une montagne toute couverte d'arbres chargés de feuilles, ou un*

Inventeur, Ingénieux et sensible qui enseigna tout aux Romains ses vainqueurs et qui longtemps après sa ruine et Celle de l'Empire Romain a servi encor à tirer l'Europe moderne de la^d grossière ignorance.

Il Connoissoit Athenes mieux qu'aujourd'huy quelques voyageurs ne connoissent Rome après l'avoir vüe. Ce nombre prodigieux de statues des plus grands maitres, ces colones qui ornoient les marchez publics, ces monuments de génie et de grandeur, ce téâtre superbe et Immense bâti dans une grande place entre la ville et la citadelle où les ouvrages des Sophocles et des Euripides êtoient Ecoutez par les Pericles, et^e les Socrates, et où des^f Jeunes gens n'asistoient pas debout et en tumulte, en un mot tout ce que les atheniens avoient fait pour les arts en tous les genres Etoit présent à son Esprit. Il êtoit bien loin de penser Comme ces hommes ridiculement austères et ces faux politiques qui blâment encor les atheniens d'avoir été trop somptueux dans leurs Jeux publics, et qui ne savent pas que Cette magnificence même enrichissoit Athenes En attirant dans son sein une foule d'Etrangers qui venoient l'admirer et prendre chez elle des leçons de vertu et d'Eloquence.

Vous L'engageâtes^g madame cet homme d'un Esprit presque universel à traduire avec une fidélité pleine d'Elégance et de force L'Iphigenie en Tauride d'Euripide, on la représenta dans une fête qu'il eût l'honneur de donner à vôtre a. S., fête digne de Celle qui la recevoit et de celuy qui en faisoit les honneurs, vous y

---

Dieu qui lance au loin ses traits, ou les sommets des rochers frapés souvent de la foudre. Non-seulement cette langue avoit l'avantage de remplir d'un mot l'imagination; mais chaque terme, comme on sçait, avoit une mélodie marquée, & charmoit l'oreille, tandis qu'il étaloit à l'esprit de grandes peintures. Voilà pourquoi toute traduction d'un poëte grec est toujours faible, sèche & indigente. C'est du caillou & de la brique avec quoi on veut imiter des palais de porphire. Cependant M. de Malesieu, par des efforts que produisoit un entousiasme subit, & par un récit véhément, sembloit suppléer à la pauvreté de la langue, & mettre dans sa déclamation toute l'âme des grands hommes d'Athènes.

^{d} modern editions *sa*
^{e} EDI followed by *par*
^{f} EDI *de*
^{g} modern editions *engageâtes*

VOLTAIRE'S DEDICATION OF *ORESTE*

représentiez Iphigenie. Je fus témoin de ce spectacle, Je n'avois alors nulle habitude de notre téâtre françois, Il ne m'entra pas dans la tête qu'on pût méler de la galanterie dans ce sujet tragique. Je me livray aux moeurs et aux coutumes de la Grece d'autant plus aisément qu'à peine J'en connoissois d'autres, J'admiray L'antique dans toutte sa noble simplicité. Ce fut là ce qui me donna la première Idée de faire la Tragédie d'Œdipe sans même avoir lû celle de Corneille. Je Commençay pour*h* m'essayer en traduisant la fameuse scène de Sophocle qui contient la Double Confidence de Jocaste et d'Œdipe. Je la lus à quelques uns de mes amis qui fréquentoient les spectacles, et à quelques acteurs, ils m'assurèrent que ce morceau ne pouroit Jamais réussir en France, il m'exhortèrent à lire Corneille qui l'avoit soigneusement Evité, et me dirent tous que si je ne mettois à son Exemple un*i* Intrigue amoureuse dans Œdipe Les Comédiens même ne pouroient pas se Charger de mon ouvrage. Je lûs donc l'Œdipe de Corneille qui sans être mise*j* au rang de Cinna et de Polieucte avoit pourtant*k* beaucoup de réputation. J'avoue que je fus révolté d'un bout à l'autre, mais il falut céder à l'exemple et à la mauvaise coutume. J'introduisis au milieu de la terreur de Ce Chef d'oeuvre de l'antiquité non pas une Intrigue d'amour, l'idée m'en paroissoit trop choquante, mais au moins le ressouvenir d'une passion Eteinte. Je ne répéteray point ce que J'ay dit ailleurs, sur ce sujet *l*pour la quelle seule J'avois osé Composer toute la pièce. J'eus assez de fermeté pour ne me point rendre, je ne fus regardé que Comme un jeune homme opiniâtre et je répéteray encore pour faire voir quel êtoit le préjugé de notre nation qu'un acteur nommé Quinaut qui d'ailleurs avoit de l'esprit dès qu'il falloit Jouer cette scène telle qu'elle êtoit pour me punir de ma témérité et pour votre A. S. se souvient.*l*

---

b EDI *par*
i EDI *une*
j EDI *mies*
k modern editions followed by *alors*
l the copyist made several obvious mistakes in this passage, which Voltaire struck out, replacing it by *votre* on one page and again *votre altesse s. se souvient* continuing as shown in all editions.

Votre altesse s. se souvient que J'eus l'honneur de lire Œdipe devant elle. La scène de Sophocle ne fut assurément pas Condamnée à ce tribunal, mais vous et M. le Cardinal de Polignac et Mr de Malesieu et tout ce qui Composoit votre Cour vous me blâmâtes universellement et avec très grande raison d'avoir prononcé le mot d'amour dans un ouvrage où Sophocle avoit si bien réussi sans ce malheureux ornement Etranger; et ce qui seul avoit fait recevoir ma pièce étoit[m] précisément le seul défaut que vous Condamnâtes.

Les comédiens Jouèrent à regret l'Œdipe[n] dont ils n'espéroient rien, le public fut entierrement de vôtre avis, tout ce qui étoit dans le goust de Sophocle fut aplaudi généralement et ce qui ressentoit un peu la passion de l'amour fut Condamné de tous les critiques Eclairez. En effet madame quelle place pour la galanterie que le parricide et l'inceste qui désolent une famille, et la Contagion qui ravage un pays, et quel exemple plus frappant du ridicule de notre téâtre et du pouvoir de l'habitude, que Corneille d'un côté qui fait dire à Thesée, *quelque ravage affreux qu'étale icy la peste l'absence aux vrais amants est encor plus funeste*, et moy qui soixante ans après luy vient faire parler une vieille Jocaste d'un viel amour; et tout cela pour complaire au goût le plus fade et le plus faux qui ait Jamais [o]corrompu la littérature[o].

Qu'une Phedre dont le caractère est le plus téâtral qu'on ait Jamais vû et qui est presque la seule que l'antiquité ait représentée amoureuse, qu'une Phedre disje Etale les fureurs de cette passion funeste, qu'une Roxane dans l'oisiveté du serrail s'abandonne à l'amour et à la Jalousie, qu'Ariane se plaigne au ciel et à la terre d'une Infidélité Cruelle, qu'Orosmane tue ce qu'il adore, tout cela est vrayement tragique, l'amour furieux, criminel, malheureux suivis de remords, arrache de nobles larmes. [p]Point de milieu:

---

[m] EDI *fut*
[n] MS first reading *la pièce* altered by Voltaire.
[o] MS1 first reading *dominé une nation* altered by Voltaire.
[p] MS added by Voltaire between the lines to replace *larmes* struck out.

VOLTAIRE'S DEDICATION OF *ORESTE*

il faut ou que l'amour domine en tiran ou qu'il ne paraisse pas, il n'est point fait pour la seconde place.*ᵖ* Mais que Neron se Cache derrière une Tapisserie pour Entendre les discours de sa maitresse, et de son rival, mais que le vieux Mithridate se serve d'une ruse Comique pour savoir le secret d'une Jeune personne aimée par ses deux Enfans, mais que Maxime même dans la pièce de Cinna si remplie de bautez mâles et vrayes ne découvre en lâche une Conspiration si Importante, que par ce qu'il est Imbécillement amoureux d'une femme dont il devoit Connoitre la passion pour Cinna, et qu'on dise*ᑫ* pour raison . . . . . *L'amour rend tout permis, un véritable amant ne conoit point d'amis*, mais qu'un vieux Sertorius aime Je ne sçay quelle Viriate et qu'il soit assasiné par Perpenna, amoureux de Cette Espagnole, Tout cela est petit, et puérile. Il le faut dire hardiment; et ces petitesses nous mettroient prodigieusement au dessous des atheniens, si nos grands maitres n'avoient racheté ces défauts qui sont de notre nation, par les sublimes beautez qui sont uniquement de leur génie. Une Chose à mon sens assez Etrange c'est que les grands poètes Tragiques d'Athenes ayent si souvent traitté des sujets où la nature Etale Tout ce qu'elle a de touchant, une Electre, une Iphigenie, Une Merope, un Alcmeon, et que nos grands modernes Négligeant de tels sujets n'ayent presque traité que l'amour qui est souvent plus propre à la Comédie qu'à la tragédie. Ils ont crû quelques fois annoblir cet amour par la politique, mais un amour qui n'est pas furieux est froid, et une politique qui n'est pas une ambition forcenée est plus froide encore. Des raisonements politiques sont bons *ʳ*dans Polibe, dans Machiavel*ʳ*, la galanterie est à sa place dans la Comédie *ˢ*et dans des contes*ˢ*. Mais rien de tout cela *ᵗ*n'est digne de la gravité et de la grandeur de la tragédie*ᵗ*. Le goust de la galanterie avoit dans la tragédie prévalu au point qu'une grande princesse qui par son Esprit et par son rang

---

ᑫ modern editions *donne*
ʳ MS first reading *dans un livre* altered by Voltaire.
ˢ MS added by Voltaire between the lines.
ᵗ MS first reading *n'est tragique* altered by Voltaire.

sembloit en quelque sorte Excusable de Croire que tout le monde devoit penser Comme elle, imagina qu'un adieu de Titus et de Berenice êtoit un sujet tragique*.* Elle le donna à traitter aux deux*ʷ* maitres de la scène. Aucun des deux n'avoit Jamais fait de pièce dans la quelle L'amour n'eût Joué un principal ou un second rôle, mais l'un n'avoit Jamais parlé au Coeur que dans les seules scènes du Cid qu'il avoit Imitées de l'espagnol, l'autre toujours Elégant et tendre Etoit Eloquent en*ˣ* tous les genres, et savant dans cet art Enchanteur de tirer de la plus petite scituation les sentiments les plus passionez*ʸ*. Aussy le premier fit de Titus et de Berenice un des plus mauvais ouvrages qu'on Connoisse au téâtre, l'autre trouva le secret d'intéresser pendant cinq actes sans autre fonds que ces paroles, *Je vous aime et Je vous quitte*. C'étoit à la vérité une pastorale entre un Empereur, une reine et un Roy, et une pastorale cent fois moins Tragique que les scènes Intéressantes du pastor fido. Ce succez avoit persuadé tout le public et tous les auteurs que l'amour seul devoit être à Jamais L'âme de touttes les tragédies.

Ce ne fut que dans un âge plus mûr que cet homme Eloquent Comprit qu'il êtoit capable de mieux faire et qu'il se répentit d'avoir affaibli la scène par Tant de déclarations d'amour, par tant de sentiments de Jalousie et de coqueterie plus dignes comme j'ay déjà osé le dire de Menandre que de Sophocle et d'Euripide; Il Composa son Chef d'oeuvre d'Athalie; mais quand il se fut ainsy détrompé luy même, le public ne le fut pas encore. On ne pût Imaginer qu'une femme, un Enfant, et un prêtre, pussent former une tragédie Intéressante. L'ouvrage le plus aprochant de la perfection qui soit Jamais sorti de la main des hommes, resta longtemps méprisé, et son Illustre autheur mourut avec le Chagrin d'avoir vû son siècle Eclairé mais Corrompu ne pas rendre Justice à son Chef d'oeuvre.

ᵘ MS first reading *étoit* altered by Voltaire, partly in the margin.
ᵛ MS first reading *de tragédie* altered by Voltaire.

ʷ MS followed by *grands* struck out by Voltaire.
ˣ EDI *dans*
ʸ EDI *délicats*

VOLTAIRE'S DEDICATION OF ORESTE

Il est certain que si ce grand homme avoit vécu et s'il avoit Cultivé un talent qui seul avoit fait sa fortune et sa gloire et qu'il ne devoit pas abandonner, il eût rendu au téâtre son ancienne pureté, il n'eût point avili par des amours de ruelle les grands sujets de l'antiquité. Il avoit Commencé l'Iphigenie en Tauride et la galanterie n'entroit point dans son plan, il n'eût Jamais rendu amoureux n'y Agamemnon, n'y Oreste, n'y Electre, n'y Telephonte, n'y Ajax, mais ayant malheureusement quitté le téâtre avant[z] de l'épurer, tous ceux qui le suivirent imitèrent et outrèrent ses défauts sans atteindre à aucune de ses bautez. La morale des opera de Quinaut entra dans presque toutes les scènes tragiques. Tantôt c'est un Alcibiade qui avoue que *dans ces[aa] tendres moments il a toujours Eprouvé qu'un mortel peut goûter un Bonheur achevé.* Tantôt c'est une Amestris qui dit que *la fille d'un grand Roy brûle d'un feu secret sans honte et sans éffroy.* Icy un Agnonide *de la belle Crisis en tout lieu suit les pas, adorateur constant de ses divins appas.* Le féroce Arminius ce deffenseur de la Germanie proteste qu'[bb]il vient lire son sort dans les yeux d'Ismenie[bb], et vient dans le Camp de Varus pour voir [bb]si les beaux yeux de cette Isménie daignent luy montrer leur tendresse ordinaire[bb]. Dans Amasis qui n'est autre Chose que la Mérope chargée d'épisodes romanesques, une Jeune héroine qui depuis trois Jours a vû un moment dans une maison de Campagne un Jeune Inconnu dont elle est Eprise, s'écrie noblement[cc] *C'est ce même Inconnu pour mon repos hélas autant qu'il le devoit il ne se cacha pas et pour quelques moments qu'il s'offrit à ma vue Je le vis, J'en rougis, mon âme en fut Emue.*[dd] Dans Athenais un prince de Perse se déguise pour aller voir sa maitresse à la Cour d'un Empereur Romain. On croit lire enfin les romans de mademoiselle[ee] Scudery qui peignoit des bourgeois de Paris[ff] sous le nom des héros de l'antiquité.

[z] modern editions followed by *que*
[aa] modern editions *ses*
[bb] ED1 in italics
[cc] MS this word was added by Voltaire, but was replaced in ED1 by *avec bienséance*
[dd] MS in the margin against this quotation Voltaire wrote 'Vers'.
[ee] modern editions followed by *de*
[ff] MS followed by *de sa Connoissance* struck out by Voltaire.

Pour achever de fortifier la nation dans ce goût détestable[gg] il arriva par malheur que M. de Longepierre, très zêlé pour l'antiquité mais qui ne connoissoit pas assez notre téâtre et qui ne travailloit pas assez ses vers, fit représenter son Electre. Il faut avouer qu'elle étoit dans le goust antique; une froide et malheureuse Intrigue ne défiguroit pas ce sujet terrible, la pièce étoit simple et sans Episode, voilà ce qui luy valoit avec raison la faveur déclarée de tant de personnes de la première Considération qui Espéroient qu'enfin cette simplicité prétieuse qui avoit fait le mérite des grands hommes[hh] d'Athenes pouroit être bien reçue à Paris, [i]où elle avoit été si négligée[i].

Vous étiez madame aussy bien que feu madame la princesse de Conty à la tête de ceux qui se flattoient de Cette Espérance, mais malheureusem[t] Les défauts de la pièce françoise l'Emportèrent si fort sur les beautez qu'il avoit Empruntées de la Grece que vous avouâtes à la représentation que c'étoit une statue de Proxitelé[ii] défigurée par un moderne[jj]. Vous eûtes le Courage d'abandonner ce qui en éffet n'étoit pas digne d'être soutenu[kk]; sachant très bien[ll] que la faveur prodiguée aux mauvais ouvrages [s]est aussi contraire aux progrès de l'esprit que le déchainement contre les bons[s]. Mais la Chutte de cette Electre fit en même temps grand tort aux partisants de l'antiquité, on se prévalut très mal à propos des défauts de la Copie contre le mérite de l'original, et pour achever de Corrompre le goust de la nation on se persuada qu'il étoit Impossible de soutenir sans une Intrigue amoureuse et sans des avantures romanesques ces sujets que les Grecs n'avoient Jamais déshonorés par de tels Episodes; on prétendit qu'on pouvoit admirer les Grecs dans la lecture, mais qu'il étoit Impossible de les imiter sans être Condamné par son siècle. Etrange contradic-

[gg] EDI followed by *& qui nous rend ridicules aux yeux de tous les étrangers sensés*
[hh] EDI *génies*
[ii] EDI corrected to Praxitele
[jj] MS first reading *Copiste* altered by Voltaire.
[kk] MS followed by *par V. a.* struck out by Voltaire.
[ll] MS followed by *que rien n'est plus contraire aux progrès des arts* struck out by Voltaire.

VOLTAIRE'S DEDICATION OF ORESTE

tion, car si en effet la lecture en plait Comment la représentation en peut elle déplaire?

Il ne faut pas Je l'avoue s'attacher à imiter ce que les anciens avoient de défectueux et de faible, il est même très vraisemblable que les défauts où ils tombèrent furent relevez de leur Temps. Je suis persuadé madame que les bons Esprits d'Athenes Condamnèrent Comme vous, quelques répétitions, quelques déclamations dont Sophocle avoit Chargée son Electre, ^{mm}ils durent remarquer qu'il ne fouilloit pas assez dans le cœur humain. J'avoueray encor qu'il y a^{mm} des beautez propres^{nn} à la langue grecque^{oo}, aux mœurs, au Climat, au temps, qu'il seroit ridicule de vouloir transplanter parmy nous. Je n'ay point Copié l'Electre de Sophocle, il s'en faut beaucoup. J'en ay pris autant que ^{pp}je l'ay^{pp} pû tout L'Esprit et toutte la substance. Les fêtes que célébroient Egiste et Clitemnestre, et qu'ils appelloient les festins d'Agamemnon, l'arrivée D'Oreste et de Pilade, l'urne dans la quelle on croit que sont renfermées les cendres D'Oreste, l'annau d'Agamemnon, le Caractère d'Electre, celuy D'Iphise qui est précisément la Crisotemis de Sophocle, ^{qq}et surtout^{qq} les remords de Clitemnestre, tout est puisé dans la tragédie grecque. Car lorsque celuy qui fait à Clitemnestre le récit de la prétendue mort d'Oreste luy dit, *eh quoy madame cette mort vous afflige?* Clitemnestre répond, *Je suis mère et par là malheureuse, une mère quoy qu'outragée ne peut hair son sang*^{rr}. Voilà ce qui fut aplaudi chez le peuple, le plus Judicieux et le plus sensible de la terre, voilà ce que J'ay vû senti par tous les bons Juges de notre nation, ^{ss}et c'est ce qui doit Confondre la malheureuse critique de ceux qui ne connoissant n'y le cœur humain n'y le téatre disoient que Clitemnestre est un caractère *louche*. Le Contraire eût été affreux,

---

^{mm} MS first reading *J'avoueray encor qu'il y a même* altered by Voltaire.
^{nn} EDI followed by *non seulement*
^{oo} EDI followed by *mais*
^{pp} modern editions *j'ai*
^{qq} MS first reading *enfin* altered by Voltaire.

^{rr} EDI followed by *elle cherche même à se justifier devant Electre du meurtre d'Agamemnon: elle plaint sa fille, & Euripide a poussé encore plus loin que Sophocle l'attendrissement & les larmes de Clitemnestre.*
^{ss} not in the editions.

ils ne savoient pas que*ss* rien n'est*tt* plus dans la nature qu'une femme, criminelle envers son Epoux, et qui se laisse attendrir par ses enfans, qui reçoit*uu* la pitié dans son Cœur altier et farouche, qui s'irrite, qui reprend la dureté de son Caractère quand on luy fait des reproches trop violents, et qui s'apaise ensuitte par les soumissions et par les larmes. Le germe de ce personnage étoit dans Sophocle*vv*, et je l'ay dévelopé. Il n'apartient qu'à l'ignorance et à la présomption qui en est la suitte de dire qu'il n'y a rien à imiter dans *ww*Sophocle et dans Homere*ww*. *ʹ*Il n'y a point de bauté dont on ne trouve chez eux les semences*ʹ*.

Je me suis Imposé sur tout la loy de ne pas m'écarter de cette simplicité tant recommandée ʹpar les Grecsʹ et si difficile à saisir. C'étoit*xx* là le vray caractère de l'invention et du génie, c'est*yy* l'essence du téatre. Un personnage Etranger qui dans l'Œdipe ou dans l'Electre feroit un grand rôle, qui détourneroit sur luy l'attention seroit un monstre aux yeux de quiconque connoit les anciens ʹet la nature dont ils ont été les premiers peintresʹ. L'art et le génie Consistent à trouver tout dans son sujet, et non pas à Chercher hors de son sujet. Mais Comment imiter cette pompe et cette magnificence vraymant tragique des vers de Sophocle? cette Elégance, cette pureté, ce naturel, sans quoy un ouvrage (bien fait d'ailleurs) seroit un mauvais ouvrage?

J'ay donné au moins à ma nation quelque idée d'une Tragédie sans amour, sans Confidents, sans Episodes; le petit nombre des partisans du bon goust m'en sçait gré, les autres ne reviennent qu'à la longue quand la fureur de party, l'injustice de la persécution, et les Ténèbres de l'ignorance, sont dissipées. C'est à vous madame à Conserver les Etincelles qui restent encore parmy nous de cette lumière prétieuse que les anciens nous ont transmise. Nous leur devons tout, aucun art n'est né parmy nous, tout y a été transplanté, mais la Terre qui porte ces fruits Etrangers

---

tt ED1 followed by *en effet*
uu MS1 first reading *laisse entrer* altered by Voltaire.
vv ED1 followed by *& dans Euripide*
ww ED1 *les anciens*
xx MS1 first reading *c'est* altered by Voltaire.
yy ED1 c'étoit

VOLTAIRE'S DEDICATION OF *ORESTE*

s'épuise et se lasse, et l'ancienne barbarie aidée de la frivolité perceroit encor quelque fois malgré la culture; les disciples D'Athenes et de Rome deviendroient des gots et des vandales, amollis par les moeurs des sibarites, sans cette protection Eclairée et attentive des personnes de votre rang. Quand la nature leur a donné ou du génie ou l'amour du génie, elles encouragent notre nation qui est plus faitte pour imiter que pour Inventer, et qui Cherche toujours dans le sang de ses maitres les leçons et les Exemples dont elle a besoin.

Tout ce que je désire Madame c'est qu'il se trouve quelque génie qui achève ce que j'ay Ebauché, qui tire le teâtre de cette molesse affetée[zz] où il est plongé, qui le rende respectable Aux esprits les plus austères, digne [aaa]des baux Jours[aaa] d'Athenes, digne[bbb] du très petit nombre de Chef d'oeuvres que nous avons et enfin du suffrage d'un esprit telque le vôtre et de ceux qui peuvent vous ressembler.

[zz] EDI *& de cette afféterie*
[aaa] modern editions *du théâtre*

[bbb] MSI first reading *et* altered by Voltaire.

19

A propos d'une lettre inconnue de Voltaire

par Enrico Straub

Voltaire écrit le 8 décembre 1773 à son ami et ancien secrétaire, l'Italien Cosimo Alessandro Collini (1727-1806), un billet de quelques lignes dont le contenu indique qu'il accompagnait une lettre de remerciements destinée à un traducteur inconnu de sa *Henriade* en italien. Cette lettre ne nous a pas été conservée, de sorte qu'on ne sait rien de certain sur la traduction, sur son auteur et sur les relations de celui-ci avec Voltaire. Le court billet n'apporte aucun éclaircissement qui nous permette de voir plus clair; en voici le texte: 'Je vous adresse, mon cher ami, la Lettre que je dois à celui qui m'a fait l'honneur de traduire la Henriade en italien. J'écris bien rarement; mais quand j'écris mes dernières volontés je pense à vous' (Best.17576). Dans son commentaire Theodore Besterman nomme quatre traducteurs qui pourraient en être les destinataires. Il s'agit de Giovanni Marenzi, d'un Ceretesi, de Tommaso Medini et d'un certain Villa. Il ne peut pourtant pas dire avec certitude auquel des quatre traducteurs la lettre était adressée.

Le matériel dont nous disposons ne nous apporte en fait aucun indice qui permette d'identifier le traducteur et son œuvre. Collini, à qui Voltaire a envoyé la lettre et qui par conséquent doit avoir servi d'intermédiaire entre le traducteur et l'auteur, ne donne aucune information utilisable dans les papiers qu'il a laissés. Dans les passages où il évoque sa collaboration avec Voltaire, et dans sa correspondance avec lui, il ne désigne pas le traducteur par son nom. La lettre[1] de Collini datée du 16 novembre 1773

[1] Côme Alexandre Collini, *Mon séjour auprès de Voltaire* (Paris 1807). Ce livre contient un choix très arbitraire de la correspondance entre

donne pour tout renseignement qu'un compatriote italien s'est adressé à lui pour le prier de faire parvenir ses œuvres à Voltaire, et, parmi elles, une traduction de la *Henriade* en vers italiens; la lettre révèle en outre que Collini a fait l'envoi le même jour encore, de Mannheim (Best.17539). Il garde cependant le silence sur le nom de son compatriote italien et ne donne aucune indication sur ses relations avec lui[2]. De qui était donc cette traduction de la *Henriade* envoyée à Voltaire par Collini en automne 1773?

Parmi les cinq traductions italiennes connues jusqu'à cet automne 1773, quatre sont à rejeter d'emblée, soit qu'elles aient été faites avant l'époque qui nous intéresse — en ce cas Voltaire après si longtemps ne serait pas revenu sur ce sujet pour remercier l'auteur — soit qu'il en ait déjà parlé dans des lettres que nous avons conservées. Il serait alors invraisemblable que Voltaire ait envoyé une seconde lettre de remerciements par l'intermédiaire de Collini.

La traduction, aujourd'hui inconnue, d'un certain Nenci se trouve déjà mentionnée, avec des louanges, dans une lettre[3] datant du 18 octobre 1739.

Voltaire ne peut vraisemblablement pas avoir reçu la traduction partielle de Francesco Corsetti, qui avait paru en 1745 en appendice à une anthologie d'élégies latines, en 1773 seulement, c'est-à-dire vingt-huit années après sa parution[4].

Collini et Voltaire. Ainsi la lettre mentionnée est donnée écourtée et faussement datée du 16 novembre 1770. Le contenu indique pourtant indubitablement qu'elle n'a été écrite que le 16 novembre 1773; cf. la datation exacte de Best.17539.

[2] une remarque de Collini sur la lettre adressée à Voltaire, dans *Mon séjour*, garde le même silence sur le nom du traducteur. A notre grand étonnement il mentionne là l'existence de plusieurs traductions de la *Henriade*, et il cite même six lignes de celle, autrement inconnue, de Nenci, qu'il considère comme la meilleure.

[3] Best.1991; depuis la publication m. Besterman a identifié le destinataire de cette lettre: Roberto Ignazio Solaro di Breglio. Cf. également Best.2257.

[4] cf. aussi Theodore Besterman, 'A Provisional bibliography of Italian editions and translations of Voltaire' *Studies on Voltaire and the eighteenth century* (1961), xviii.263-306, no.85.

LETTRE INCONNUE DE VOLTAIRE

Giovanni Marenzi envoie le 28 septembre 1769 un manuscrit de sa traduction à Voltaire, et celui-ci l'en remercie dès le 12 février 1770[5].

D'après des documents épistolaires, la traduction d'un chevalier Ceretesi est parvenue entre les mains de Voltaire, sous la forme d'un manuscrit transmis par Claret de La Tourette, en 1770 déjà[6].

La supposition que Voltaire adressait sa lettre de remerciement à Tommaso Medini s'avère aussi impossible, car la traduction de celui-ci est datée de 1774, elle est donc postérieure à la lettre de Voltaire. Le fait que Voltaire envoie directement à Medini une lettre détaillée (Best.18112) sur sa traduction le 9 décembre 1774, une année presque exactement après son billet à Collini, confirme encore notre idée que Medini ne peut pas être le traducteur en question.

La traduction de la *Henriade* que nous recherchons ne peut donc être que celle qui a paru à Neuchâtel en 1772, sur laquelle le traducteur porte le nom de Antigono de Villa[7]. Une autre édition de cette même traduction semble avoir été imprimée la même année à Florence[8]. La chronologie des faits vient confirmer cette supposition: cette traduction paraît en 1772, Collini la reçoit du traducteur et la fait parvenir en novembre 1773 à Voltaire, qui répond au début de décembre 1773.

Un fait nouveau vient, sinon confirmer, du moins fortement renforcer cette supposition: c'est une lettre de Voltaire inconnue jusqu'à nos jours. Elle ne nous est parvenue que sous la forme d'une copie qui semble avec une forte probabilité reproduire cette lettre qui nous manquait. Voici ce texte:

---

[5] Best.14942 (Marenzi à Voltaire); Best.15151 (Voltaire à Marenzi).

[6] Best.15090 (à Claret de La Tourette); Best.15438 (Claret de La Tourette à Voltaire); Best.16269 (à Claret de La Tourette).

[7] *L'Enriade, poema eroico del Signor de Voltaire*, tradotto in versi italiani dal Signor Antigono de Villa, professore d'Anatomia e belle Lettere nell'Accademia di Berlino (Neuchâtel 1772).

[8] *L'Enriade di Voltaire, tradotta in versi italiani da Antigono de Villa* (Firenze, Carlieri, 1772). Indication d'après Melzi, mais invérifiable.

Copie de la lettre de Mr. de Voltaire écrite à Mr. Docteur Antoine Valli, qui a traduit en italien l'Henriade.

Monsieur

Un vielliard de quatrevingt ans, malade et presque aveugle, a oublié son âge et ses maux pour lire votre Henriade italienne. Je vous remercie de l'avoir embellie. La facilité de vôtre stile fera croire un jour, que vôtre ouvrage est l'original et que le mien est la copie. Agréez la reconnaissance un peu laconique d'un homme, qui n'est pas en état d'écrire une longue lettre, ni même de la dicter. L'esprit est prompt mais la chair est faible. J'ai l'honneur d'être etc.
Voltaire

Ce texte se trouve parmi les papiers que Giacomo Casanova a laissés, et qui sont conservés dans les archives du château des comtes de Waldstein à Duchcov[9] en Tchécoslovaquie, château où le libertin a vécu de 1785 à 1798, année de sa mort. Le texte de la lettre n'offre dans sa brièveté et la généralité de son contenu — la date et le nom du destinataire manquent d'ailleurs dans la copie — aucun indice directement utilisable pour la classer.

On peut pourtant situer à peu près exactement l'époque où la lettre a été écrite; elle coïncide avec celle où Voltaire doit avoir écrit la lettre de remerciement qu'il a transmise à Collini. Voltaire, né le 21 novembre 1694, se désigne comme octogénaire, il doit donc avoir écrit ses lignes vers 1774. Le billet envoyé à Collini pour accompagner la lettre que nous recherchons a été rédigé à la fin de 1773. La proximité de ces dates nous incline à croire qu'il s'agit bien de la lettre que Collini était prié de transmettre.

L'en-tête donné par le copiste indique comme destinataire et traducteur de la *Henriade* un docteur Antoine Valli, et non pas, comme l'indiquaient les éditions de Neuchâtel et Florence, Anti-

---

[9] autrefois Dux en Bohème. Depuis 1920 les manuscrits originaux sont dans les archives d'état à Mnichovo Hradiště, Tchécoslovaquie; cote: U15-21 (b). Des doubles photocopiés se trouvent à Duchcov.

gono de Villa. En fait il s'agit là d'un pseudonyme[10] sous lequel un savant florentin nommé Valli a fait paraître sa traduction. L'en-tête de la copie donne donc son nom exact au destinataire: Antoine Valli.

On ne sait rien de certain sur ce personnage ni sur ses relations avec Voltaire. Sa préface de la *Enriade* italienne ne nous apprend rien non plus sur lui-même. Le frontispice le désigne comme 'Professore d'Anatomia e belle Lettere nell'Accademia di Berlino'. Comme il ne se trouve pas parmi les membres de l'Académie des sciences, nous pouvons supposer qu'il a professé dans la Ritter-Akademie de Berlin, institution destinée aux fils de la noblesse. On comprendrait alors qu'il ait été désigné dans le frontispice comme 'professore', étant donné que les adhérents de l'Académie des sciences étaient normalement appelés 'membres'. Il est probable que Valli a pris contact avec son compatriote Collini pendant le séjour de celui-ci à Berlin et Potsdam en 1750-1753. Il semblerait alors naturel qu'il s'adresse plus tard à l'ancien secrétaire de Voltaire pour faire parvenir, par cet intermédiaire, sa traduction au patriarche de Ferney.

Si vraisemblables et persuasives que soient ces explications apportées à la lettre de Voltaire, on pourra toujours douter de l'authenticité du texte, tant qu'on n'en trouvera pas le manuscrit original. La copie serait plus digne de foi si l'on pouvait reconstituer le chemin que le texte de la lettre doit avoir fait de Voltaire jusqu'à Casanova, et surtout s'il était possible de connaître les conditions dans lesquelles le texte du manuscrit original a été copié.

La copie se trouve sur le dos d'un bulletin en langue française qui n'est écrit que jusqu'au tiers et où sont notés minutieusement des événements concernant la vie politique et mondaine de la cour

---

[10] G[aetano] Melzi, *Dizionario di opere anonime e pseudonime di scrittori italiani* (Milano 1848), i.66; Emil Weller, *Lexicon pseudonymorum* (Regensburg 1886), p.36; Marino Parenti, *Dizionario dei luoghi di stampa falsi, inventati o supposti* (Firenze 1951), p.151. Malheureusement Melzi ne donne pas les sources de son indication; Weller et Parenti la reprennent telle qu'elle est.

de Paris. Il est daté du 25 mai 1774 et représente le dernier d'une série de vingt-deux rapports du même genre, écrits anonymement et sans nom de destinataire à partir du 24 octobre 1773, de Versailles, Choisy-le-Roi et Paris. Ce bulletin ne contribue pourtant pas à éclairer les circonstances dans lesquelles la copie a été faite; rien dans son contenu n'implique de lien entre elle et ce rapport, et de plus l'écriture du bulletin n'est pas la même que celle de la copie de Voltaire. L'auteur de la copie n'est donc certainement pas celui du bulletin, ceci malgré la proximité étonnante des deux dates: décembre 1773 et mai 1774. On peut aussi supposer que la copie a été ajoutée ultérieurement, peut-être parce que le papier manquait. Le fait qu'elle a été écrite sur la dernière feuille des vingt-deux rapports, qui probablement se trouvait juste en haut, nous incline aussi à le croire.

La supposition que Casanova lui-même aurait ajouté ces lignes ne peut être maintenue, car elles ne sont pas de sa main. Il est très probable qu'il n'était même pas, à l'origine, le destinataire de ces rapports français; il semble au contraire qu'ils soient venus plus tard en sa possession, portant déjà la copie de la lettre de Voltaire. Rien n'indique dans ses œuvres, dans ce qui reste de sa correspondance, ni dans tout ce qu'il nous a laissé, comment et pourquoi il a reçu cette copie.

A l'époque où ont été transcrits les rapports et la copie, Casanova habitait à Trieste (novembre 1772-septembre 1774) et faisait encore de longs et fréquents voyages à travers toute l'Europe, jusqu'à ce qu'il s'établisse en 1785 définitivement au château des Waldstein à Duchcov. Il paraît peu probable qu'il se soit chargé, pendant ses voyages peu commodes, de ces documents qui — à la différence de ses lettres — ne touchaient pas directement à sa personne, et qui n'ont pas trouvé d'écho dans son œuvre pourtant si variée.

Nous supposons qu'il a reçu ces rapports français avec la copie de la lettre de Voltaire d'un de ses nombreux et savants correspondants, à l'époque où il s'occupait particulièrement d'études historiques à Duchcov. Ces textes lui venaient éventuellement de

LETTRE INCONNUE DE VOLTAIRE

son vieil ami le comte Max Joseph Lamberg (1729-1792); celui-ci pendant ses nombreux voyages avait passé trois ans à Paris, où en 1757 ou 1758 Casanova avait fait sa connaissance. De 1767 jusqu'à sa mort, Lamberg resta en contact épistolaire avec notre libertin, l'informant selon son propre témoignage sur tous les événements littéraires[11]. Les lettres — plus de 360 à l'origine, dont par malheur seulement 173 nous sont parvenues — prouvent que Lamberg avait à plusieurs reprises envoyé à son ami des documents littéraires intéressants, parmi lesquels des textes de Voltaire[12]. Malheureusement la correspondance conservée ne mentionne pas la lettre de remerciement à Antonio Valli, dont la copie n'est même pas de la plume de Lamberg.

Dans quelles conditions la lettre de Voltaire a été recopiée et comment elle est parvenue parmi les papiers de Casanova, ces points restent obscurs comme auparavant; cependant la découverte de ce texte n'est pas sans intérêt parce qu'il semble parfaitement remplir une lacune dans la correspondance de Voltaire.

---

[11] Giacomo Casanova, *Correspondance avec J. F. Opiz*, éd. Fr. Khol et Otto Pick (Leipzig 1913), i.103 (Casanova à Opiz, 1 avril 1793).

[12] *Casanova und Graf Lamberg. Unveröffentlichte Briefe des Grafen Max Lamberg*, éd. Gustav Gugitz (Wien &c. 1935), pp.41 (Lamberg à Casanova, 12 avril 1773), 137 (Lamberg à Casanova, 6 février 1790).

Voltaire and Seneca
by Stephen Werner

> [Ils ont dit] qu'il y a de grands rapports entre Sénèque et Voltaire.
> Tant mieux pour l'un et pour l'autre; et je ne crois pas qu'on fît un mauvais compliment au plus fameux de nos aristarques, si on lui disait qu'il y a de grands rapports entre Voltaire, Sénèque et lui.
> Diderot, *Essai sur les règnes de Claude et de Néron.*

Roman antiquity was an important source of inspiration for eighteenth-century French literature. Voltaire, it is well known, owed a considerable debt to Horace, Virgil and Lucretius. Yet another influence on his thought—one which is generally overlooked—could well have been the Roman Stoic statesman and philosopher, Lucius Annaeus Seneca. For Voltaire, as for a significant number of his contemporaries, Seneca was a writer to be turned to for encouragement and guidance, and even, upon occasion, for inspiration.

The importance of Seneca to French writing in the middle ages and in the sixteenth century has long been recognized[1]. It is only now, however, that we are beginning to appreciate how firm a hold he had on the minds of eighteenth-century *philosophes* and on the century in which they lived. Rousseau's first discourse,

---

[1] the question of Seneca's influence on the medieval period is discussed by Anne Marie Marthe Smit, *Contribution à l'étude de la connaissance de l'antiquité au moyen âge* (Leiden 1934). For Seneca and the Renaissance see *Les Tragédies de Sénèque et le théâtre de la Renaissance*, ed. Jean Jacquet (Paris 1964).

for example, abounds in praises of this Stoic; and so do his letters to Voltaire[2]. Jean Jacques, wrote Diderot, 'nous rappele Sénèque en cent endroits et ne doit pas une ligne à Cicéron' (A.-T.iii.234). We know that Montesquieu had read Seneca early in life[3]; moreover, the *Esprit des lois* contains this enthusiastic tribute to the austere wisdom of the Stoics: 'Les diverses sectes de philosophie chez les anciens pouvoient être considérées comme des espèces de religion. Il n'y en a jamais eu dont les principes fussent plus dignes de l'homme, et plus propres à former des gens de bien, que celle des Stoïciens'[4].

Le Système de la nature, Holbach's masterpiece, derives not only from Lucretius but also from Seneca[5]; and one of Holbach's disciples, La Grange, spent eighteen years in translating the *Omnia opera* into French. La Mettrie composed an *Anti-Sénèque*, or *Essai sur le bonheur*. There were others, too, like Chamfort[6] or mme Du Châtelet[7], who used the Roman philosopher's writings for their own ends. It was Diderot though, who, among

---

[2] there remains much to be done on the Seneca-Rousseau relationship. For earlier studies see, for example, Leon Hermann, 'Jean-Jacques Rousseau, traducteur de Sénèque', *Annales de la Société Jean-Jacques Rousseau* (1920-1921), xiii.215-224; G. Pire 'De l'influence de Sénèque sur les théories pédagogiques de Jean-Jacques Rousseau', *Annales de la Société Jean-Jacques Rousseau* (1953-1955), xxxiii.51-92; K. S. Tchang, *Les Sources antiques de Jean-Jacques Rousseau sur l'éducation* (Paris 1919). See also Best.6289, where Rousseau quotes *De providentia*.

[3] see the useful study by L. M. Levin, *The Political Doctrine of Montesquieu's Esprit des Lois: Its Classical Background* (New York 1936). Montesquieu's education at the Collège de Juilly is discussed by Pierre Barrière, *Un Grand Provincial: Charles-Louis de Secondat, Baron de la Brède et de Montesquieu* (Bordeaux 1946). Also of value are M. W. Rombout's *La Conception stoïcienne du bonheur chez Montesquieu* (Leiden 1958) and Johann Albrecht von Rantzau, 'Politische Wirkungen antiker Vorstellungen bei Montesquieu', *Antike und Abendland* (1956), v.107-120.

[4] *Œuvres complètes*, ed. Roger Callois (Paris 1951), ii.721-722.

[5] a study of the Holbach-Seneca relationship is being undertaken by the present author. There are relevant suggestions in Henry Guerlac's 'Three eighteenth-century social philosophers', *Daedalus* (1958), lxxxvii.8-24'.

[6] see Alain Michel's 'Vauvenargues et le stoïcisme latin', *Cahiers de l'Association Guillaume Budé* (1964-1965), i.95-102.

[7] *Discours sur le bonheur*, ed. Robert Mauzi (Paris 1961), p.3.

eighteenth-century minds, understood Seneca best. He was confident, late in life, of having found a kindred spirit in him: 'Après avoir lu Sénèque, suis-je le même que j'étais avant que de le lire — cela n'est pas, cela ne se peut', he exclaimed[8]. The Encyclopedist regretted not having discovered Seneca earlier but made up for this neglect by writing the *Essai sur les règnes de Claude et de Néron*, that curiously revealing essay on the Stoic's life and work. Here may be found some of the most discerning remarks ever written on the Roman moralist[9].

Voltaire, too, was inevitably attracted to writers like Horace, Lucretius and Seneca for it might be said that they best represented the finer qualities of *Romanitas*. Seneca, of whose complete works Voltaire owned no fewer than three copies[10], had much in common with enlightenment philosophers: he was a practical moralist, concerned above all with ethics and the daily conduct of men. Voltaire's classical interests are described in 'Education', an article which appears in the *Dictionnaire philosophique*: 'Je vous ai fait lire autrefois Despautère et Cicéron, les vers de Commire et de Virgile, le *Pédagogue chrétien* et Sénèque, les *Psaumes* de David en latin de cuisine, et les odes d'Horace.... En un mot, j'ai fait ce que j'ai pu pour vous bien élever' (M.xviii.471). Voltaire had been introduced to the great Latin writers when still a young man. One might indeed say that the *philosophe* had two educations and they were almost simultaneous. He attended the Jesuit Lycée Louis-le-grand and frequented the Société du Temple, a centre of libertine scepticism.

The Jesuit teachers at Louis-le-grand were ardent humanists whose instruction had a moral and cultural aim. 'L'antiquité païenne elle-même', it has been noted, 'devait servir à propager

---

[8] Herbert Dieckmann, *Inventaire du fonds Vandeul et les inédits de Diderot* (Geneva 1951), p.257.

[9] for Diderot and Seneca consult Fritz Schalk, *Diderots Essai über Claudius und Nero* (Nordrhein-Westfalen 1954). Also Douglas A. Bonneville, *Diderot's Vie de Sénèque* (University of Florida Monographs xix: Gainesville 1966). See the review of Bonneville's book by Stephen Werner, *Diderot studies* (1968), x.335-337.

[10] *Studies on Voltaire* (1959), ix.230.

la foi chrétienne'[11]. The chief Roman author studied in eighteenth-century Jesuit schools was Cicero, admired for the beauty of his Latin prose and for the ideas of such works as the *Tusculan disputations* and *De finibus*. Other authors read included Caesar, Sallust, Livy, Valerius Maximus and Seneca[12]. The main poets read were Ovid, Horace, and Virgil; but students at Louis-le-grand had a chance to read extracts from such differing poets as Tibullus, Catullus, Martial, Propertius, Juvenal and Persius, and they also read choruses from Seneca's tragedies (Dupont-Ferrier, i.133). His plays, adapted as they were from the Greek, were looked on as models of dramatic art (i.225). These works were to leave a firm imprint on the mind of Voltaire.

The Jesuit fathers, writes an historian of that order, had a 'vive sympathie envers le "bon homme Epictète", "le plus homme de bien de tout le paganisme", envers Sénèque et Plutarque'[13]. 'La fréquentation des Stoïques fournira à nos éducateurs des lieux communs pour leurs developments moraux, accusera sans doute l'aspect volontaire de leur conception de la vertu', it has been observed[14]. Seneca was traditionally held in high esteem by the Jesuits and had been especially honoured in the sixteenth century. Stoic exhortations on the need to bear suffering and to master one's passions were well-suited to a nation torn by religious and civil wars. Less esteemed in the eighteenth century than in earlier times, Seneca's writings were still a staple of Catholic education. Voltaire's teachers at Louis-le-grand did not forget

---

[11] Gustave Dupont-Ferrier, *Du collège de Clermont au lycée Louis-le-grand* (Paris 1921), i.231.

[12] *ibid.*, p.133. See also André Schimberg, *L'Education morale dans les collèges de la compagnie de Jésus en France sous l'ancien régime* (Paris 1913), pp.148-149.

[13] François de Dainville, *Les Jésuites et l'éducation de la société française* (Paris 1940), p.245.

[14] *ibid.*, p.245. The subject of Stoicism and sixteenth-century France is admirably treated by Léontine Zanta, *La Renaissance du stoïcisme au XVIe siècle* (Paris 1914). See also Henri Busson, *La Pensée religieuse française de Charron à Pascal* (Paris 1933) and J. Dedieu, 'Les Origines de la morale indépendante', *Revue pratique d'apologétique* (1909), viii.401-423, 579-598.

that of all pagan authors Seneca was the one most firmly admired by the church—'our Seneca' Tertullian had indeed called him.

The Roman Stoic is of unquestioned importance in the study of the Jesuit school theatre. The Jesuits, unlike Calvin or Rousseau, accorded a special place to the theatre. Plays had, they said, a civilizing mission: they fostered piety and protected young people from vice. Each teacher of rhetoric at Louis-le-grand was required to write a tragedy in Latin every year. Students would themselves compose similar plays as exercises. These school-dramas took their themes from the Bible, the lives and legends of the saints, and profane history. But the style in which they were couched was consciously Senecan: 'La langue des pièces est habituellement vive et concise; le vers iambique, dont elle se sert, à l'exemple de Sénèque, se prête heureusement au dialogue' (Dupont-Ferrier, i.291).

Since he was an exceptionally gifted student, Voltaire was asked to write such plays and was strongly influenced in this task by two of his teachers at the school: Gabriel Franc Le Jay (1657-1734) and Charles Porée (1675-1745), both ardent admirers of Seneca. Father Le Jay, it is said, 'avait fait une étude attentive du style de Sénèque le tragique. Il se sert avec une certaine adresse des façons de dire de Sénèque'[15]. *Damoclès*, one of Le Jay's plays, was in fact directly taken from Seneca. *Père* Porée, Voltaire's other teacher, was described as a 'passé Sénèque' (Pierron, p.90). Porée's views on the function of the theatre are set forth in the prologue to his *Philedonus sive juvenis voluptarius:* 'Quelle est notre fin? Divertir? Nous cherchons un autre avantage, mais c'est au ciel à convertir'[16]. It is difficult to determine which plays of Seneca Voltaire studied while at the Collège. What is certain, however, is that he knew their form and dramatic sweep and that they were to govern the style of his own early work for the theatre. Moreover, the young *philosophe*, hostile as he was to

---

[15] Alexis Pierron, *Voltaire et ses maîtres* (Paris 1866), p.106.

[16] quoted by L. V. Goufflot, *Le Théâtre au collège du moyen âge à nos jours* (Paris 1907), p.201.

many aspects of Jesuit education, rarely failed to wax enthusiastic about their theatre. The school-theatre, he wrote to Bianchi in 1763, constituted nothing less than the best part of a Catholic education (Best.9336).

At the time of Voltaire the Jesuits wished to impart, then, what might be called a Christian humanism. Through writers like Horace and Seneca they stressed the inborn dignity of human nature. They attempted to see all things in relation to the soul for they believed that it was through the soul that man could perfect his humanity. The Jesuits sang the glory of god through the resoundingly pagan world of the Roman moralists and poets.

But at the same time that Voltaire was a pupil of the Jesuits he was also heir to a more pronounced secular tradition, that of the Société du Temple. It was there, George Havens writes[17], that Voltaire 'sharpened his gift for repartee and ironic wit, developed his natural tendency toward religious skepticism, practiced the graceful art of badinage and light society verse, and formed his literary taste'. Poets of the Société were hostile to orthodoxy and metaphysics and took their inspiration from Horace and Lucretius. They rejected the notion of the immortality of the soul and clung to the traditional themes of seventeenth-century libertine poets: elegiac musings on the shortness of life, the instability of all that lives and the certain decay of beauty. They also spoke, however, of the difficulties of prolonging life's pleasures. Their poetry takes on, at times, a stoical attitude which would seem at best a very diluted philosophy of Seneca. Theirs was a tempered epicureanism; it blended the high purpose of Lucretius, the gaiety of Epicurus, and the resignation of Seneca.

In the years before 1734 Voltaire, when concerned at all with Seneca, is chiefly interested in the plays, their influence on French theatre, in particular. The *Lettres sur Œdipe* (1719) point out that Seneca's *Hippolytus* left a deep imprint on Racine's *Phèdre*

[17] in his edition of *Candide* (New York 1951), p.xv.

and that the last act of Corneille's *Œdipe* is a close translation of Seneca's play of the same name[18]. The *philosophe* (who was also of course to write about Œdipus) is a classicist who speaks with reverence of the great tragedians of antiquity.

The years from 1734 to 1738, however, were a time of reeducation. Voltaire the classical poet was gradually becoming Voltaire the *philosophe* and his writings reveal this change. The poems of that time hark back to the stock themes of the Société du Temple, many of them classical in inspiration. There are verses in praise of pleasure, stoical musings on death and, Norman Torrey writes, 'many a pagan precept to fling in the face of theology'[19]. When Voltaire quotes ancient authors he uses more often than not a Horatian tag[20]. He was drawn to Horace's easy patrician philosophy and to his mellow scepticism.

As he comes increasingly under the influence of Horace—a writer whose nature closely resembled his own—he also begins to grow more aware of the philosophical and moral aspects of Seneca's writings. 'Le Stoïcisme', Jean Marmier has reminded us, 'puise ses formules chez Horace aussi bien que chez Sénèque'[21]. Voltaire's *Epîtres*, like Horace's own *Epistulae* or the *Epistulae morales* of Seneca, are patrician in mood. Following Seneca and Horace, Voltaire's moral precepts are condensed into memorably gnomic phrases. There are verses on the unhappiness of kings, the vanity of human wishes and the inevitability of death. What is to be found in the *Epîtres* (in addition to increasingly

---

[18] M.ii.28. See also M.xxxi.188. The article of H. G. Franq, 'Les Malheurs d'Œdipe', *Revue de l'Université Laval* (1965-1966), xx.211-224, 308-317, 458-480, 560-569, 657-675, shows how the Œdipus theme was treated by Sophocles, Seneca, Corneille, Voltaire, Gide and Cocteau. Franq draws no parallels, however, between the version of Seneca and that of Voltaire.

[19] *The Spirit of Voltaire* (New York 1938), p.21.

[20] Raymond Naves, *Le Goût de Voltaire* (Paris 1938). Naves collected 139 different quotations from Horace in the works of Voltaire. This is more than from any other Latin poet, including Virgil. Best.xcix.107-114 lists several times as many from the correspondence alone.

[21] *Horace en France au dix-septième siècle* (Paris 1962), p.37.

sophisticated ideas on freewill, the immortality of the soul, and the relationship between church and state) is a mild, almost gentle stoicism. Voltaire blends the counsel of Horace and the freethinking libertine poets with reminiscences of Lucretius and Seneca.

The art of Seneca and Horace—like that of Voltaire—was not cut off from life. It showed that reasonableness and sense of proportion which is acquired through living[22]. It was practical, free from any fanaticism which, in Voltaire's mind, would threaten the happy life. 'You taught us to follow the lessons of philosophy', the *philosophe* wrote of Horace: 'to scorn death and at the same time to savor life's gifts' (M.x.445). The good life described by Horace and Seneca, however, while surely praiseworthy, is not so austere as to be unattainable. If these writers have the severity of Lucretius they also seem to show an adaptability worthy of Epicurus. 'I am wont to cross over even into the enemy's camp, not as a deserter, but as a scout', Seneca had said (*Epist. mor.* ii.6). The Stoic sage, Horace wrote, is confident in his convictions. He bids defiance to the tyrant and the crowd alike:

> Nunc agilis fio et mersos civilibus undis
> Virtutis, verae custos rigidisque satelles[23].

Voltaire, it has been said, 'faisait quelquefois du stoïcisme comme M. Jourdain faisait de la prose'[24]. This view is perhaps simplistic. What is certain, however, is that before going to England Voltaire's poems express a gentle philosophy of stoicism. They are characterized by 'pensées justes' on a variety of moral subjects. They reflect the influence of Horace and Seneca. Voltaire chooses from these writers, though, ideas which are closest

---

[22] Seneca was familiar with Horace and quoted him directly on a number of occasions—in the *Apocolocynthosis* (xiii.3), in the *Letters* (lxxxvi.13; cxix.13; cxx.20) and in the choruses of the tragedies.

[23] *Epistulae*, I.i.16-17. See also Cicero, *De finibus*, III.xx.68. Also *De officiis*, I.vii.22. An interesting parallel may be drawn with Seneca's *De consolatione ad Helviam*, xii.4, where the Roman speaks of the 'strict and virile school of Stoic philosophy'.

[24] Eugène Rovillain, 'Rapports probables entre le Zadig de Voltaire et la pensée stoïcienne', *PMLA* (1937), lii.374-389.

to his temperament. He rejects the arbitrary and severe 'stoïcisme de la raison' (that of Epictetus)[25] and is attracted to what could be called a 'stoïcisme du cœur' (Seneca and Horace)[26]. The *Epîtres* show that tempered philosophy which was always to be a part of Voltaire's life (M.x.217):

> A son état mesurant ses désirs
> Selon les temps se faire des plaisirs
> Et suivre enfin, conduit par la nature,
> Tantôt Socrate, et tantôt Epicure.

From 1758 to 1762 Voltaire reshaped his philosophy of ideas into a philosophy of action. Once again the influence of Seneca is apparent. *Candide* provides a good example. Pococurante, at one point in the tale, contemptuously speaks of 'des recueils de sermons qui, tous ensemble, ne valent pas une page de Sénèque' (M.xxi.204).

The young Candide is gullible and optimistic. But in his travels he has seen peaceful towns razed, old men impaled and maidens violated. The innocent are burned at the stake. Maturity brings with it a warm stoicism. It is clear that life is demanding and will always be so. How could it be otherwise? Seneca might have asked. For Voltaire, as for Seneca, wisdom consists in accepting, forthrightly and with courage, our condition as men. Idle speculation about the nature of the universe is not only presumptuous, it is also vain. *Candide* teaches us to learn to conduct our lives in accordance with nature and to realize our potential for virtue through society and friends. We will thus be able to begin living as philosophers.

The theme of ennui—the *taedium vitae* of classical moralists—is an important one in *Candide*. Men are, as both Horace and Seneca liked to observe, naturally inconstant and dissatisfied.

---

[25] these terms were used by Alain Michel, p.101.

[26] the Epicurean aspects of Seneca's thought were studied by H. Mutschmann, 'Seneca und Epikur', *Zeitschrift für Klassische Philologie* (1915), p.321.

'Everyone hurries his life on and suffers from a yearning for the future and a weariness of the present', Seneca had warned (*De brevitate vitae*, vii.8). Men are like drivers in a chariot race, Horace said; each driver has his eyes set on the horse before him and forgets about those he has passed (*Satires*, I.i.113). It seems that no one is happy in *Candide*: the wealthy want more silver plate, the Jesuits more converts, and the Bulgars more captives. We are discontented, Voltaire advises us, because we do not know what is best for us. We are continuously driven off the right course by fantastic and artificial desires which, in our unenlightened state, we take to be natural needs.

Like his classical teachers Voltaire suggests that to master life we must first master ourselves. We must follow the rules nature has set down for right living. Friends, for example, *Candide* says, make life tolerable. No good thing is pleasant to possess, Seneca had already stated, without friends to share it[27]. The wise man, the Stoics were fond of asserting, was never a private man. Also important is meaningful work and the sense of fulfilment it provides. It is thus that Eldorado and its life of self-indulgent idleness leads to stultification. As Seneca had previously noted, tranquility can never come from irresponsibility. The Pococurante episode in *Candide* suggests that contentment has little to do with wealth or education either. It depends rather upon a mind purged of fear and unnatural desires. It is inseparable from a healthy body bent on purposeful work. Happiness—Voltaire

---

[27] Seneca, *Epist. mor.*, v.4: 'Hoc primum philosophia promittit, sensum communem, humanitatem et congregationem'. The *philosophes*, of course, focused attention upon our inherent need for social intercourse. The *Encyclopédie*, for example, was not the effort of a lone compiler but of a society of men of letters whose aim was the betterment of mankind and the wide dissemination of knowledge. Cf. the articles 'Isoler', 'Epicurisme', 'Droit naturel' and 'Stylite', among others. For the Encyclopedists, as for Seneca, man was a social being, a single part of one body of humanity. The further man carries the work of moral improvement in himself, they felt, the stronger will he feel himself drawn to society. See Edward Zeller, *Stoics, Epicureans, and Sceptics* (London 1892), pp.310-331, for a general discussion of this subject.

and Seneca would probably have agreed—cannot be divorced from friends and worthwhile social activity.

During the later years of his life Voltaire was often to come back to Seneca. In 1763, for example, he quotes the *Epistulae morales* in a letter to mme Du Deffand: 'Etes-vous de l'avis de Mécène qui disait, que je sois gouteux, sourd et aveugle, pourvu que je vive, tout va bien?' (Best.10551). A letter written the following year makes use of the same quotation (Best.11028). What especially interested Voltaire at this time, however, was the *Troades*, Seneca's dramatization of the suffering of the captive Trojan women. The play, like *Hercules furens*, *Medea* and *Phaedra*, was modelled on Euripides and is, in the opinion of not a few, one of the Roman Stoic's finest tragedies. Voltaire was particularly fond of citing—and did so with increasing frequency—Seneca's moving lines on death and annihilation:

> Can it be true that we utterly die?
> Is there no part of us left, when the soul
> At the final breath-flicker soars into the air,
> Mingling with cloudland so soon as the torch
> Lays fingers of fire on the corpse lying bare?...
> After our death there is naught? Death is naught;
> The mere finishing goal of a race quickly run....
> The way into hell and the cruel king's realm
> And Cerberus guarding the perilous gate
> Are idlest of gossip and meaningless words—
> A fable that sounds like a feverish dream.
> Dost thou ask where thou liest when death sets thee free?
> Thou shalt lie where things lie that have not been born.[28]

In the *Traité sur la tolérance*, for example, the *philosophe* seems to be haunted by the wild beauty of these verses. The mere fact that ancient actors were permitted to declaim such statements on the stage, he asserts, is proof of Roman tolerance and their

---

[28] the translation is that of J. Wight Duff, *A Literary history of Rome in the silver age* (London 1964), p.214. Cf. *Troades* 378-381, 397-398, 402-408.

religious freedom (M.xxv.43). 'Deorum offensae diis curae; c'est aux dieux à se soucier des offenses faites aux dieux', Voltaire nostalgically reminds us (M.xxv.43). The same theme is repeated in a lively chapter of *Dieu et les hommes* (M.xxviii.155) and also in numerous letters[29]. It is brought up again in *De l'âme*. In the *Commentaire sur le livre des délits et des peines* it is a major idea: 'Nul peuple', Voltaire writes, 'ne fut plus religieux; mais il était trop sage et trop grand pour descendre à punir de vains discours ou des opinions philosophiques' (M.xxv.548).

Voltaire also drew on Seneca for several articles in the *Dictionnaire philosophique* (1764). Both 'Polythéisme' and 'Idolâtrie', for example, mention him. Voltaire speaks of ancient religion and the clear and lofty idea the Romans had of a supreme being before their simple faith had been corrupted by priestly imposters. The same idea is discussed in 'Idole'. The *philosophe* alludes to Rome and Greece in order more successfully to cast discredit on the church. As further proof of what he considers the unreliability of Christian tradition, he mockingly describes a series of letters said to have been exchanged between Seneca and st Paul ('Christianisme' and 'Paul'). The inference to be drawn from the observation that this 'correspondence' was spurious is easily recognized.

The anticlericalism of another article, 'Superstition', was also markedly influenced by Seneca. 'Mal' derives from the Stoic's *Epistulae morales*, celebrating as it does the notion of the sacredness of man to his fellow men—*homo res sacra homini*. It is an idea which Seneca had frequently expressed. 'Enfer' commends the religious tolerance of the ancient Romans and cites as evidence of this understanding the now familiar lines from Seneca's *Troades* (M.xviii.541):

> Le palais de Pluton, son portier à trois têtes,
> Les couleuvres d'enfer à mordre toujours prêtes,
> Les Styx, le Phlegéton, sont des contes d'enfants
> Des songes importuns, des mots vides de sens.

---
[29] Best. 11045, 15709, 15752, 15780.

VOLTAIRE AND SENECA

Voltaire also put to good use the Roman's *Naturales quaestiones*, one of the most frequently read books on the natural sciences in the middle ages, especially favoured by Roger Bacon. In a well known chapter on comets (VII.xxii)—a theme which for obvious reasons was to find great favour in the Enlightenment—Seneca had sought to discredit the false notions of earlier writers on that subject. He declared (II.cclvi) that speculative ideas must be subject to experimental verification and affirmed the beauty of disinterested research ('Quod, inquis, eris pretium operae? Quo nullum maius est, nosse naturam') and the boundless progress of reason.

The *Quaestiones*, Voltaire suggested, is a work in praise of empirical inquiry and the free discussion of scientific evidence (Seneca had indeed said[30] that he had written this work in order to free mankind from unfounded fears and from superstition). Various passages from this curious encyclopedia of ancient cosmology were to leave a mark on Voltaire's own *Lettre sur la prétendue comète* (1773), a work which harks back to Bayle's *Pensées diverses sur la comète*. Not unexpectedly, Voltaire's discussion of comets leads to an attack on obscurantism in general. Although he declares the Roman's theories on comets to be outmoded, he also shows that the latter's high moral purpose and devotion to truth cannot be questioned. Seneca had sought reliable data for his theories. He discarded hearsay and rumour and stated fairly the points of conflicting interpretations. His impartiality even caused him to reject the explanations of his own Stoic school when he found them wanting. Empiricism, then, is for Voltaire a powerful weapon against ignorance and superstition and Seneca is a prestigious witness to the rightness of that method[31].

Looking back on this history of Voltaire's indebtedness to Seneca certain features of it seem to emerge. Voltaire's attitude

---

[30] II.cclv. Cf. A-T iii.358-363.

[31] Seneca, Voltaire wrote, is to be honoured and praised for having realized that a time would come when people would be astonished at the ignorance of his own age. This idea is repeated in 'Cyrus', in the *Dictionnaire philosophique*.

towards the Stoics is not simple. He unquestionably admired their admonitions to live simply and in accordance with nature. He had harsh words, however, for their arrogance, their affected disdain for pleasure and honours. He associated early Stoicism (that of Zeno, for example) with Jansenism and the extravagant rigours a *philosophe* would despise. The lesson of teaching mankind to overcome the accidents of pain and sorrow could, in Voltaire's opinion, be a costly one. Such peace, he implied, was often achieved at the expense of life itself[32].

Seneca, though, was only nominally a Stoic. Influenced as he was by Epicurus and Lucretius, to say nothing of Democritus, he found much to criticize in the austerity of his Stoic predecessors. In many pages of the *Epistulae morales*, for instance, he takes them to task for their dogmatism and inhumanity: 'To enable yourself to meet death, you may expect not encouragement or cheer from those who try to make you believe, by means of their hair-splitting logic, that death is no evil. For I take pleasure, excellent Lucilius, in poking fun at the absurdities of the Greeks, of which, to my continual surprise, I have not succeeded in ridding myself. Our master Zeno uses a syllogism like this: "No death is glorious; but death is glorious; therefore death is no evil". A cure, Zeno! I have been freed from fear; henceforth I shall not hesitate to bare my neck on the scaffold. Will you not utter sterner words instead of rousing a dying man to laughter?'[33]

If the Stoics did not provide the *philosophes* with a complete attitude towards life, they did, among other things, however, introduce a principle that proved to be a turning point in the

---

[32] see, for example, the seventh *Discours* (1737), M.ix.421. 'L'Ecole de Zénon, dans sa fière ignorance, Prit jadis pour vertu l'insensibilité'. In *La Mort de César* Voltaire notes that Cato must have had a 'cœur d'airain' to have preferred death to that most precious of life's gifts, friendship. Stoics, the *philosophe* remarked on numerous occasions, were vain, even pompous. Cf. fifth *Discours*: 'Voilà votre portrait, Stoïques abusés; vous voulez changer l'homme et vous le détruisez' (M.ix.412).

[33] Seneca, *Epistulae morales*, lxxxii.9. Cf. lxxi.32. Another attack on the early Stoics may be found in Cicero, *De finibus*, iii.4.

history of ethical, political and religious thought—and one which was to have a remarkable career in the Enlightenment. This notion, Ernst Cassirer writes[34], was a belief in the fundamental equality of all men. Indeed, it was held that all good men, whatever their social or geographical position, were citizens of the same world. It was a concept to be developed by some of the more distinguished forerunners of the French Enlightenment and to be perfected in the *Encyclopédie*. 'Un honneste homme', said Cyrano de Bergerac, 'n'est ni Alleman, ni Espagnol, il est Citoyen du Monde et sa patrie est partout'.[35] Today's philosophers, Voltaire affirmed, are isolated, do not help each other, and die in misery. 'Ce n'était point ainsi qu'en usaient les stoïciens et les épicuriens: ils étaient frères, ils faisaient un corps; et les philosophes d'au-d'hui sont des fauves qu'on tue l'une après l'autre' (Best.12614).

Naturally drawn to classical thought, Voltaire came to Seneca through Horace, the chief influence in his early poetical career. Voltaire's youthful poems are decidedly Horatian in spirit. They have that mixture of moral commonplace, philosophic generalization and exhortation which we associate with the Roman poet. There are lines on the necessity to seize the present moment and the undesirability of caring too much for wealth. The young Voltaire advises resignation. It is a time when he is attracted to the theatre and to Seneca's plays. He is drawn not so much to their philosophic content as to their style, above all their connection with French classical theatre. By 1758 Voltaire has given up the aristocratic stance of the *Epîtres* to become a philosopher of action. *Candide* and the *Dictionnaire philosophique* are rich in references to Seneca. In the later years of Voltaire's life Seneca comes to stand for a philosopher of action. His *Troades*, for example, bears witness to his courage, to his hatred of superstitious fanaticism. A letter to mme Du Deffand begins, characteristically,

---

[34] *The Myth of the state* (New York 1955), p.126.
[35] *Lettre contre les frondeurs*, ed. La Chèvre, ii.280. See also Pierre Bayle's article 'Usson' in the *Dictionnaire historique et critique*: 'Je ne suis ni Français, ni Allemand, ni Anglais, ni Espagnol ... je suis citoyen du monde.'

with the *philosophes*'s favourite verses from the *Troades*, lines which had assumed an ever-increasing importance in Voltaire's mind. 'Le néant a du bon', Voltaire concludes, 'consolons-nous, nous en tâterons' (Best.11045). The *Naturales quaestiones* portrays Seneca as an enlightened advocate of reason and experimental truth. For those of the Enlightenment, these works indicate the Roman Stoic's far-sighted philosophical vision.

It might well be said that Voltaire was drawn to Seneca out of a love for philosophy and ethics. As Seneca adapted the teachings of Epicurus and Democritus from the Greek so did Voltaire accept the precepts of Seneca from the Latin. Although the Roman Stoic did not have for Voltaire the enduring pertinence he held for Diderot or Rousseau, he was, nevertheless, a noteworthy classical influence. 'Il faut du stoïcisme dans plus d'une occurrence', Voltaire wrote to Bertrand; 'mais je n'adopte des stoïques que les principes qui laissent l'âme sensible aux douceurs de l'amitié, et qui avouent que la douleur est un mal' (Best.5859). Seneca had advocated modesty, submission to the laws of nature and courage. He had thus helped provide Voltaire with the consolations of philosophy. With the passage of time this lesson was to stand him in increasingly good stead.

Aaron Hill's translation of Voltaire's Alzire

by Donald Schier

In all, Hill translated four of Voltaire's tragedies: *Zaïre (Zara)*, *Alzire (Alzira)*, *Mérope* and *La Mort de César (Roman revenge)*. The Parisian successes especially of the first two of these plays made them desirable theatrical properties and confirmed the general opinion that the plays were masterpieces and Voltaire the greatest genius of tragedy. Hill's flattery of Voltaire was probably in large measure the expression of his honest opinion: 'I found you born for no one country, by the embracing wideness of your sentiments; for, since you *think* for all mankind, all ages, and all languages, will claim the merit of your genius' (Best.1043). It is true that Hill later came to have a much less favourable opinion of Voltaire. He thought *La Mort de César* maligned the Roman emperor; and his English patriotism was outraged by the preface to Voltaire's *Mérope*, which denied to the English not only genius in painting and music but also in tragedy. However this disaffection was still in the future at the time of *Alzire*.

The translation was very hastily put together, as we learn from another passage of the same letter: 'I was already got to a *retreat*, in which I bury my town purposes, when, about three weeks since, the *French Alzira* was, first, sent down to me by my bookseller; and now the actors (perfect in their parts) are ready to begin its representation: this charge against myself I send you for two reasons; such a precipitation will excuse the *faults* in my own version, and convince you of my zeal to save you from duller'.

Hill's version was indeed 'acted on June 18, 1736, at Lincoln's-Inn-Fields, and had a run of nine nights'[1]—a respectable showing at that time. Dorothy Brewster says little about the merits of the translation, merely remarking that *Alzire* was translated 'rather more freely than the earlier play' *[Zaïre]* and that Hill occasionally improved on Voltaire (pp.146-147). Richard Cumberland, however, with true Regency gusto, damns the English version of the play completely: 'To naturalize a tragedy of this description became a matter of importance, and this task was undertaken and executed by Mr. Aaron Hill. Would that, for the credit of British taste and talent, it had fallen into better hands! It is pretty certain that it could not have fallen into worse; for whether we consider it as a translation, or as an adaptation to our stage, nothing could so ill have accomplished either purpose, as the puerile, bombastic thing produced by him under the name of *Alzira*; in which he has notoriously intermixed his own turgid insipidity, but has allowed all the spirit of his great original completely to evaporate'[2].

The first general impression the modern reader has of Hill's translation is that he has systematically obscured Voltaire's purpose in writing the play—a purpose clearly set forth in the *Discours préliminaire*: 'On a tâché dans cette tragédie, toute d'invention et d'une espèce assez neuve, de faire voir combien le véritable esprit de la religion l'emporte sur les vertus de la nature' (M.iii. 379).

Voltaire also wanted to show that the highest achievement of religion is to lead mankind to the deistic virtues of forgiveness and toleration, and in his play this dogmatic intent—broadened to contrast the clemency of true religion to the ferocity both of Zamore the man of nature and the Catholic Spaniards—is clearly the essential element. Ronald Ridgway[3] says: 'Tout porte à croire

---

[1] Dorothy Brewster, *Aaron Hill* (New York 1913), p.145.

[2] R. Cumberland, ed. *The British drama* (London 1817), vol.xiv, p.xii (*Alzira* is at pp.1-50).

[3] *La Propagande philosophique dans les tragédies de Voltaire* (Studies on Voltaire, xv: 1961), pp.104-105.

qu'en écrivant *Alzire*, Voltaire considérait sérieusement que le théâtre pourrait servir de temple à la nouvelle religion bâtie sur les ruines du christianisme ... avec *Alzire* la scène devient en quelque sorte une église; église déiste, où l'on prêche la bonne morale et adore le dieu de l'humanité'.

Hill cared more about the people, and more about the purely stagy qualities of the tragedy, than about the lesson of the play. He could not omit the religious argument, for it is built into the structure of the play; but he could and usually did minimize or distort it[4]. In act I, scene i, for instance, Voltaire begins by establishing the difference between the *conquistador* Gusman[5] and the virtuous Alvarez, who is his own spokesman in the play. As they discuss the principles upon which Spanish rule should be founded, Alvarez says:

> Ah! mon fils, que je hais ces rigueurs tyranniques!
> Les pouvez-vous aimer ces forfaits politiques,
> Vous, chrétien, vous choisi pour régner désormais
> Sur des chrétiens nouveaux au nom d'un Dieu de paix?
> Vos yeux ne sont-ils pas assouvis des ravages
> Que de ce continent dépeuplent les rivages?
> Des bords de l'Orient n'étais-je donc venu
> Dans un monde idolâtre, à l'Europe inconnu,
> Que pour voir abhorrer, sous ce brûlant tropique,

---

[4] the scene of the action is Peru. Don Carlos has succeeded his father, don Alvarez, as governor. He loves Alzira, who, with her father Ezmont, has been converted to Christianity. She however loves Zamor who, unknown to her, has been captured by the Spaniards. Alvarez frees the captives and discovers that it is Zamor who had saved his life. Zamor is determined to be revenged on Carlos whom he does not know to be Alvarez's son. Zamor and Alzira meet only after her marriage to Carlos. Zamor now learns that Carlos is the son of Alvarez whom he reveres; nevertheless he bursts into a council meeting and wounds Carlos. Alzira and Zamor are arrested. Carlos is carried in; with his dying breath he forgives Zamor, announces that henceforth the Indians will not be slaves but will be ruled by law, and gives Alzira to Zamor. Zamor is overwhelmed by this example of true Christianity.

[5] in Voltaire's text Carlos is called Gusman; Ezmont, Montèze; and Zamor, Zamore.

Et le nom d'Europe et le nom catholique?
Ah! Dieu nous envoyait, quand de nous il fit choix,
Pour annoncer son nom, pour faire aimer ses lois:
Et nous, de ces climats destructeurs implacables,
Nous, et d'or et de sang toujours insatiables,
Déserteurs de ces lois qu'il fallait enseigner,
Nous égorgeons ce peuple au lieu de le gagner.
Par nous tout est en sang, par nous tout est en poudre,
Et nous n'avons du ciel imité que la foudre.

This is not the complete speech; however if we make a careful examination of this fragment and of the corresponding English text it will become clear how Hill muffles Voltaire's message. Here is Alvarez's speech in Hill's English:

Away, my son, with these detested schemes!
Perish such politic reproach of rule!
Are we made captains in our Maker's cause,
 O'er these new Christians called to stretch his name,
His peaceful name! and shall we unprovok'd,
Bear murders which our holy cheats presume
To mispronounce his injur's altar's due?
Shall we dispeople realms, and kill to save?
Such, if the fruits of Spain's religious care,
I, from the distant bounds of our old world,
Have to this new one stretch'd a Saviour's name,
To make it hateful to one half the globe,
Because no mercy grac'd the other's zeal.
No, my misguided Carlos, the broad eye
Of one Creator takes in all mankind:
His laws expand the heart; and we, who thus
Wou'd by destruction propagate belief,
And mix with blood and gold religion's growth,
Stamp in these Indians' honest breasts a scorn
Of all we teach, from what they see we do.

HILL'S TRANSLATION OF *ALZIRE*

In length the two passages are very close: the translation is two lines longer than the original. However, in every line Voltaire is sharply focused and incisive where Hill is diffuse. For 'Les pouvez-vous aimer ces forfaits politiques', we have the nearly meaningless 'Perish such politic reproach of rule!' The next two lines of French become five remarkably inept English ones. The stretching of the name is a poor figure (to which Hill complacently returns a few lines later) and it is psychologically inconceivable that a Catholic and a Spaniard, even a deistic Spaniard like Alvarez, should refer to his priests as 'holy cheats'. This attack on Catholic priests is not in the French text at all; throughout the play Voltaire is careful not to make explicit the link between religious belief and the savagery of the Spaniards. Of course he often makes this and similar points elsewhere in his works, but such an attack uttered in this play would have created a scandal that would probably have obscured his real intention. So in his next two lines Voltaire again makes no mention of religious fanaticism while Hill is explicit in the rather Pope-ish line, 'Shall we dispeople realms and kill to save?' Voltaire's next four lines are rendered by five of fairly tortuous construction in Hill. Voltaire's straightforward couplet, 'Ah! Dieu nous envoyait, quand de nous il fit choix / Pour annoncer son nom, pour faire aimer ses lois' is not rendered at all. Instead we have the dubious figure of the creator's broad eye and a weak generalization. Finally Voltaire brings together blood-lust and the lust for gold and sets them up as opposite to the law of god. He finds the epigrammatic formulation, 'Nous égorgeons ce peuple au lieu de le gagner', and insists again on the un-Christian actions of the Spaniards: 'Et nous n'avons du ciel imité que la foudre'. In contrast, Hill's last five lines are weak and general. We 'Wou'd by destruction propagate belief' is perhaps not bad, but 'And mix with blood and gold religion's growth' is not only feeble but blurs the contrast which the whole speech is supposed to have made. The 'Indians' honest breasts' provoke incongruous images of a sturdy yeomanry and the Roast Beef of Old England, and there is a copybook platitudinousness about 'a scorn / Of all we teach from what they see we do' quite aside from the stylistic infelicities of the line.

A similar analysis could be made of any pair of fairly extended passages. Hill's text continually produces the same effect of heavy-footed diffuseness. The insensitiveness Hill shows in the case of the 'holy cheats' in the passage quoted, often reappears. When Voltaire uses the word *chrétien* in this play it is always in a serious and elevated sense; he never makes the word ironic as Hill does here (I.v):

ALZIRE
Qui peut se déguiser pourrait trahir sa foi;
C'est un art de l'Europe; il n'est pas fait pour moi.

ALZIRA
She who can hide her purpose can betray:
And that's a Christian virtue I've not learnt.

Where Voltaire, speaking of the marriage of Gusman and Alzire, imagines the heavenly host taking part in the ceremony like the angels in some Italian baroque painting (I.ii):

MONTEZE
Va, je crois voir des cieux les peuples éternels
Descendre de leur sphère, et se joindre aux mortels

Hill is Protestant, even Calvinistic:

EZMONT
Summon the reverend choir, prepare the rites.

Voltaire introduces a number of notes into his text to defend the factual correctness of certain statements. Thus in order to show that there are human qualities which unite all mankind Voltaire introduces into his play mention of an Indian legend (II.iv):

HILL'S TRANSLATION OF *ALZIRE*

ZAMORE
Souviens-toi du jour épouvantable
Où ce fier Espagnol, terrible, invulnérable,
Renversa, détruisit jusqu'en leurs fondements
Ces murs que du Soleil ont bâtis les enfants;

and underlines his intentions with this note: 'Les Péruviens, qui avaient leurs fables comme les peuples de notre continent, croyaient que leur premier inca, qui bâtit Cusco, était le fils du soleil.'

Hill omits the note as he omits them all, and obscures the purpose behind the mention of the legend:

ZAMOR
Bethink thee of the black, the awful day
When that vile Spaniard Carlos, curse the name!
Invulnerable or to sword or shame
O'erturned those walls, which time when young saw built
By earth attracted, children of the sun.

On the other hand Hill goes too far in converting Zamor at the end of the play. Again in a note, Voltaire specifically denies that the scene shows a miraculous conversion: 'Ceux qui ont prétendu que c'est ici une conversion miraculeuse se sont trompés. Zamore est changé en ce qu'il s'attendrit pour son ennemi. Il commence à respecter le christianisme; une conversion subite serait ridicule en de telles circonstances' (M.iii.435).

In keeping with this conception Zamore's answer to his enemy's noble gestures is carefully tentative (v.vii):

Je demeure immobile, égaré, confondu.
Quoi donc, les vrais Chrétiens auraient tant de vertu?
Ah! la loi qui t'oblige à cet effort suprême,
Je commence à le croire, est la loi d'un Dieu même.
J'ai connu l'amitié, la constance, la foi;
Mais tant de grandeur d'âme est au-dessus de moi;

51

Tant de vertu m'accable, et son charme m'attire,
Honteux d'être vengé, je t'aime et je t'admire.

In Hill's version the calculated tentativeness gives way to immediate conviction:

I stand immoveable—confused,—astonish'd!
If these are Christian virtues, I am Christian.
The faith that can inspire this gen'rous change,
Must be divine—and glows with all its God.
—Friendship, and constancy, and right, and pity,
All these were lessons I had learnt before.
But this unnatural grandeur of the soul
Is more than mortal; and out-reaches virtue.
It draws—it charms—it binds me to be Christian.
It bids me blush at my remember'd rashness:
Curse my revenge—and pay thee all my love.

The translation tends to be wordier than the French original. In part this was no doubt the result of Hill's choice of iambic pentameter blank verse as his medium, but it is the result of his effort not merely to translate but also to adapt the play. He usually tries to give a Shakespearean ring and a Shakespearean denseness to Voltaire's lucid alexandrines; the effect achieved, more often than not, is simply one of prolixity. This is what Cumberland called Hill's 'turgid insipidity', and an example of it occurs at the beginning of the fourth act where a five-line monologue spoken by Voltaire's Gusman becomes a fourteen-line tirade in English:

GUSMAN *(seul)*

Quoi! n'être point vengé!
Aimer, me repentir, être réduit encore
A l'horreur d'envier le destin de Zamore,
D'un de ces vils mortels en Europe ignorés
Qu'à peine du nom d'homme on aurait honorés...
Que vois-je! Alzire! ô ciel!

HILL'S TRANSLATION OF *ALZIRE*

D. CARLOS *(alone)*
And—must I coldly then to pensive piety
Give up the livelier joys of wish'd revenge?
Must I repel the guardian cares of jealousy,
And slacken every reign to rival love?
Must I reduce my hopes beneath a savage?
And poorly envy such a wretch as Zamor?
A coarse luxuriance of spontaneous virtue;
A shoot of rambling, fierce, offensive freedom;
Nature's wild growth—strong but unprun'd, in daring?
A rough, raw, woodman of this rugged clime;
Illit'rate in the arts of polish'd life:
And who, in Europe, where the fair can judge,
Wou'd hardly, in our courts, be call'd a man!
—She comes! Alzira comes! — unwish'd — yet charming.

This inflation is a usual procedure of Hill's: where Montèze's narrative (v.i) has twenty-four lines in Voltaire's text, Ezmont's has thirty-four in Hill's; Alzire's monologue (iv.v) has sixteen lines in Voltaire and twenty-four in Hill.

Hill also adapts by changing the manners of the play. The customs of the English stage, and those of society as well, sanctioned his making Voltaire's Zamore much more of a Hotspur than the original, and allowed Hill to put expressions into his mouth that would never have been tolerated on the other side of the Channel (ii.iv).

MONTEZE
Puisse-tu mieux connaître, ô malheureux Zamore,
Les vertus de l'Europe et le Dieu qu'elle adore.

ZAMORE
Quelles vertus! cruel! les tyrans de ces lieux
T'ont fait esclave en tout, t'ont arraché tes dieux.

This becomes:

EZMONT
May'st thou, unhappy Zamor, learn to know
And, knowing, to confess, in Europe's right,
Her gods should be ador'd, her sons obey'd!

ZAMOR
Obey'd! Hell blast 'em! — What, these sons of rapine?

An amusing example of this adaptation occurs in the recognition scene between Zamore and Alzire (III.iv). Voltaire has Alzire faint chastely into the arms of her *suivante*, Elmire, while Hill allows her to fall forthrightly into Zamor's.

When Hill adds lines to Voltaire's text, it is always with the intention of heightening the effect. Thus these verses of Zamor's (v):

> Yet he must die; my hand not err'd so far,
> But he must die; and when he does, my soul
> Shall snatch th'expected moment, hovering, watchful,
> And hunt him in revenge from star to star.

have no equivalents in French. Alzire's speech (v.v) is also completely changed by Hill, but here the reason is not very clear:

> Venge-toi, venge un fils, mais sans me soupçonner.
> Epouse de Gusman, ce nom seul doit t'apprendre
> Que loin de le trahir, je l'aurais su défendre.
> J'ai respecté ton fils, et ce cœur gémissant
> Lui conserva sa foi, même en le haïssant etc.

In English she says

> Wondrous old virtue! obstinately kind!
> Thou, singly just, amidst a race of thieves!
> 'Twere to be base as they are, could I stoop
> To deprecate a vengeance duly thine.
> For thy son's blood be mine the willing sacrifice.
> All I require is but escape from slander;

HILL'S TRANSLATION OF *ALZIRE*

> From poor suspicions of a guilt I scorn.
> Carlos, tho' hated, was a hated husband
> Whence even my hatred ow'd his life defence etc.

Certain of Hill's additions are not without poetic charm. Miss Brewster points out (p.147) the lines

> My taste of time is gone, and life to me
> Is but an evening's walk, in rain and darkness

which are authentic if minor poetry, and they have no source in Voltaire. So too Voltaire's lines (IV.iii)

> Fatigués de carnage et de sang enivrés,
> Les tyrans de la terre au sommeil sont livrés —

are more concrete and pictorial in Hill's English:

> Wearied by slaughter, and unwash'd from blood,
> The world's proud spoilers all lie hush'd in sleep.

Such improvement is by no means usual, however. While Hill can occasionally do better than Voltaire, more often he is much, much worse (IV.iv):

> Ce Dieu, ce destructeur des dieux de mes ancêtres
> T'arrachent à Zamore et te donne des maîtres?

> Shall gods, who rob the gods of our forefathers
> Shall these obtrude a lord, and blast a lover?

Or again (II.iv):

> [Que peuvent tes amis]
> Contre ces fiers géants, ces tyrans de la terre
> De fer étincelants, armés de leur tonnerre
> Qui s'élancent sur nous aussi prompts que les vents?

> How can thy naked, untrain'd warriors conquer?
> Unequally oppos'd to iron men:
> To woundless bosoms, coated o'er with safety!
> And arm'd with missive thunders in their hand
> That stream deaths on us swifter than the winds?

55

Hill made certain other alterations in Voltaire's play which are changes of form rather than changes of language. He follows English custom in ending each act with a rhymed couplet. He omits the French scene divisions at the entrance or exit of any important character, but, at least in the text of the *British drama*, each act is headed 'scene 1', although in no case is there a scene 2. In II.ii, when Zamore inquires about Montèze (Le verrai-je?) Hill includes Alzire (And shall I see 'em?). So also in Zamore's monologue (II.iii) Voltaire adds to the suspense before the forthcoming recognition scene by keeping Zamore uncertain as to whether Alzire is nearby. Hill does not; his Zamor knows (how?) that Alzire is with her father.

Voltaire was curiously non-committal about the fate of his plays at Hill's hands. He noted in the case of *Zaïre* the marked tendency on Hill's part to overdo certain scenes (Brewster, p.143, n.85). In a letter to Raynal written after the publication of Hill's very free adaptation of *Mérope* with its hostile Advertisement, he says wryly: 'Je connois de réputation Aaron Hill. C'est un digne anglois. Il nous pille et il dit du mal de ceux qu'il vole' (Best.3428). Although no comments of his on the play itself seem to have come down to us, Voltaire did express some dissatisfaction with the prologue and epilogue which he received separately (Best.1096). Presumably he was irritated by these lines in the prologue:

> 'tis Britain's claim,
> To hold no second place in taste or fame.
> In arts and arms alike victorious known
> Whate'er deserves her choice she makes her own.

Considering his very adequate knowledge of English, it is a pity that Voltaire has left us no critique of Hill's translation. It would certainly have been interesting to know whether Voltaire felt, as the present writer does, that Hill's principal unfaithfulness as a translator was not merely in the words but in the tone and emphasis of his English version.

HILL'S TRANSLATION OF *ALZIRE*

Hill's translation of *Alzire* is barely readable today—less readable, in the present writer's opinion than Voltaire's play. Shakespeareanized French tragedy is neither flesh nor fish. At least in Hill's hands it lacks much of the dignity, the economy and the discipline of classic tragedy. A few flowers of rather dubious rhetoric do not compensate for what is missing. Cumberland rightly said of Hill that he 'has allowed all the spirit of his great original completely to evaporate'. As it stands, *Alzira* is a good example of the subtlety of the relationships upon which the effect of a work of art depends. No one can be unaware of Voltaire's propagandistic intent, while Hill's English version, in which the changes are relatively few, produces very little of the same effect. His characters go through the same motions as Voltaire's; to a large extent they even say the same things; but the effect of the two plays is widely dissimilar. *Traduttore, traditore.* It does not seem useful to speculate on why Hill wrote what he did; probably the deist message seemed much less urgent in London than in Paris; undoubtedly too Hill himself was far less sensitive than Voltaire to the poetry of religion. In the end *Alzira* was not *Alzire*, and the play that Ridgway (p.102) describes as the essential document for an understanding of Voltaire's theatrical message became in English merely a standard bit of mock-heroic fustian.

Voltaire and Humphry Clinker

by E. T. Helmick

Any consideration of the work of Tobias Smollett must take into account the many kinds of writing he did during various periods in his life. His earliest work was in the picaresque novel, or perhaps more properly, the rogue romance[1]. A long middle period in his career was devoted to criticism, translation, and the editing and writing of history. And finally came *Humphry Clinker*, generally accepted as his masterpiece. One thing that books about Smollett have in common (aside from their dedications to Chauncey Brewster Tinker) is the insistence that his last novel is different in almost every way from its predecessors. Steeves (p.131) begins the analysis of Smollett's novels with the words, 'always excepting *Humphry Clinker*', and previous critics seem to agree that Smollett had developed by this time a more mellow attitude, a subtler wit, more interest in history and philosophy, less reliance on stock characters, and an ability to plot a complex story.

The reasons for this development are seldom given by critics; those who discuss the matter often find it a 'rare, unexpected, and inexplicable miracle'[2]. Knapp (p.321) says it is emphatically not this, but rather the 'logical culmination of the rich maturing of Smollett's art and personality'. He adds that this conclusion is obvious to anyone who reads Smollett's works with insight.

---

[1] Harrison Steeves, *Before Jane Austen* (New York &c., 1965), p.131.

[2] this is Lewis Knapp's summary of other critics' views in *Tobias Smollett* (Princeton 1949), p.16.

Louis Martz assigns a more specific cause: the years spent in compiling and editing history, he says, gave Smollett new approaches, made him more aware of political and economic conditions, and, most of all, improved the order and precision of his style. Another critic, Harrison Steeves (p.148), does not agree with Martz. According to him, the years between *Peregrine Pickle* (1751) and *Humphry Clinker* (1771) were spent in 'soul-destroying and unrewarded hack work'. Further, he warns that all of Smollett's fiction shows a highly complex inheritance.

Following this cue, without disregarding a degree of miracle or the benefits that can come from experience in writing and editing[3], I suggest that there was another influence at work on Smollett's writing—his translations of Voltaire. In many ways Smollett's later attitudes are similar to Voltaire's, and *Humphry Clinker* contains some parallels to *Candide*, in particular, that are worth noting.

Many of the similarities between Voltaire and Smollett, of course, raise no question of influence. Their earliest works of fiction, *Zadig* and *Roderick Random*, were published in the same year. Both were primarily vehicles for satire, and both sold well. The two authors were, in fact, the best-sellers of the time. And although critics debate whether either man ever developed a formal system of philosophy, they are certain that both adopted the ideas of the materialist psychology of the time, including, in Donald Bruce's words, 'Locke's evaluation of the effects of upbringing and worldly circumstance, Hume's informed scepticism, Hartley's study of the mechanics of emotion and conduct, Montesquieu's awareness of the force of climate and situation'[4]. Voltaire added English philosophy to his knowledge of French philosophy during his exile in England from 1726 to 1728;

---

[3] George Sherburn 'The Restoration and eighteenth century' in *The Literary History of England*, ed. A. C. Baugh *et al.*, p.963, offers another source for *Humphry Clinker*: the 'poetical epistles of the witty and popular *New Bath guide* by Christopher Anstey'.

[4] *Radical doctor Smollett* (Boston 1965), p.45.

VOLTAIRE AND *HUMPHRY CLINKER*

Smollett learned his materialist outlook from the faculty at the School of medicine in Glasgow, where everything was explained in the language of the new science (Bruce, p.23). With such basic similarities in background and philosophy, it is not surprising that the two men respected each other and that Smollett chose to spend four years translating and annotating the works of Voltaire.

This work was important to the study of Smollett for several reasons. First, it is in his notes to the translation that Smollett gives the only direct statement of many of his ideas. (His letters are about trivial matters.) In these notes, for example, he tells of his admiration for Hume, his scorn for the Cambridge neo-Platonists, and his approval of Voltaire's explanation of sensory perception. He says of this last idea that it is 'expressly the doctrine of Aristotle. The soul has no knowledge but that which it acquires through the senses'[5]. Comments on religion, too, are explicit: 'All the mischiefs of religious zeal are, we apprehend, deducible from the single doctrine of faith, implying that our eternal happiness or misery depends on our believing or disbelieving certain tenets, concerning which the faculty of reason cannot be exercised' (ix.81). Finally, during his work as Voltaire's translator, Smollett seems to have learned from one of the masters of prose style much that helped to make *Humphry Clinker* one of the masterpieces of English fiction[6].

Several new ideas and techniques in *Humphry Clinker*—not discoverable in *Roderick Random*—might well derive from Voltaire. The latter thought, for example, that external circumstances change man's temperament. In one passage he remarks that even the weather conditions man's state of mind, 'tant nous sommes machines, et tant nos âmes dépendent de l'action des corps' (xxii.19). And Matthew Bramble echoes in *Humphry Clinker*, 'I have perceived that my opinion of mankind, like mercury in

---

[5] *The Works of Voltaire* (Paris &c., 1901), xviii.141.

[6] this is George Sherburn's evaluation.

the thermometer, rises and falls according to the variations of the weather'[7].

In this last novel the basis for humour changes: in the earlier books, Smollett had used mostly humour of situation, almost invariably physical. Now he uses humorous characters and a much subtler ironic tone. Donald Bruce points out an anecdote at the end of *Humphry Clinker* that has 'all the guile and deadly surface innocence of Voltaire' (p.127). Lismahago, telling of the savages' rejection of the Christian religion, shows only their eminent reason. Not only Smollett's technique, but incident as well, may owe something to Voltaire here, especially to a scene in *L'Ingénu* in which a Huron Indian makes Christianity look foolish[8]. That Smollett agreed with Voltaire on the subject we know; he added a note to his translation that the church, particularly the medieval church, had retarded rather than advanced civilization. This is an important theme of *Candide*, of course.

Even more revealing than these general similarities are several specific passages from *Candide* which are paralleled in *Humphry Clinker*. In *Candide*, Martin tells of his supposed Socinianism, then discusses Manichean sects (Works, i.147) in Humphry Clinker (pp.198-199) Tabitha and Lismahago talk of the Athanasian creed, then of Indians who worship the great principles of good and evil. Lismahago is far more subtle and individual—an original, Smollett calls him—than the author's earlier caricatures. His comments on the political, religious, and social life of England recall the comments of Candide on the countries he visits. His account of the torture of Murphy by the Indians is much like the torture of Cunegonde by the Bulgarians in the fourth chapter of *Candide*. Both authors find racial distinctions during the travels of their heroes. Candide remarks that 'The natives of Europe seem to have their veins filled with milk only; but fire and vitriol

---

[7] *Humphry Clinker* (New York 1960), p.98.

[8] this story is retold in Will Durant, *The Story of Philosophy* (New York 1964), pp.210-211.

VOLTAIRE AND *HUMPHRY CLINKER*

circulate in those of the inhabitants of Mount Atlas and the neighboring provinces' (i.99). And Matthew Bramble writes, 'The spirit of rambling and adventure has been always peculiar to the natives of Scotland' (*Humphry Clinker*, p.277). Not only racial, but class characterization is common to both. However, for both a proper education can solve all the problems here. When Humphry Clinker is discovered to be the son of Matthew Bramble, much is made of the education he has had in spite of this former station; in *Candide*, the parallel is in Cacambo's remark dismissing the imaginations of 'persons who have not received a proper education' (i.120).

Perhaps, though, if translating the works of Voltaire effected any change in Smollett's writing, it was chiefly in his style. Voltaire's use of language is notable for its restraint and simplicity. In his prose romances, particularly, he shows to advantage his ironic style. And in *Candide*, says one critic, his style is closest to perfection: 'Voltaire never dwells too long on a point, stays to laugh at what he has said, elucidates or comments on his own jokes, guffaws over them, or exaggerates their form'[9]. Smollett has moved toward this style by the time of *Humphry Clinker*, creating a better novel than his others because his prose moves swiftly forward. A count of the words in the sentences on two pages in *Roderick Random* shows forty-four words to be the average; in *Humphry Clinker*, sentences average close to thirty words. Louis Martz thinks conciseness is significant: 'The generally recognized superiority of Humphry Clinker over the novels of the early period rests, I believe, in large part, on superior precision, economy, and clarity of style'[10].

It is imperative that we do not make too much of the comparison between the works of Smollett and those of Voltaire—or anyone else. Smollett is, most importantly, what he would have called an original. Even in his own time critics recognized that

---

[9] 'Voltaire', *Encyclopedia Britannica* (Chicago 1964), xxiii.251.

[10] *The Later career of Tobias Smollett* (New Haven 1942), p.16.

although Fielding, Richardson, and others had their imitators, Smollett was inimitable; by the same token, he is not derivative. But perhaps his studies of Voltaire helped him to come close to that finest satire which he described as 'the very essence of peevish Delicacy inflamed to a poetical Orgasm.[11]'

[11] *The Letters of Tobias Smollett*, ed. Edward S. Noyes (Cambridge, Mass. 1926), p.61.

Turgot et Vergennes contre la lettre de Voltaire à Boncerf

par J. Vercruysse

Le samedi 24 février 1776 le bourreau brûlait publiquement en vertu d'une sentence rendue la veille par le Parlement de Paris *Les Inconvéniens des droits féodaux*[1]. Dénoncé par le prince de Conti, cet ouvrage avait sévèrement été critiqué par l'avocat-général Séguier. Mandé et sommé de s'expliquer, l'éditeur Valade nomma le censeur et l'auteur: Pierre François de Boncerf[2].

Né à Chasaulx en 1745, le jeune homme avait fait ses études à Besançon avant d'entrer aux Finances. L'ayant remarqué, Turgot l'avait chargé d'un travail sur la nature du domaine et son aliénabilité. Ses vues sur la féodalité plurent au ministre qui le poussa à les publier. La disgrâce de Turgot entraîna celle de son commis: Boncerf se retira en Normandie. La Révolution le ramena dans la capitale; nommé officier municipal, il fut aussi chargé de l'administration des biens des Orléans. En 1792 Boncerf faillit être condamné à mort; il se retira alors à Saint-Cyran où il

---

[1] *Arrest de la cour de parlement* (23 février 1776). L'édition visée était celle portant les marques de Londres et Paris, Valade, de iv.70 pp. Deux autres éditions avec les mêmes marques comptent respectivement 48 et iv.72 pp. Citons encore celle de Londres de 72 pp., une autre sans mention de lieu et de date de iv.46 pp. et celle de 1791 comptant [iv].viii. 90 pp.

[2] cf. 'Préface historique' des *Inconvéniens* (Paris 1791), *Récit et réfutation de quelques calomnies* [1791], *Précis de la défense du citoyen Boncerf* (Paris an II), trois écrits de Boncerf; F. Delacroix, 'Le Procès de Boncerf en 1776', *Mémoires de la société d'émulation du Doubs* (1887), ii.328-348; C. Thuriet, 'Boncerf. Portrait historique', *Les Annales franc-comtoises* (1902), xiv. 219-238; etc.

mourut au début de 1794. A la suite de l'exécution de l'arrêt, une délégation du parlement se rendit à Versailles; le roi lui marqua sa satisfaction mais déclara que son désir était qu'il ne fût donné aucune suite à l'arrêt et le 4 mars il écrivit en ce sens au premier président[3].

L'attachement de Voltaire pour les réformes de Turgot est suffisamment connu pour qu'on s'y arrête ici. De Ferney, il fit connaître le 8 mars sa sympathie à Boncerf (Best.18839). Jusqu'ici il a été admis que cette lettre fut imprimée pour la première fois dans l'édition de Kehl (lxiii.200-201); la découverte de documents inédits nous oblige à reconsidérer cette opinion. Ils sont en effet formels sur ce point: la lettre de Voltaire à Boncerf a été *imprimée* peu après sa réception à Paris mais l'édition fut aussitôt retirée[4]. Elle circula néanmoins en manuscrit. M. Besterman possède une copie contemporaine qui fit partie des papiers Suard. La marquise Du Deffand écrit pour sa part à Walpole le 21 mars[5]: 'Je vais faire copier une lettre de Voltaire qu'il a envoyée à M. de Malesherbes, où vous verrez qu'il soutient bien son caractère; c'est à propos d'un arrêt du parlement qui a condamné au feu un livre intitulé, *Contre les droits féodaux*'.

Ladite lettre était accompagnée de cette curieuse 'Lettre de l'Editeur': 'Je m'empresse, Monsieur, de vous faire part de la charmante lettre de M. de Voltaire à notre digne patriote. Mon amour et mon zèle pour mon Roi et pour le sublime M. Turgot et pour ma patrie sont des devoirs qui m'engagent à la rendre publique, et je crois ne pouvoir mieux faire que de vous l'adresser; je ne doute nullement de votre exactitude et de votre vigilance

---

[3] on trouvera ce texte dans les *Œuvres* de Turgot, éd. G. Schelle (Paris 1923), v.271. Pour une relation des événements, cf. *Mémoires secrets* (Londres 1778), ix.58-60, 62-66, 68, et S. P. Hardy, *Mes loisirs ou journal d'événemens* (Paris, Bibliothèque nationale, MS.fr.6682, pp.178, 179, 183, 184, 186, 201 et 207).

[4] nous n'avons trouvé aucun exemplaire. Boncerf réimprima cette lettre en 1791 dans ses *Inconvéniens*, pp.78-79.

[5] voir les notes de Best.18839. Il faut évidemment lire 'Boncerf' pour 'Malesherbes'.

pour remplir mes vues qui je crois ne tendent qu'à graver de nouveau dans le cœur des vrais Français leur tendresse et leur amour pour notre jeune monarque, à chérir et à immortaliser M. Turgot et ajouter des lauriers de gloire à la couronne que M. de Voltaire a si noblement mérités. Je suis, Monsieur, etc. R.D.B.'

Nous ignorons si cette 'Lettre de l'Editeur' est de Boncerf lui-même, mais dans sa préface des *Inconvéniens* (Paris 1791) pp.iv-v, il s'est livré à quelques considérations fort intéressantes sur la lettre de Voltaire: 'Voltaire ne garda point le silence dans cette circonstance [l'affaire de 1776]: ce génie immortel, qui a tant contribué à préparer la révolution, écrivit un grand nombre de lettres à différentes personnes avec qui il étoit en correspondance, ainsi qu'à l'Auteur; elles sont imprimées dans la grande édition de ses œuvres; la plus étendue de ces lettres est sous le nom du R. P. Policarpe, Prieur des Bernardins de Chésery; on la joint ici, en déclarant cependant qu'elle fut faite sous les yeux de Voltaire par M. Christin, de Saint-Claude, actuellement Député à l'Assemblée Nationale, ami et convive habituel de Voltaire, et depuis son exécuteur testamentaire. On verra jusqu'à quel point il en avoit pris le style. Cet Ecrit, et plusieurs autres de la même main, ont été imprimés sous le nom de Voltaire, sans que le public se soit apperçu d'aucune différence de style'. Selon Boncerf donc la parternité de la *Lettre du révérend père Polycarpe prieur des bernardins de Chézery à m. l'avocat général Séguier* devrait donc être retirée à Voltaire et donnée à son fidèle correspondant Gabriel Frédéric Christin (1744-1799), ami et compatriote de Boncerf[6].

Meister inséra la lettre de Voltaire dans sa *Correspondance littéraire*[7]: elle connut donc une certaine publicité. Mais les ministres

---

[6] cette *Lettre* a été publiée pour la première fois, sans commentaires, dans l'édition de Kehl (xlix.362-369). Boncerf ne fait pas mention de l'*Autre lettre d'un bénédictin de Franche-Comté à m. l'avocat-général Séguier*. La supercherie a été signalée aussi par Weiss, *Biographie universelle* (Paris 1854), viii.233, et A. Robert, E. Bourloton et G. Cougny, *Dictionnaire des parlementaires français* (Paris 1891), ii.110.

[7] *Correspondance littéraire*, éd. M. Tourneux, xi.369-370.

se montrèrent particulièrement soucieux de prévenir une publication dans les gazettes de Hollande.

Les lettres de Turgot, Vergennes, Desnoyers et Boncerf sont intéressantes à plus d'un titre. Outre le fait qu'elles affirment clairement l'impression de la lettre et son retrait, elles révèlent l'appréhension de Turgot devant sa diffusion. Déjà en conflit avec le parlement[8], le ministre ne tenait pas, sans doute, à l'aggraver inutilement. Ensuite, il est amusant de voir comment les diplomates ont interprété les faits: entre la lettre de Turgot à Vergennes et celle du chargé d'affaires à La Haye aux principaux gazetiers hollandais, s'étend un monde de nuances fort curieuses. Enfin, nonobstant les nombreuses interventions et condamnations antérieures et même un certain discrédit qui avaient frappé ces gazettes, on constate qu'elles représentaient néanmoins une réalité dont il fallait tenir compte[9]. C'est dans cette perspective qu'il faut lire la lettre[10] de Turgot à Vergennes:

A Versailles le 21 mars 1776

Je sais, Monsieur, que vous avés bien voulu renvoyer au Sr Renet de Beaurepaire la copie imprimée de la Lettre de M. De Voltaire a l'auteur de la brochure sur les droits féodaux que ce jeune homme avoit fait imprimer par étourderie et dont il a heureusement retiré les exemplaires. Je vous prie d'en recevoir tous mes remercimens. Comme on pourroit bien tenter de faire insérer cette Lettre dans les Gazettes étrangères, je vous serois infiniment obligé de vouloir bien donner les ordres les plus précis pour l'en empêcher. J'ai l'honneur d'etre avec un tres parfait attachement, Monsieur, votre très humble et très obeissant serviteur

Turgot

---

[8] cf. E. Faure, *La Disgrâce de Turgot* (Paris 1961). Le 30 janvier le parlement avait ordonné la suppression de *Bénissons le ministre*; le 3 mai, *Le monarque accompli* subit le même sort.

[9] E. Hatin, *Les Gazettes de Hollande et la presse clandestine aux XVIIe et XVIIIe siècles* (Paris 1865), pp.96-101. Pour l'attitude de Voltaire, cf. notre 'Voltaire et la Hollande' (*Studies on Voltaire*, xlvi: 1966), pp.170-172.

[10] Paris, Ministère des affaires étrangères, Archives: Correspondance politique, Hollande 528, f.256.

LA LETTRE DE VOLTAIRE A BONCERF

Le ministre des affaires étrangères répondit le lendemain à son collègue, l'assurant que des instructions seraient données à l'ambassade de France à La Haye (f.258). Le 24, il écrit au chargé d'affaires, l'abbé Desnoyers (f.259): 'On a imprimé en dernier lieu à paris (biffé: en france), M, une lettre de m. de Voltaire addressée à l'auteur de la brochure sur les droits féodaux; mais l'editeur de cette lettre en a retiré tous les exemplaires en vertu d'ordres superieurs. Cependant comme il est possible qu'il en existe encore quelques uns ou qu'on en ait tiré des copies, et qu'on les ait fait passer à l'etranger (biffé: en hollande) pour les faire inserer dans les gazettes ou autres feuilles periodiques (biffé: feuilles publiques), vous voudrez bien prendre (biffé: faire toutes les démarches) toutes les précautions qui dépendront de vous pour empecher (biffé: prévenir la publication) cette insertion. je vous recommande trés particulierement cet objet, et vous voudrez bien me mander toutes les démarches que vous aurez faites pour le remplir avec succes'.

Six jours plus tard Desnoyers écrivait à son tour cette lettre aux principaux gazetiers (f.302):

Monsieur, à la haye le 30 mars 1776

Je suis chargé de prévenir la demande qui pourroit vous être faite d'insérer dans vos feuilles une Lettre de M. de Voltaire à l'auteur de la Brochure sur *les Droits féodaux*. Quelques Personnes qui possédoient cet Ecrit à Paris l'ont refusé à un Imprimeur, et se flattent qu'il restera entre leurs mains dans l'état où il est. Cependant la Crainte que quelques Copies ne pénètrent plus loin que Paris, m'engage d'après les Instructions que j'ai reçues, à vous prier, non seulement de me renvoyer ce qui vous parviendroit de semblable, mais encore de soustraire, par la sagesse de vos Conseils, les Libraires de votre connoissance, et qui doivent avoir en vous la même confiance que moi, au péril et au peu de profit de violer les Loix de la prudence particulière et de la Justice publique. Je vous aurai, Monsieur, une véritable obligation de contribuer ainsi à un Service que je crois rendre dans cette Occasion à plusieurs Personnes à la fois

J'ai l'honneur d'être avec une parfaite Considération, Monsieur, votre &c

Desnoyers.

Le 2 avril (ff.308-309) le chargé d'affaires pouvait assurer Vergennes que ses instructions avaient été suivies. Puisqu'il n'y avait pas eu de délit les pouvoirs publics n'avaient pas été alertés. Il ajoutait en post scriptum: 'La Lettre de M. Voltaire du 8 mars, Monseigneur, avoit effectivement été envoyée aux Gazetiers des différentes Villes de hollande. J'en ai la preuve dans la remise et l'Envoi qui m'en sont déja faits dans l'instant de la part de quelques uns d'entre eux que les autres imiteront. Votre Excellence connoit cette Lettre et l'a jugée, ainsi que tout ce qui peut y avoir politiquement trait'. Il ajoutait effectivement à sa réponse la copie d'une lettre adressée dès le 21 mars par Boncerf à Pierre Gosse, éditeur de la *Gazette de La Haye*, et remise donc par celui-ci à l'ambassade. Cette lettre[11] est connue (Best.18878). G. Schelle note à son sujet: 'Cette lettre fut communiquée à notre ambassade à La Haye et par elle aux libraires de la ville'. La lettre de Desnoyers à Vergennes infirme complètement ce propos. Boncerf agit de sa propre initiative, inspiré peut-être par Turgot. Pour compléter notre dossier nous donnons ici la lettre de Boncerf:

On a abusé de ma Confiance, Monsieur, pour prendre Copie d'une Lettre que m'a écrit M. de Voltaire le 8 de ce mois. On a poussé l'indiscrétion jusqu'à la faire imprimer. J'en ai été informé à temps, et j'ai fait enlever l'Edition; Néanmoins il est possible qu'il soit échappé à mes recherches quelques Exemplaires ou Copies. J'ai l'honneur de vous informer de ce fait et de vous prier de ne point donner place dans votre ouvrage à cette Lettre, si elle vous étoit adressée. Ce seroit aller contre l'intention de l'Auteur

---

[11] f.257; une autre copie figure dans la série France M.D.1882, f.116. C'est cette dernière qui a été publiée par G. Schelle (v.271) et m. Besterman; elle ne présente aucune différence notable avec celle qui figure dans la Correspondance politique.

et la mienne, et je puis vous l'assurer contre celle du Gouvernement.

Je suis avec un parfait dévouement Monsieur, Votre très humble et très obéissant serviteur   Boncerf

Mr Gosse Junior et fils à la Haye

Pour terminer, il nous reste à dire quelques mots sur l'attitude des autres gazettes hollandaises. Les *Gazette d'Amsterdam* et *Gazette d'Utrecht* se contentèrent d'une simple relation des événements (Suppléments aux nos. xix et xxii des 5 et 15 mars de la première; nos. 19, 21, 22, et Suppléments aux nos. 21, 22, 25 et 31 des 5, 12, 15, 16 mars et 12 avril 1776 de la seconde). Seul le journal de Leyde, les *Nouvelles extraordinaires de divers endroits*, rédigé par Elie Luzac, livra quelques commentaires très favorables à la brochure de Boncerf (nos 19, 20, 21, 22, 25, 30, 35 des 5, 8, 12, 15, 26 mars, 12, 30 avril).

Madame Denis et Ximenès ou la nièce aristarque

par J. Vercruysse

Si l'étude de nombreux écrivains qui vécurent dans l'entourage de Voltaire permet de mesurer l'influence qu'il a exercée sur leurs œuvres, elle met souvent au jour également des éléments biographiques nouveaux. Dans cette dernière perspective, nous voudrions évoquer ici un chapitre peu connu des relations de madame Denis et du marquis de Ximenès, en l'occurrence, la critique qu'elle fit d'une de ses tragédies, *Epicharis ou la mort de Néron*.

Né à Paris le 26 février (le 28 selon d'autres) 1726, Augustin Marie de Ximenès fut d'abord militaire: mousquetaire puis guidon de gendarmerie, il prit part à la bataille de Fontenoy et devint par la suite mestre de camp dans la cavalerie. Des raisons de santé et de fortune le poussèrent à vendre sa charge en 1747 et il se mit à écrire. Ami de la Clairon, il fit bientôt la connaissance de Voltaire, auquel, malgré quelques orages, il resta toujours attaché.

L'œuvre littéraire du marquis est assez diverse et quelconque: quatre tragédies, une dizaine de poèmes, des essais sur Racine et Boileau qui lui valurent les critiques de Prevost d'Exmes et de Cubières et une foule de petites pièces en tous genres. Malgré ses origines aristocratiques, Ximenès sut parfaitement s'adapter à tous les régimes politiques: 'doyen des poètes sans culottes' comme il se proclamait lui-même sous la Révolution, il rima aussi bien pour les Théophilanthropes que pour l'Empire et la

Restauration. Ximenès qui avait épousé en 1768 Angélique Jourdan, mourut à Paris le 31 mai 1817[1].

Ses contemporains l'ont jugé diversement. Autrèpe disait de lui, selon Chamfort[2], 'C'est un homme qui aime mieux la pluie que le beau temps, et qui, entendant chanter le rossignol, dit: ah! la vilaine bête!'. Beaumarchais, Ségur, Palissot, La Harpe[3] lui ont marqué quelque sympathie mais Mably le nomme le 'niais de Voltaire' (Correspondance littéraire, décembre 1782, xiii.234). Les auteurs du périodique, faisant écho aux propos de Diderot[4] l'accusent d'être un plagiaire, un aventurier, bête et malpropre (15 décembre 1772, x.125-126).

Voilà pour le personnage dont madame Denis s'éprit un moment, et pour lequel, malgré certains événements, elle garda longtemps quelque affection. De son aveu[5] nous savons qu'en 1755 elle était fort liée depuis dix ans avec la mère du marquis; cette amitié justifiait la présence du tragédien dans son entourage mais nous ne savons rien de leurs premières relations. Dans une lettre du 4 janvier 1751 à Darget (Best.3757), Voltaire fait état de bruits circulant à Paris au sujet d'un mariage possible entre sa nièce et le marquis. Remarquons cependant que dans le chapitre qu'il a consacré à la 'Conduite de madame Denis en l'absence de son oncle', Longchamp[6] qui fait allusion à ses liaisons avec un

---

[1] notice biographique (autobiographique dit Beuchot) dans les Additions et corrections au Dictionnaire des théâtres de Paris (Paris 1756), vii.746-747; J. M. Quérard, La France littéraire (Paris 1839), x.548-551; Nouvelle biographie générale (Paris 1846), xlvi.883-884.

[2] 'Caractères et anecdotes' Œuvres principales (Paris 1960), pp.160-161.

[3] Beaumarchais fut sensible à des vers élogieux (Correspondance littéraire, mars 1785, xiv.155-156), tout comme Ségur, Œuvres diverses (Paris 1819), pp.335-337; Palissot fut quelque temps en froid avec lui à propos de La Dunciade, mais lui réserva une notice élogieuse dans ses 'Mémoires sur la littérature', Œuvres complètes (Paris 1809), ii.471-482, v.437-439. Pour La Harpe, cf. A. Jovicevich, Correspondance inédite (Paris 1965), pp.96, 104, 107.

[4] Salon de 1765; Salons, éd. J. Seznec et J. Adhémar (Oxford 1960), ii.185. Cf. également sa notice sur don Carlos (A-T viii.430-438).

[5] Best.5781 (à Malesherbes, 25 août 1755).

[6] Mémoires sur Voltaire (Paris 1826), ii.299-307.

certain Griff, musicien allemand 'd'une stature colossale', un marquis gênois auquel elle doit 100 louis et l'envoyé de Frédéric, Hamont, ne parle point de Ximenès. Quoi qu'il en soit, les rumeurs d'un mariage persistent (Best.3945), fondées sur des visites fréquentes. Mais Voltaire reste sceptique dans sa lettre à Darget du 11 février 1752 (Best.4193).

Puis vint *Epicharis*. Transformant au gré de son imagination les historiens anciens[7], Ximenès tira de la vie de cette célèbre conspiratrice les éléments d'une tragédie qu'il soumit à l'examen de madame Denis et de son oncle. Dans la correspondance de 1751 (13 mars, mai et juin-juillet, Best.3832, 3879 et 3927), on trouve des allusions à l'envoi d'une tragédie à Berlin. Mais il faudra attendre un an avant que Voltaire ne s'explique clairement: 'Vous m'annoncez', écrit-il à Ximenès le 29 août 1752, 'une nouvelle qui me fait grand plaisir. Vous allez croire que c'est du duc de Foix que je veux parler. Point du tout, c'est de Neron. Je suis bien plus flatté pour l'honneur de l'art, que vous vouliez bien être des nôtres, que je ne suis séduit par un de ces succez passagers dont le public ne rend pas plus raison que de ses caprices. Honorez votre confrairie de votre nom, montrez que les français vont à la gloire par tous les chemins. Il y avait des vers extrêmement beaux dans votre ouvrage. Plus votre génie s'est développé, et plus vous vous êtes senti en état de bâtir un édifice régulier avec les matériaux que vous amassez. Je souhaite me trouver à Paris quand vous gratifierez le public de votre tragédie'[8].

Epicharis ou la mort de Néron fut représentée au Théâtre français le 2 janvier 1753 (*Mercure de France*, février 1753, p.180). La

[7] Tacite, *Annales*, xv.51, 57; Dion Cassius, *Historia romana*, lxii.27; Polyaenus, *Strategemata*, viii.62. Gabriel Legouvé (1764-1812) fit représenter le 15 pluviôse de l'an II (3 février 1794) *Epicharis et Néron*, tragédie qui ne présente aucun rapport avec celle de Ximenès.

[8] Best.4374. Les *Mémoires secrets* (11 février 1762, i.44) qui n'apprécient guère le marquis, ajoutent: 'On a longtemps cru que M. de Voltaire retouchoit les ouvrages de M. de Ximenès'.

pièce, nous apprend la notice déjà citée des *Additions*, 'fut jouée sans indulgence et sans retour. Le Parterre trouva le rôle de Néron trop fort, & les autres trop foibles. L'Auteur fut de l'avis du Parterre & voua la pièce à l'oubli: elle n'est point imprimée'. Plus d'un demi-siècle plus tard, Ximenès en publia un très court fragment, la première scène de l'acte II, et la lettre de Voltaire dans un *Choix de poésies anciennes ou inédites* (Paris 1806), pp.18-21. Les critiques sont fort rares. Les journaux ne firent pas mention de la tragédie; madame Denis se contenta d'une remarque laconique dans sa lettre du 8 janvier à Chenevières (Best.4514): 'Le marquis de Chymene a fait une belle culbute'. Voltaire garda un silence prudent. L'unique jugement quelque peu étendu que nous connaissions est une *Lettre à monsieur F**. sur la tragédie d'Epicaris* (Paris 1753, 22 pp.) adressée à Fréron par l'obscur Sébastien Gazon-Dourxigné.

Selon l'auteur, cet échec prouve, une fois de plus, que souvent 'un obstacle invincible pour réüssir en tout genre' est le résultat du mérite. Cependant, '*Epicaris* n'est pas une excellente tragédie; mais il s'en faut bien qu'elle soit aussi faible que des gens mal intentionnés ou des esprits prévenus voudroient le persuader. Les vrais connaisseurs dont le suffrage est preferable à celui de la multitude, lui ont rendu plus de justice; & pour prouver qu'elle en est digne, il me suffira, Monsieur, de vous en rappeler le précis Scene par Scéne' (p.5). C'est ce qu'il fait en citant de mémoire ci et là quelques vers; aucune appréciation si ce n'est dans la conclusion: 'si la tragédie d'*Epicaris* est défectueuse à quelques égards, c'est plutôt par le choix du sujet qui est presque intraitable, que par la manière dont elle est conduite, ou par la poësie du stile. Quant aux caractères, il faut avouer qu'ils ne sont pas tous d'une égale force.... La versification est la partie la mieux traitée: elle est presque toujours élégante, pure, poëtique, harmonieuse; & si ce brillant coloris eut été repandu sur un meilleur fonds, l'ouvrage, malgré la cabale, auroit infailliblement réussi' (pp.19-20). Au reste, le mérite de la brochure de Gazon-Dourxigné ne consiste pas dans l'expression de l'avis d'un homme de lettres par ailleurs fort médiocre, mais bien dans le résumé de la pièce; elle est de plus notre unique source complète.

L'échec de cette tragédie n'entama cependant point les bonnes relations de la nièce et du militaire homme de lettres. Ainsi, lorsque celui-ci songe à poser sa candidature à l'Académie, encouragé et appuyé par Voltaire (Best.5228, 5241, 5243), madame Denis écrit de Colmar à Thibouville le 27 août 1754 (Best.5268): 'j'en serais fâchée. Ce serait une seconde imprudence. Si j'étais à Paris, je ferais l'impossible pour l'en empêcher'. Installé un an plus tard à Prangin, Voltaire envoie au marquis les 'plus sincères compliments' de sa nièce (Best.5419). Mais un événement malencontreux allait compromettre, du moins pour un certain temps, ces bonnes relations.

Madame Denis avait constaté la disparition d'un manuscrit de l'*Histoire de la guerre de 1741* confié à sa garde. Aussitôt elle accuse Ximenès de l'avoir volé: 'J'ai cru Chymène un insencé, mais non pas un fripon à pendre', écrit-elle à Argental le 24 août 1755 (Best.5779). Affirmation gratuite répétée le lendemain dans trois lettres (Best.5781, 5782, 5783). Voltaire ne l'apprend que le 6 septembre (Best.5803). Pendant ce temps, mis au courant des graves accusations lancées contre lui, Ximenès entreprend de se justifier. Il écrit à madame Denis une lettre dont le texte est malheureusement perdu; mais on connaît cependant la teneur par une lettre de Voltaire à Argental en date du 10 (Best.5814): 'Et que pensez vous de la belle lettre de Chimène à madame Denis? et de la manière dont ce misérable ose parler de vous? Touttes ces horreurs, touttes ces bassesses, touttes ces insolences sont elles concevables?' Mais le même jour, Voltaire écrit à Thieriot (Best.5817) que Ximenès n'est pas l'auteur du vol; il pourra se disculper d'une 'accusation si odieuse'. Cependant il maintient ses premières déclarations dans la lettre qu'il écrit le 12 à Argental (Best.5822). Pressenti pour une enquête, Malesherbes avait déjà fait savoir (Best.5794) qu'il ne disposait d'aucune preuve contre Ximenès, propos qu'il confirmera à madame Denis le 21 septembre (Best.5847). Le rapport de l'inspecteur

Hémery adressé à Berryer le 30 août[9] ne mentionne même pas le marquis.

Finalement le rôle de Ximenès s'était limité, selon Voltaire, à savoir 'comment ces mémoires informes et défigurez ont été imprimez en partie' (Best.6050). L'incident était clos. Beuchot, dans sa notice que nous avons déjà citée, affirme que pour le prix de sa rentrée en grâce, le marquis aurait accepté de laisser imprimer son nom au bas des *Lettres sur la Nouvelle Héloïse*. Il écrivit la première et la dernière ligne de la première lettre sans plus. Ximenès jouit à nouveau de l'estime de l'oncle et de la nièce: les lettres des 30 décembre 1761 et 28 février 1762 (Best.9444, 9554) qu'elle écrivit à Lekain ne permettent pas d'en douter. Puis, au fil des années, les relations avec madame Denis iront en s'amenuisant sans perdre cependant de leur affabilité. Dix ans plus tard, Voltaire présentera encore les compliments de sa nièce (25 septembre 1772, 15 octobre 1773; Best.16868, 17497).

Chose curieuse, vers la même époque les auteurs de la *Correspondance littéraire* (15 décembre 1772, x.125) félicitaient madame Denis d'avoir échappé deux fois au 'péril' d'un mariage avec Ximenès dont le seul but était, selon les auteurs, de capter l'héritage du vieil oncle. Propos gratuit qui s'insère parfaitement dans le ton méchant que le périodique ne cessa de tenir contre le marquis.

Voyons maintenant le rôle d'aristarque joué par madame Denis à propos de la tragédie de son soupirant. Ses notes autographes[10] sont de deux sortes: des corrections du texte et des remarques d'ordre général. Ces dernières peuvent se ramener aux points suivants: l'intérêt du spectateur doit être ménagé par le développement continu des caractères et des faits. En ce sens, il convient de bien lier les scènes, d'éviter les invraisemblances et

---

[9] M.xv.151-152. Cinquante ans plus tard, Collini maintenait la thèse du vol sans toutefois nommer le marquis; *Mon séjour auprès de Voltaire* (Paris 1807), p.152. E. Ritter, 'Le Marquis de Ximenez, Voltaire et Rousseau', *Annales de la Société Jean-Jacques Rousseau* (Genève 1916-1917), xi.195-200.

[10] Bibliothèque nationale, N.acq.fr. 24344, ff.1-12. Texte calligraphié de l'acte I et des scènes 1 à 3 de l'acte II.

inconvenances de caractère et de situation. Les personnages doivent être nobles et l'on évitera d'accorder trop d'importance aux personnages secondaires. Enfin, la passion dominera dans les propos; le romanesque, la froideur et les inutilités seront proscrits. Ces principes de la nièce, est-il besoin de les souligner, reflètent fidèlement ceux de l'oncle[11].

Ces judicieux conseils furent-ils écoutés? Pour répondre à cette question nous ne disposons que du résumé de Gazon-Dourxigné et de la scène publiée par Ximenès en 1806. Leur examen permet toutefois de constater que le texte du manuscrit a été modifié considérablement. Ainsi, par exemple, Ximenès a fondu en une seule les scènes 1 et 2 de l'acte I de la version manuscrite. En supprimant dans cette même version la scène 3, l'auteur est allé plus loin que le conseillait madame Denis. La comparaison des textes de la scène 4 (MS) devenue la deuxième à la scène, montre que la critique a été suivie: l'intervention d'Epicharis dans la discussion qui oppose Pison et Thraseas (qui a remplacé Rutile), relève considérablement la scène et elle permet d'éviter de la sorte les écueils justement signalés par madame Denis. C'est cette scène que Ximenès a publiée en 1806 mais il la situe au début du deuxième acte. Au reste, la confrontation des vers cités par Gazon-Dourxigné et ceux de 1806 montre que celui-ci a modifié et poli son texte par la suite, peut-être en vue de la publication.

Enfin, la scène 5 du manuscrit, qui terminait le premier acte, a disparu également. Là encore, devant l'ampleur des critiques, l'auteur a dépassé les intentions de son aristarque en éliminant ces répliques d'ailleurs durement jugées. Ximenès ajouta un monologue d'Epicharis, méditant sur les moyens d'éviter à Drusus un parricide, sans lui découvrir sa naissance (il est le fruit des amours de Néron et d'Epicharis), ni trahir les Romains. C'était, on ne peut plus, entortiller les faits.

L'examen de la première scène du deuxième acte telle que la rapporte le résumé montre que le marquis a maintenu l'essentiel

---

[11] R. Naves, *Le Goût de Voltaire* (Paris 1938), pp.260-294.

du fond et de la forme de sa version manuscrite. Par contre, de nombreuses modifications de texte ayant été suggérées pour la scène suivante, et Gazon-Dourxigné ne citant aucun vers, la confrontation est impossible; le déroulement des faits n'a subi aucun changement.

Enfin, nous dirons que la scène 3 du manuscrit a été modifiée et reportée au début du quatrième acte; Ximenès a augmenté la scène 2 d'un monologue de Poppée qui déplore les rigueurs de son sort et de Néron. En résumé, nous constatons donc que dans l'ensemble Ximenès a entendu et suivi les critiques de madame Denis, et qu'il les a dépassées plus d'une fois. Il est impossible de juger dans quelle mesure l'auteur a tenu compte des critiques de style puisque nous ne disposons que d'un résumé et peu de textes.

Nous reproduisons ici le texte des notes autographes de madame Denis tel quel. Nous l'avons ponctué là où son intelligence s'avérait difficile. Afin d'éviter les longueurs, nous avons résumé les passages qui n'ont donné lieu à aucune remarque; les mots imprimés entre parenthèses sont biffés sur le manuscrit.

Nous commencerons par cette remarque liminaire et générale: 'Ordinairement, on commence par mettre une tragédie en prose avant de la mettre en vers, c'est ainsy qu'en usoit le celebre Racine, mais on a commencé au contraire par mettre celle-cy en vers [prose] et l'on ne la presente aujourd huy en prose, que pour qu'on juge plus aisement de la conduite de cet ouvrage; on a voulu le destituer de ces agrements qu'on doit a la poësie, qui eblouissent quelque fois et qui par là ressemblent asses a ces feux qui n'eclairent que pour conduire dans le precipice'.

Le rideau s'ouvre sur un monologue d'Epicharis: elle crie sa colère contre Néron qu'elle hait après l'avoir aimé. Cette première scène ne soulève aucune critique. C'est dans la scène suivante, qui réunit l'héroïne et sa confidente Phénice, qu'apparaissent les premières corrections. Epicharis révèle ses désirs de vengeance; Phénice s'en prend à Poppée, ce qui lui vaut cette réplique:

MADAME DENIS ET XIMENES

'La fille d'Othon n'est point l'objet de ma haine. Je ne puis ni envier son sort, ni la punir de mes maux: ceux qu'elle endure peut-être, m'en vangent assez. Ce n'est point sur elle que doivent tomber mes coups: c'est Néron seul qu'il faut immoler (tu ne connois pas encore tous ses crimes: apprends tous mes malheurs Phénice. ... Nous fumes tous deux unis par un secret hymenée: Néron impatient alloit le publier), lorsque sa mere luy ouvrit les routes du trone (des Cesars), en forçant Claude de lui donner sa fille. Je me sacrifiay moi même à ses intérêts[12], a ceux de sa grandeur future que présageoit mon amour, & qu'avoit préparée l'artifice d'Agrippine. Je consentis à un hymen qui promettoit à mon amant l'Empire du monde[13]: ... Neron seul me suffisoit ... Je dédaignai l'Univers[14]. Satisfaite du cœur de l'ingrat qui m'abandonne, contente de la foi qu'il m'avoit jurée, (et qu'il viole), heureuse alors[15] par l'espérance de voir un jour mon fils couronné par son pere devenir l'appui du Trone des Cesars[16] ... conçois l'excès de ma douleur et de ma honte ... Octavie n'est plus ... Neron me trahit ... il épouse Poppée ... et je pourrois endurer qu'il plaçât sans crainte sa nouvelle amante dans un rang qui m'étoit si bien dû! Et je laisserois mon fils privé pour jamais des droits de sa naissance[17], ramper loin du Trone et de sa mere! ... Dans un état, puis je[18] vivre un seul instant, et vivre sans être vangée? ô mon fils! sans l'amour qui m'attache à toi, je rougirois de voir encore la lumiere'.

Cette tirade lui paraissant trop longue, madame Denis l'interrompt par cette remarque de Phénice: 'Vous me faites fremir

---

[12] madame Denis note entre les lignes: 'cela est trop sec, il faut de la passion et surtout de la chaleur'.
[13] idem: 'tout cela est trop sec et trop froi'.
[14] idem: 'elle couchoit donc avec lui depuis ce mariage rompu; on ne sinteresse point a une catin'.
[15] idem: 'je vous dis quelle couchoit avec lui et je ne le veux pas'.
[16] idem: 'elle ne doit point parler la de son fils ce nest pas sa place'.
[17] idem: 'fi la vilaine de vouloir monter sur le trone dun monstre qui vient de tuer sa femme pour laisser la place libre'.
[18] idem: 'linteres qu'on prendra a Epicaris dans le reste de la piece depand de cette'.

dans quels dangers Mme allez vous vous plonger? ah fuiez plus tot un ingrat.' Madame Denis fait enchaîner par Epicharis:

'moi fuire? non fenice, et sil faut que je meurs, je veux du moins expier le crime davoir aimé neron (ce monstre) en delivrant rome de sa barbarie tu ne connois pas a quel point il moutrage; mon secret peut seul me justifier a tes yeux, et je n'ai plus la force de te le cacher. je fus unie a Neron par un secret himenée; dans ce temps il etoit vertueux, son amour impatient alloit le publier lors qu'Agrippine sa Mere lui ouvrit les routes du trone en forçant claude de lui donner sa fille. juge des combats qu'eprouva ma tendresse; il faloit renoncer a mon epoux pour jamais, ou ne le conserver quand lui fermant le chemin du trone; perdre ma gloire, ou nuire a la siene. lamour que jus pour lui lemporta sur mon embition. je lui rendis ses sermens, je me servis de lempire que javois sur son coeur pour le [pr]ier daccepter la main doctavie, enfin je sacrifiai tout a sa grandeur, trop heureuse de faire regner sur le monde lobget qui regnoit sur mon coeur; je me livrois (du moins) donc a la douce esperence de meriter du moins la confiance et lestime de lamant que jadorois, (au prix de tant damour il me banit, moutrage; un amour effrené le porte à immoler octavie pour mettre poppée sur le trone et sans doute pour me braver davantage [un mot illisible] et tu pourois encor topposer a ma vengence,) ah comme je fus trompée, autrefois lamour de la terre, le cruel en est devenu leffroi. victimes de sa fureur, sa mere et son frere nont pu lassouvir. pour prix du trone quil tient doctavie, il vient encor de limmoler et sans doute pour me braver davantage (encor). non contant de moutrager et de me banir, son amour effrené y place poppee; ah mon fils sans lamour qui mattache a toi je rougirois de voir encor la lumiere'.

Le déroulement ultérieur de la scène n'est pas critiqué. Nous noterons toutefois les remarques suivantes, d'abord ces retouches à une réplique de Phénice: 'Que dites vous, Madame, et quel peut être ce fils (qui m'est encore inconnu? quel est son sort?)? pourquoi un mistere si profond nous en a t'il jusqu'ici derobé la connoissance? Neron vous a t'il paru redoutable a son sang meme? Le poursuivroit il enfin?. . .' Ensuite à la réponse d'Epicharis, dont voici le texte primitif:

'Il ne le connoit point. Ma douleur se plait à déposer mes secrets dans ton sein: ton amitie la partage et l'adoucit: apprens toutes mes infortunes.

Mon fils[19] fut elevé à Sparte. Je confiai son enfance et le secret de ses jours à Probus: J'attendois que Neron devenu Maitre du monde, et fidèle à sa promesse lui rendit son nom et ses droits; quand la fureur d'Agrippine, par un coup de sa politique sanglante, voulut perdre ce fils encore méconnu. Sa fureur fut vaine, et Probus déroba la victime au fer des assassins trompés qui furent eux mêmes, bientôt après, punis d'un crime qu'ils n'avoient point achevé. Mon fils survêquit à leur rage qu'éprouva le fils de Galba. Mon fils luy même, depuis ce tems, sous le nom de Drusus, chéri de Galba qui se croit son père, devient sous mes yeux, sa plus chere esperance, celle de Rome et la mienne.'

Sur le manuscrit cette tirade est biffée verticalement et madame Denis l'a refaite dans la marge:

'il ne le connois pas, mon fils fut elevé a Sparte. notre hymen secret nous obligea de cacher ce gage de notre amour. nous confiames tous deux son enfance a probus dans le dessein de le rappeller un jour pres de nous. (quand nous pourions declarer notre hymen) espoir vin et trompeur. Octavie presante un trone a Neron, ma tendresse pour lui le force d'y monter, elle eut sa main, phenice, mais je possedois encor son cœur. Neron me jura mille fois de faire monter un jour ce fils au trone des Cesars.

privée de mon epoux, eloignée de mon fils, la certitude detre toujours aimée de Neron me consoloit de voir octavie sur le trone, et celle de voir un jour regner mon fils me remplissoit de joie. quand tout a coup une fureur secrete qui sans doute venoit dagrippine[20] voulut perdre cet enfant encor inconnu; peut etre cette femme (craignoit elle) embitieuse craignoit elle quil ne me

---

[19] idem: 'il ne le connoit point'.   [20] cette proposition est entre parenthèses dans le texte.

donna trop dempire sur le coeur de neron. quoi quil en soit des assassins cruels furent envoiés pour immoler mon fils. probus qui laimoit, voulant scauver la victime leur livra le fils de galba. cet enfant elevé pres du mien perit de la main de ces barbares; et mon fils survequit a leur rage. ces cruels trompés furent eux memes punis d'un crime quils navoient point achevés. mon fils depuis ce temps elevé sous le nom de drusus, chery de galba qui se croit son pere, devient sous mes yeux sa plus chere esperance, celle de Rome, et la miene.'

Plus loin, les propos de Phénice et d'Epicharis ont également été remaniés; voici pour la confidente: 'Par quel motif secret que je ne puis concevoir, (Neron n'estil pas informe du) (navez vous pas informê Neron du) sort de son fils?' En regard, madame Denis a abrégé la question: 'par quel motif secret'. La réponse d'Epicharis telle que la donne Ximenès est biffée de trois traits; en voici le texte: 'Vingt fois j'ai voulu l'en instruire: vingt fois ma frayeur plus forte m'a fermé la bouche. J'ai vu Néron courir dans la carrière des crimes, s'en applanir les chemins, démentir ses premieres années, m'ôter son cœur enfin ... J'ai craint de parler alors ... Aujourd'hui je crains d'ôter à mon fils une erreur qui doit lui être chere. Je crains de lui apprendre quil est mon fils, et que Neron est son pere: je crains surtout de perdre, en le recouvrant, l'appui de Galba'.

Résumons la suite: l'héroïne fait l'éloge de Galba et souligne l'opportunité qu'il y a de garder le secret pour Drusus. Notons deux corrections minimes: madame Denis a biffé un terme qualifiant l'ambition de Galba et a remplacé 'sang' par 'fils'. En fait, cette réponse a été refaite comme la précédente par la nièce de Voltaire: 'probus lexigea de moi; il sentit qu'une puissance inconnue vouloit la mort de mon fils, et que si sa perte etoit resolue il ne pouvoit une seconde fois le garentir du trepas. pour concerver cet obget si cher a mon coeur, il me fit encevelir ce mistere dans le secret le plus profond, et neron crut que mon fils netoit plus. (je m'y pretai dautant) pouvais je le detromper lors que ce barbare oubliant tous mes bienfaits, sapplanissoit deja le chemin du crime, dementoit ses premieres années, enfin m'otoit son coeur pour adorer poppée dont il est abboré; dans letat terrible ou ma reduit le sort jai cru devoir epargner a drusus la peine de partager les douleurs de sa Mere, et de ne voir qu'avec orreur le sang dont il est né; jai craint surtout en lui decouvrant sa naissance de perdre lappui de galba, ce romain incorruptible &'.

Un signe renvoie alors au texte de Ximenès et une note ajoute: 'jusqua la fin de la scene'. La scène s'achève sur une question de Phénice: Epicharis ne craint-elle pas les soupçons, et leurs conséquences, de Néron? L'héroïne répond qu'il y a encore des Romains vertueux tels que Pison et Rutile qui lui prêteront leur concours pour accomplir ses desseins.

La scène 3 fait d'abord l'objet d'une appréciation générale: 'Vous dites dans la scene precedante que galba est un des principaux chefs de la conspiration et vous n'en dites pas un seul mot dans cette scene cy; je ne puis me preter a cela: il me semble que pison dit beaucoup des grands mots qui ne signifient rien. il ne compte pas conspirer au commencement de la scene, il sy determine a la fin et je ne scai pour quoi. Si epicaris lui disoit que galba a une armée, quil comande les gardes de neron, et quil sera a la teste des conjurés, laction commenceroit a se developer et pison auroit un motif (une raison) valable pour prendre la resolution de faire perir neron plus tot quil ne comtoit. deplus ne pouvant parler de drusus, galba dans cette scene tient sa place et vous ne devez pas perdre une minute se personage de vue. du reste epicaris et pison ce font tous deux de tres beaux complimens (qui me font songer) comme la pucelle et dunois[21]: retranchez les. cela est bon dans st real[22] mais déplacé et froid dans une tragedie'.

En effet, Epicharis et Pison se font des compliments sur leur civisme; elle engage Pison à se révolter contre Néron. Deux phrases ont été supprimées dans sa tirade; le texte biffé est illisible.

---

[21] allusion au chant iv (M.ix.75-92).
[22] ce point de vue est également celui de Voltaire déjà exprimé dans une lettre du 6 janvier 1736 à Olivet (Best.946). Par la suite, l'oncle ne cessera de répéter ce jugement: cf. M.xiv.131; Best.3928, 4240, 6902.

Pison reconnaît qu'Epicharis joue un rôle déterminant dans la rébellion, et il se prépare à prendre ses dispositions. Ces propos terminent la scène 3. Un 'Retrouvez vous icy' a été remplacé par 'rejoignons nous'. La scène 4 qui met en présence Rutile et Pison est précédée d'une remarque générale: 'le premier deffauts de cette scene est detre entre deux personages subalternes, il faut donc quelle ne soit que scene de passage, cest la p^{ere} regle du theatre. rutile qui offre le trone a pison petit personage dans la piece fera rire jen suis sure, puisque cest epicaris, galba et drusus qui sont les grands conjurez et sur qui sarretent tous les regards. cette scene seroit siflée. les complimens quils se font sont insoutenables, en un mot ils ne doivent parler que de galba, peu et dutou de la crainte ou ils sont que galba (passage conjecturé) ne laisse lempire pour drusus son fils. cela prepare la scene suivante ou vous devez rassembler toutes vos forces. quel que soit le role de pison on ne dira jamais quil est foible par ce que personne ne sen soucie, et quil nest quun instrument des grands conjurez. mais si le role de drusus est mauvais il fera ecrouler la piece'.

Puisque l'on peut facilement déduire l'objet de cette conversation, il est inutile d'en reproduire le texte. Pour cette scène nous signalerons encore la seule critique directe de cette réponse de Rutile: 'Vous seul pourriés rappeller l'heureux siecle d'Auguste en faisant voir, sur le trône des Cesars, un homme qui reünit comme lui, toutes les vertus nécessaires, pour commander heureusement. Prévenez l'effet des brigues qui pourroient s'oposer à vôtre elevation. Galba dans les Gaules à la tête de son armée, (a une faction puissante), dont il est adoré. . . .' Madame Denis note en marge: : 'cecy peut être supprimé, si cela fait longueur'

Au début de la scène 5, on notera une nouvelle remarque générale, reprenant en substance les propos de Pison, Rutile et Drusus:

'ce n'est point a pison a parler le p^{er}, cest a drusus, vous sçavez qu'un acteur ne peut venir sur la scene sans un motif quel quil soit. es ce drusus qui vient de son propre mouvement? es ce pison qui la envoié chercher? ce ne peut etre pison, car il aurait du le dire a epicaris, et cest ce que nous ne voulons pas; cest donc drusus qui vient les trouver; en ce cas il faut quil dise pourquoi. (il faut que) pison doit marquer a drusus la crainte ou il est quil ne veuille envahir lempire. cela donnera occasion a drusus de repondre de belles choses sur la liberté qui seroient (sont) incipides dans la bouche de pison. il me semble que drusus devroit aussi dans cette scene parler de poppée, pleindre une personne aussi vertueuse detre livrée a un (barb[are]) monstre comme neron, cela commenceroit a interesser pour elle, songez que personne n'en a encor rien dit. et quelle doit paroitre au second acte; il doit la demander pour unique recompence.

Dans le discours de Pison, nous signalerons deux légères corrections: madame Denis a remplacé un 'pour' avec 'par', et le copiste lui-même a substitué 'joug' à 'sang'. Ce discours de Drusus:

'J'ai trop longtems devoré mes affronts. Trop longtems l'univers a gemi sous le joug impérieux des Nerons: Il faut en exterminer les restes criminels. Je ne crains point de (mourir) m'ouvrir devant vous, et nos périls communs doivent reünir nos coeurs. La Garde Prétorienne m'est confiée. Les armées, sous les ordres de Vindex et de mon pere, sont occupées loins de Rome. Le Tiran n'a pour sa défense que des soldats étrangers vendus à son courroux, et enrichis des depouilles de nos principaux Citoyens. Leur fidelité n'est point à l'épreuve des promesses dont on peut les éblouir, et je crois que je puis, sans me flater, vous promettre aujourd'hui, que le monde sera sans Tirans, et Poppée sans Diadême.'

Ce discours entraîne la remarque suivante de madame Denis: 'ils faut que les armées soient pres de Rome, du reste ce que drusus dit sur les moiens quil prendra pour immoler neron me paroit bien'.

Enfin, pour terminer le premier acte nous citerons encore trois appréciations sur ces répliques consécutives; Pison répondant à Drusus: 'Que Rome soit aussi sans maitre. unissons-nous, Seigneur, pour le bien commun; travaillons uniquement pour (votre) nôtre gloire et pour la Republique', le critique note: '[un mot illisible] mauvais'. Drusus enchaîne: 'Je n'ai d'autre dessein (aujourd'huy) que de punir les cruautés de Néron, et d'affranchir Poppée et le monde d'un esclavage que je ne puis plus suporter'. D'où la critique: 'cest mauvais'. Enfin, Pison répond: 'Epicaris nous est nécessaire. sa vertu et son crédit lui ont donné des amis. son Parti est puissant et capable de nous vanger, si nous succombons, et d'achever ce que nous aurons eu du moins la gloire de commencer'.

A côté du nom de Pison, madame Denis a écrit: 'tres mauvais'. En outre, nous noterons cette remarque: '*epicaris nous est necessaire* ou aviez vous donc lesprit? cest le chef de la Conspiration, cest elle qui y a engagé galba, voila une belle decouverte'.

Le deuxième acte s'ouvre sur une conversation entre Néron et Tigellin. L'empereur lui rappelle brièvement toutes les difficultés qu'il a vaincues: son frère, sa mère, son épouse, les sujets séditieux 'Citoyens ingrats, tous ont péri sous le fer qu'ils aiguisoient contre moy'. Approuvant ce discours, le confident demande cependant si l'attitude d'Epicaris ne l'inquiète pas. Néron le rassure: ne l'aime-t-elle pas? En outre, il a pris ses précautions.

La deuxième scène met en présence Poppée et l'empereur. Non sans inquiétude, il lui proclame son amour dans un long discours. Poppée répond: '(De quels doutes cruels vous m'accablez!) ah! Seigneur, pardonnez a (lisez mieux dans) une ame tourmentee tour à tour de vos soupçons (cruels), des inquietudes de votre amour (madame Denis ajoute: et des trouble que notre hymene eleve dans lempire) enfin des milles (ces trois mots ajoutés) craintes que je ne puis vaincre ni dissimuler'.

Madame Denis note à ce sujet: 'poppée ne doit jamais mentir n'y faire entendre a neron quelle laime; elle seroit odieuse au (dieux) au spectateur: prenez bien garde a cela'.

Les craintes de Poppée étonnent Néron; elle s'explique: 'Vous en avez trop repandu; et c'est en vain que vous croyés trouver votre sureté sur un trône entouré de morts. Ce n'est que par l'amour qu'on peut regner sans effroi. ne bravez point le desespoir d'un peuple qui adoroit octavie, celui d'Epicaris qui vous a tout sacrifié, et a qui vous deviez peut etre plus qu'a Octavie.

Soyez touché de ses larmes'. Cette réplique attire d'abord ce commentaire: 'puis que le mariage etoit secret je crois que poppée ne doit point scavoir ce que neron doit a epicaris mais elle peut dire', puis madame Denis refait la réplique de Poppée: 'ne bravez point le desespoir d'un peuple qui adoroit Octavie, Epicaris a un grand parti dans rome; elle vous aima: aiez pitie de ses larmes, songez que les debris, les morts, le sang sont les routes par les quelles vous avez passé pour me faire arriver au trone. les romains peuvent m'en punir et jattire sur vous leur haine'.

Voici la réponse de Néron: 'Est ce à vous de me montrer ce que je lui dois? Vous, pour qui j'ay tout fait, voudriés vous m'en punir? songez que les debris, les morts, le sang vous ont ouvert les routes du trone, et que les pleurs mêmes d'Epicaris sont un nouveau triomphe pour vous. . .'. Madame Denis note en regard: 'je ferois commencer la les soupcons de neron sans nomer drusus. poppée sen deffendroit; il lui nomeroit drusus et elle partiroit de la (pour lui) pour promettre a neron de lepouser'. La réplique de Poppée a été légèrement corrigée: l'exemple d'Epicharis devient celui d'Octavie et la 'haine' des Romains le cède à leur 'vengeance'.

Le déroulement de la scène suscite encore cette réflexion d'ordre général: 'plus je reflechis, plus je sens que (pour moi) je prendrois mon parti dans cette scene de faire soupconner drusus par neron; poppée lui fut promise, elle consentit à lepouser, il est tout simple que neron le soubconne et pour lors la fraieur ou se soubçon geteroit poppée lui feroit promettre a Neron de lepouser pour lui prouver quelle naime point drusus. il faut quelle le deffende avec chaleur, quelle lui fasse bien entendre quil est son suget le plus fidelle, que la sureté de sa vie depend de lui. Reflechissez a cet idée et a mesure que vous ferez la scene, nous en resonerons. pour moi, je ne vois pas mieux et je suis presque sure que ce p^{er} soupçon geté sur drusus au second acte rendra son role plus interessant pendand toute la piece'.

Nous citerons aussi cette réplique, corrigée, de Néron: 'Tant de détours sont superflus. Je lis dans votre coeur. (Je perce à travers toutes ces craintes forcées) . . . Ce n'est point le rang que je vous offre qui vous paroit odieux; c'est celui qui veut le partage avec vous; C'est ma tendresse que vous detestez: C'est ma main que vous refusez: C'est mon amour que vous dédaignez... ingrate, vôtre seule crainte est de faire mon bonheur... quelle étoit ma credulité! (J'ai cru trouver en vous un coeur comme le mien. Mes sentimens m'assuroient des vôtres: Je jugeois de vôtre sincérité par la mienne... malheureux!) ainsi, tant de soins, tant d'hommages, tant de bienfaits'...

La scène s'achève sur un ultimatum adressé par l'empereur à Poppée. La troisième scène met en présence Poppée et Iras, sa suivante. Celle-ci comprend mal les réticences de sa maîtresse; pour les justifier, la favorite rappelle ce que fut sa vie, et elle ne veut pas trahir Drusus. Signalons deux corrections mineures: parmi les états qui 'empoisonnent' la vie de Galba, madame Denis a supprimé 'la contrainte' et substitue 'épouser' à 'exposer' ce qui est plus logique. Poppée trouve que sa situation est presque symbolique (un 'cher amant' est également biffé).

Le texte manuscrit s'arrête au milieu de la réplique étonnée d'Iras, mettant ainsi un terme aux critiques de madame Denis. Malgré leur caractère judicieux, répétons-le, la tragédie de son soupirant échoua. Elles n'auraient pas suffi d'ailleurs à sauver un texte dont les extraits que nous avons présentés ici prouvent suffisamment la médiocrité.

The Structure and meaning of the
Lettres persanes
by Robert F. O'Reilly

Introduction

Critics have usually viewed Montesquieu's early literary production as a prelude to his *magnum opus*, *L'Esprit des lois*. Studies which relate the *Lettres persanes* to the evolution of Montesquieu's thought are valuable, as are source studies which situate this novel in a particular literary tradition or in the history of ideas. Such scholarly pursuits are helpful in that they establish the literary, moral, and ideological atmosphere from which the work arose. However, they tend to shift the emphasis away from Montesquieu, the conscious artist and literary craftsman, who conceived and executed highly entertaining and cleverly wrought narratives.

The mid-twentieth century has seen the emergence of studies which are increasingly literary in their emphasis. Montesquieu's reference to a *chaîne secrète* in the 'Quelques Réflexions sur les *Lettres persanes*' has prompted some interesting studies of the novel. M. Roger Mercier[1] has pointed out the presence of certain episodes and ideas which, when juxtaposed, indicate a fundamental dialectic of negation and affirmation. M. Roger Laufer's examination[2] of the work is psychological and structural, and he concludes that the novel is built on a series of contrasts which

[1] 'Le Roman dans les *Lettres persanes:* structure et signification', *Revue des sciences humaines* (July-September 1962), cvii.345-356.

[2] 'La Réussite romanesque et la signification des *Lettres persanes* de Montesquieu', *RHL* (April-June 1961), lxi.180-201.

have as their focal point the enigmatic Janus-faced character of Usbek. Mrs Pauline Kra's study[3] lacks the dynamic quality of m. Laufer's, is more static in its approach and more traditional in its conclusions. For mrs Kra the *secret chain* consists of an organized thematic pattern which informs the work logically though subtly. Professor Robert Frautschi's study[4] attempts to uncover an all-pervasive tone which is part of each individual letter and which mediates between all of the letters.

Stylistic studies of the *Lettres persanes* have been productive. M. Laufer maintains that the letters are an example of *style rococo*, while Patrick Brady has demonstrated that the work possesses neo-classical attributes as well[5]. M. Pierre Nardin[6] has provided the most complete and informative stylistic study without attempting to confine the letters by a period concept. M. Nardin clearly sees that Montesquieu's style reflects the motivating ideas behind the *Lettres persanes*. The confrontation between the orient and the occident, between Persians and Parisians, is conveyed through a style which is supercharged with rhetorical devices for creating antitheses. M. Nardin's work confirms substantially the studies of Mercier and Laufer. Montesquieu's dialectic style dovetails nicely with Mercier's and Laufer's conclusion that Montesquieu's conception of the work and method are basically dialectic.

My approach to the *Lettres persanes* is also literary. Where other critics have given only a piecemeal view of the subject, I am presenting a comprehensive study of such traditional materials as epistolary method, characterization, style, and structure in an attempt to uncover a general meaning behind the letters and to reveal the cohesion of form and content in the *Lettres*

[3] 'The Invisible chain of the *Lettres persanes*', *Studies on Voltaire* (1963), xxiii.9-60.
[4] 'The Would-be invisible chain in *Les Lettres persanes*', *FR* (April 1967), xl.604-612.
[5] Roger Laufer, *Style rococo: style des lumières* (Paris 1963), p.48; Patrick Brady, 'The *Lettres persanes*—rococo or neo-classical?' *Studies on Voltaire* (1967), liii.47-77.
[6] 'La Recette stylistique des *Lettres persanes*'. *Le Français moderne* (1952-1953), xx.277-286, xxi.13-28, 101-109.

THE *LETTRES PERSANES*

persanes. The one dominant theme throughout my study is that Montesquieu was acutely aware of the craft of fiction. He began writing the *Lettres persanes* with a clear purpose and succeeded in accomplishing his goals. Although the novelistic elements of his work have been viewed as the scaffolding for social satire, he made a conscious effort to create a nexus between form and content, to combine the novelistic and the satirical.

This tendency emerges most clearly in the *Lettres persanes*. In an attempt to demonstrate Montesquieu's unremitting artistic preoccupations, I will examine the master plan of the letters as outlined in the 1721 'Introduction' and in the 1754 'Quelques réflexions sur les *Lettres persanes*'. I will then show how this plan is realized through Montesquieu's concern for various techniques of illusion, for consistent characterization, and for a closely knit structure.

Thus through an internal examination of the *Lettres persanes*, my study converges on one fixed point, an appreciation of Montesquieu's craftsmanship, which produced a work unique in its day and still meaningful for the modern reader.

1. The master-plan

When Montesquieu published the *Lettres persanes* in 1721, the epistolary novel as a fictional form was still in the infant stages. The *Lettres d'une religieuse portugaise*, published in France in 1669 and translated into English in 1678, had been extremely successful and certainly helped popularize the letter-form as a type of narrative fiction. There were also other causes for the rise of the epistolary novel such as a long tradition of using the letter-form for many kinds of subjects[7].

Beside these literary precedents social usage played an important role in the development of the epistolary novel. Letter-

[7] Charles E. Kany, *The Beginnings of the epistolary novel in France, Italy, and Spain* (Berkeley 1937), traces the development of the letter-form in France from the twelfth century through the seventeenth century.

writing in the seventeenth and eighteenth centuries had become a social institution. The example of mme de Sévigné is instructive on this point. Written in an informative and pleasing style, her letters were read aloud to friends, copied, and the originals treasured. Vivienne Mylne[8] reminds us that 'to the eighteenth-century reader there was nothing inherently improbable in someone's having kept a whole series of letters which might later be found and published. It was this fact which enabled fictional letters, like memoir-novels, to masquerade as real-life products.'

The influence of seventeenth-century literary standards on the development of criticism was another factor which shaped the development of the first-person narrative. Obstinate classicists leveled harsh artistic judgements against works which did not conform to traditional rules. These classical precepts, that were directly stated in the *arts poétiques* and put into practice in the dramatic works of the seventeenth century, explain, in part, the efforts of eighteenth-century novelists to establish the true-to-life nature of their fictions. Thus, they attempted to conform to the demi-god of classicism, *vraisemblance*. According to professor Georges May[9] this desire to satisfy the demands for verisimilitude in the novel resulted in a shift away from the episodic novels of the seventeenth century, *romans héroïques*, towards a new emphasis on realism which in turn affected the form of narrative fiction and gave impetus to the development of the first person narrative, the *roman-mémoires*.

In view of the requirement for realism it is not surprising that authors defend the authenticity of their works in an introduction. The editorial comments which accompany much eighteenth-century fiction may be amusing to the modern reader. Yet these comments had a very real and important function. They were rooted in a tradition which goes back to the rules of classical theatre, and they provided the needed justification for publishing

---

[8] *The Eighteenth-century French novel* (Manchester 1965), p.145.

[9] *Le Dilemme du roman au dix-huitième siècle* (New Haven 1963), pp.15-46.

the material at hand. Just as classical tragedy had to be anchored in historical fact, *vérité historique*, and had to observe rules of verisimilitude, eighteenth-century novelists felt the necessity of documenting and authenticating their tales by maintaining that they had drawn them from nature and from real life.

In the earliest editions of the *Lettres persanes* we see Montesquieu bowing to tradition. In an introduction in the conventional style of his time he attempts to give his letters an aura of authenticity. He assumes the mask of an anonymous editor and states that he has been copyist and translator of a number of letters entrusted to him by Persian visitors to France. He disclaims any responsibility for the contents of the letters and states further that the job of editing has only been undertaken to make the letters more palatable to western readers: 'Je ne fais donc que l'office de traducteur: toute ma peine a été de mettre l'ouvrage à nos mœurs. J'ai soulagé le lecteur du langage autant que je l'ai pu, et l'ai sauvé d'une infinité d'expressions sublimes, qui l'auroient envoyé jusque dans les nues'[10].

The justification and reasons for publication are arrived at in a rather backhanded fashion. In a burst of false modesty the translator refuses to praise the merit and usefulness of the letters whose excellence will be so obvious as to need no commentary from him: 'L'usage a permis à tout traducteur, et même au plus barbare commentateur, d'orner la tête de sa version, ou de sa glose, du panégyrique de l'original, et d'en relever l'utilité, le mérite et l'excellence. Je ne l'ai point fait; on en devinera facilement les raisons' (p.132).

Within the novel itself Montesquieu tries to maintain the illusion that he is indeed only the editor of a collection of letters, by providing in footnotes additional information such as a research scholar would do. In many cases these footnotes are factual

---

[10] *Œuvres complètes*, ed. Roger Caillois (Paris 1949), i.131. Hereafter noted only by page number. I have followed the orthography of the Pléiade edition. In quotations taken from other sources, I have modernized the spellings.

descriptions of historical significance and often enrich the text by providing valuable facts. The notes range from the simple dates of letter 92, where the death of Louis XIV is noted, to more complex descriptive and historical notations. For example, in letter 7 the footnote is descriptive, drawing a contrast between Persian and Turkish women while in letter 75 the notation has a historical significance: 'Les Mahométans ne se soucient point de prendre Venise, parce qu'ils n'y trouveroient point d'eau pour leurs purifications' (p.245). At other times the footnotes have linguistic importance, thus, stressing the role of the fictional translator mentioned in the introduction. For instance, in letter 18 the use of the word 'immaums' is explained, while in letter 27 'la ville du Soleil' is glossed as Ispahan (p.171). The fictional editor's role emerges most strongly in notes which are interpretative in nature. Thus the use of such words as 'apparemment' or 'peut-être' suggest an editor's comment rather than an omniscient author's: 'Ce sont apparemment les chevaliers de Malte' (p.159) and 'L'Auteur parle peut-être de l'île de Bourbon' (p.311).

Whereas the introduction and notes to the *Lettres persanes* stress the genuineness of the letters, the 'Quelques réflexions', added to the 1754 edition, make no pretence of anonymity. Montesquieu emerges as a literary critic drawing attention to points of composition and characterization. He reveals the care which went into the planning of what appeared a random collection. This literary apology was prompted ostensibly by a pamphlet published by *abbé* Gaultier in 1751, *Les Lettres persanes convaincues d'impiété*. Gaultier refused to accept the fictional veil that tried to justify a criticism of religion. Montesquieu answered Gaultier by emphasizing the true-to-life nature of his pseudo-foreign letters. However, more important than this attempt to disguise the satirical aspects of the letters, the 'Quelques réflexions' indicate an interesting change in Montesquieu's attitude towards realism. He is no longer concerned with hiding his voice behind a fictional editor but with introducing a tale whose characters and themes are realistic.

Therefore, in defending himself against Gaultier Montesquieu shifts the position of 1721. Perhaps more in sorrow than in anger he chided his readers for not understanding him and felt constrained to stress the overlooked literary aspects of the wrok. Thus he insists that his oriental observers be appreciated as artistic creations. He has made an effort to present characters and events which are psychologically sound and which correspond to models in real life. They are more than mere *porte-parole*; they are carefully planned characters whose reactions to western life are logical within the framework of their Persian origins. Montesquieu has tried to think like a Persian in his characterization of Usbek and Rica and in his portrayal of the harem. In other words, the reality of artistic creation is essential to the understanding of the novel: 'C'était un Persan qui parlait et qui devait être frappé de tout ce qu'il voyait et de tout ce qu'il entendait. Comme il trouve bizarres nos coutumes, il trouve quelquefois de la singularité dans de certaines choses de nos dogmes, parce qu'il les ignore, et il les explique mal'[11].

Montesquieu then extends the verisimilar nature of character portrayal to the entire structure of the work. The treatment of subject matter is defended on the same grounds as characterization. It is true-to-life that Rica's and Usbek's knowledge and understanding of Europe will depend upon the extent and duration of their exposure to western civilization. Montesquieu also insists that the ability of his two characters to understand or to be amazed by life in the west will be contingent upon their different personalities. Usbek and Rica will react to France as individuals with different psychologies: 'A mesure qu'ils font un plus long séjour en Europe, les mœurs de cette partie du Monde prennent dans leur tête un air moins merveilleux et moins bizarre, et ils sont plus ou moins frappés de ce bizarre et de ce merveilleux suivant la différence de leurs caractères' (p.129).

[11] *Cahiers 1716-1755*, ed. Bernard Grasset (Paris 1941), pp.197-198.

Not only does Montesquieu stress his carefully planned efforts at psychologically logical characterization, but he also indicates his thorough use of the time element and suggests the effect which Usbek's prolonged absence will have upon the outcome of the novel. The nine years which Usbek spends in Europe strengthen his knowledge of the west but weaken his iron-fisted control over the harem. The disorders within the seraglio arise as a logical result of the duration of Usbek's stay in France. Thus, the final revolt of Usbek's wives is dictated by a sense of durational realism: 'D'un autre côté, le désordre croît dans le sérail d'Asie à proportion de la longueur de l'absence d'Usbek, c'est-à-dire à mesure que la fureur augmente, et que l'amour diminue' (p.129).

Montesquieu also touches upon aesthetic theory in general by attempting to justify the use of the letter technique and to formulate a theory of the epistolary novel. To strengthen his argument he uses examples which postdate the *Lettres persanes*. In general it appears that Montesquieu felt that the epistolary method was superior to the straight narrative because it was essentially dramatic, allowed room for spontaneous digressions, and was psychologically realistic:

D'ailleurs, ces sortes de romans réussissent ordinairement, parce que l'on rend compte soi-même de sa situation actuelle; ce qui fait plus sentir les passions que tous les récits qu'on en pourrait faire, et c'est une des causes du succès de *Paméla* et des *Lettres péruviennes* (ouvrages charmants qui ont paru depuis).

Enfin dans les romans ordinaires, les digressions ne peuvent être permises que lorsqu'elles forment elles-mêmes un nouveau roman. On n'y saurait mêler de raisonnements, parce qu'aucun des personnages n'y ayant été assemblé pour raisonner, cela choquerait le dessein et la nature de l'ouvrage. Mais, dans la forme de lettre, où les acteurs ne sont pas choisis, mais forcés, et où tous les sujets qu'on traite ne sont dépendants d'aucun dessein ou d'aucun plan déjà formé, l'auteur s'est donné l'avantage de pouvoir joindre de la philosophie, de la politique et de la morale, à un roman, et de lier le tout par une chaîne secrète, et en quelque façon inconnue[12].

Just as I compared editorial comments to the concept of theatrical realism, it is not out of place to compare theories of the epistolary novel with dramatic practices. The parallels are striking. The letter-novel, like tragedy, attempts to create the illusion of reality by hiding the real author behind author-narrators who are characters in the novel and who appear to create a story through an exchange of letters. In the same way that we witness directly the actions of actors in a play, we are brought face to face with characters in the epistolary novel without the obvious intrusion of an omniscient author. The progress of a play depends upon dialogue while in the letter-novel this dialogue is simulated through an active exchange of letters between various characters. A perpetual dialogue is established which allows characters to reveal themselves and to be revealed by other characters. It was certainly in part the desire to produce dramatic realism which prompted such a writer as Montesquieu to advocate a narrative form in which action is presented rather than told[13].

Thus we see that Montesquieu chose the letter-form as an aid to verisimilitude for those readers who needed the added fictional realism of authentic letters. He reflected upon the virtue of the letter-novel. And further, he appealed to the reader to judge his work on aesthetic grounds and within the context and limitations imposed by a particular fictional world. Montesquieu's own remarks give us a clear indication of his aims in composing the letters, and a close internal examination of the work will reveal to what extent Montesquieu was successful in achieving his ends.

---

[12] *Cahiers*, pp.198-199; for a discussion of Montesquieu's awareness of the techniques of the epistolary style see F. C. Green, 'Montesquieu the novelist and some imitations of the *Lettres persanes*', *MLR* (January 1925), XX.32-42.

[13] miss Mylne points out some of the common problems shared by letter-novels and plays (pp.151-155).

II. The techniques of illusion

As was pointed out in the preceding part, the editorial framework of the novel, found in Montesquieu's 'Introduction' and pseudo-scientific apparatus, reveals the demands placed upon the eighteenth-century writer for authentic material. However, these editorial comments are only one means for producing an illusion of reality. There are the more internal literary devices which are part of the letters themselves.

Montesquieu evolved his theory of the letter-novel from his practice. The letters are an impressive example of the epistolary style he describes[14], and his efforts to portray realistic situations are on the whole successful. In a novel such as the *Lettres d'une religieuse portugaise* we hear only one voice addressing itself to someone outside the plot. Montesquieu extended and enriched the letter-form by addressing letters to other characters within the plot, such as Usbek's letters to the harem and the answers he receives from wives and eunuchs. In this more complicated form of epistolary novel not only are characters enabled to reveal their thoughts and feelings as they occur, but contrasting points of view are presented by individuals who describe the same subject.

There are several occasions where Montesquieu uses this double exposure technique effectively and in different ways. It is used for ironic contrast in letters 151 and 152 and to give a realistic explanation why the disorders in the harem have continued unchecked since the death of the chief eunuch. Approximately twenty months have passed since Usbek wrote letter 148, ordering strict disciplinary action in the harem. Narsit, the chief eunuch's successor, anticipates in no way the impending disaster and has, therefore, not carried out Usbek's measures. Letters 151

---

[14] I do not agree with professor Green's opinion that 'laudable as were his intentions Montesquieu did not produce a good novel. His theories were excellent but, like those of Diderot on the theatre, they failed when practiced by their author' (p.34).

and 152 focus on a country outing revealing the continuing sedition in the harem and Narsit's blindness. In the following quotations I have italicized certain passages to bring out ironic contrast:

| lettre CLI | Lettre CLII |
Solim à Usbek, à Paris	Narsit à Usbek, à Paris
Cependant *tes femmes ne gardent plus aucune retenue*. . . . *Il règne même parmi tes esclaves une certaine indolence pour leur devoir et pour l'observation des règles, qui me surprend*. . . . Tes femmes ont été huit jours à la campagne, à une de tes maisons les plus abandonnées. On dit que l'esclave qui en a soin a été gagné, et qu'un jour avant qu'elles n'arrivassent *il avoit fait cacher deux hommes dans un réduit de pierre qui est dans la muraille de la principale chambre, d'où ils sortoient le soir lorsque nous étions retirés*. Le vieux eunuque qui est à présent à notre tête est un imbécile, à qui l'on fait croire tout ce qu'on veut (p.365).	Roxane et Zélis ont souhaité d'aller à la campagne; je n'ai pas cru devoir le leur refuser. *Heureux Usbek! tu as des femmes fidèles et des esclaves vigilants: je commande en des lieux où la vertu semble s'être choisi un asile. Compte qu'il ne s'y passera rien que tes yeux ne puissent soutenir* (p.366).

At other times two writers discuss a philosophical problem, presenting contrary points of view. In letter 105 Rhédi defends the belief that the arts and sciences have impeded rather than furthered the development of mankind: 'je ne sais si l'utilité que l'on en retire dédommage les hommes du mauvais usage que l'on en fait tous les jours' (p.285). In letter 106 Usbek espouses Mandeville's theory in *The Fable of the bees*, anticipates Voltaire's *Le Mondain*, and takes a position which is decidedly anti-*Télémaque* when he states: 'Je suppose, Rhédi, qu'on ne souffrît dans un royaume que les arts absolument nécessaires à la culture des terres, qui sont pourtant en grand nombre, et qu'on en bannît tous ceux qui ne servent qu'à la volupté ou à la fantaisie; je le soutiens: cet état seroit un des plus misérables qu'il y eût au Monde' (p.289).

Sometimes Montesquieu has added a third voice creating a triple exposure of the same philosophical problem or event. Letters 41, 42 and 43 deal with an internal dispute in the harem. Letter 41 reveals the distorted mentality of the chief eunuch who plans to revenge himself on the black slave, Pharan, by having him castrated under the pretext that he is necessary to the harem. Letter 42 points out the true reasons for the chief eunuch's cruel project and underscores vigorously the barbarousness of castration in general:

lettre XLI
Le premier eunuque noir
à Usbek

Comme les eunuques sont extrêmement rares à présent, j'avois pensé de me servir d'un esclave noir que tu as à la campagne; mais je n'ai pu jusqu'ici le porter à souffrir qu'on le consacrât à cet emploi. *Comme je vois qu'au bout de compte c'est son avantage*, je voulus l'autre jour user à son égard d'un peu de rigueur. . . . Mais il se mit à hurler comme si on avoit voulu l'écorcher, et fit tant qu'il échappa de nos mains et évita le fatal couteau. *Je viens d'apprendre qu'il veut t'écrire pour te demander grâce, soutenant que je n'ai conçu ce dessein que par un désir insatiable de vengeance sur certaines railleries piquantes qu'il dit avoir faites de moi. Cependant je te jure par les cent mille Prophètes que je n'ai agi que pour le bien de ton service, la seule chose qui me soit chère, et hors laquelle je ne regarde rien* (p.189).

lettre XLII
Pharan à Usbek, son
souverain seigneur

Sous prétexte de quelques railleries qu'il prétend que j'ai faites sur le malheur de sa condition, il exerce sur ma tête une vengeance inépuisable. . . . *Il me destina à la garde de tes femmes sacrées, c'est-à-dire à une exécution qui seroit pour moi mille fois plus cruelle que la mort.* Ceux qui, en naissant, ont eu le malheur de recevoir de leurs cruels parents un traitement pareil se consolent peut-être sur ce qu'ils n'ont jamais connu d'autre état que le leur; mais qu'on me fasse descendre de l'humanité, et qu'on m'en prive, *je mourrois de douleur, si je ne mourois pas de cette barbarie* (p.190).

THE *LETTRES PERSANES*

Finally in letter 43 Usbek emerges as the third voice, becomes the arbiter of the dispute, reveals his expressed compassion for Pharan, and justifies our suspicions of the chief eunuch's vindictive motives: 'Recevez la joie dans votre cœur, et reconnaissez ces sacrés caractères; faites-les baiser au grand Eunuque et à l'intendant de mes jardins. Je leur défends de rien entreprendre contre vous' (p.191). Through this multiple exposure device Montesquieu not only adds variety to the text but by shifting the angle of focus between various characters, he succeeds in broadening and deepening the reader's understanding of a particular problem or event. Thus, situations which would otherwise appear simple take on the complexity of reality when viewed from several different perspectives[15].

In his continuing effort to simulate authentic situations and to vary tone, Montesquieu has used other narrative devices as well. The most common is that of dialogue or recorded conversation. There is, first of all, the indirect dialogue inherent in the letter-form which uses an exchange of letters between two or more people, for example, the harem intrigue. Secondly, there is the dialogue in which Rica or Usbek engage directly with another character such as Rica's confrontation with a missionary in letter 49 or Usbek's conversation with a casuist in letter 57. Thirdly, there are letters containing reported dialogue in which Rica and Usbek function mainly as secretaries. They relate faithfully what they have overheard, such as the conversation between two *beaux esprits* which Rica overhears through a thin partition in letter 54 or Usbek's letter concerning the papal bull *Unigenitus* in letter 101.

Another technique is that of *asides*, or interior monologue. This device enables Montesquieu to vary the epistolary style by

---

[15] Montesquieu again uses this triple exposure technique effectively in his discussion of suicide in letters 76, 77, 161. In letter 76 we are provided with Usbek's theoretical defense of suicide; in letter 77 we have a criticism of that defense by Ibben, and in letter 161 Roxane's suicide note ironically reinforces Usbek's theory by a concrete example. For a fuller discussion of the suicide question, see part IV.

allowing characters to interject their thoughts as they occur simultaneously with the event under discussion. In letter 52 Rica's portrait of vain coquettes takes on additional depths of meaning and realism as Rica reveals his own thought processes: 'Ah, bon Dieu! dis-je en moi-même, ne sentirons-nous jamais que le ridicule des autres? — C'est peut-être un bonheur, disois-je ensuite, que nous trouvions de la consolation dans la faiblesse d'autrui' (p.207). Again in letter 74 the portrait of a *grand seigneur* provokes an immediate reaction from Usbek: 'Ah! bon Dieu; dis-je en moi-même, si, lorsque j'étois à la cour de Perse je représentois ainsi, je représentois un grand sot' (p.244).

In this context we should note that Montesquieu occasionally takes advantage of a well-known convention of epistolary novels by endowing Rica and Usbek with extraordinary memories which permit them to retain and transcribe extended conversations verbatim. The sacrifice is usually one of verisimilitude in favour of the dramatic intensity and vividness provided by dialogue. Yet at times the recorded discourse in the *Lettres persanes* is carried to absurd proportions and large blocks of material become merely quoted monologues. This occurs most blatantly in four letters dealing with Rica's visit to a Parisian library. Montesquieu's onslaught on most forms of writing sacrifices both realism and dramatic intensity to his own particular prejudices.

Nevertheless, Montesquieu tries to remain discreetly within the bounds of credibility even in letters and documents which are interpolated into the text. These often treat particular areas of interest such as letter 51 on Russian customs and letter 78 on Spain. At other times these documents deal with specialized information, the knowledge of which could only come to Usbek and Rica indirectly, such as letter 130 from the 'Nouvellistes', letter 143 from a doctor, and letter 145 from a scientist. In one case, at least, it was Montesquieu's caution more than his concern for authenticity which prompted him to place the story of an actress's indiscretion with a cleric in letter form, letter 28.

THE *LETTRES PERSANES*

There are instances when Montesquieu consciously violates the realism he has set out to maintain. In letter 142 there is a mythological portrayal of John Law's administration as minister of finance. The fiction is a transparent criticism of Law and is presented as an ancient document entitled 'Fragment d'un ancien mythologiste'. Again in letter 146 Montesquieu disguises another criticism of law by situating the story 'dans les Indes': 'J'y ai vu une nation, naturellement généreuse, pervertie en un instant, depuis le dernier de ses sujets jusqu'aux plus grands, par le mauvais exemple d'un ministre' (p.361). Obviously Montesquieu was attempting to be circumspect at the expense of verisimilitude. Yet these thinly veiled references must have been only token gestures for the censors, and they certainly fooled no one.

In letter 126 a transposition of the Cellemare conspiracy occurs in which Montesquieu again consciously sacrifices realism by placing a French event of political importance in an oriental setting. There is, of course, no reason why Rica should feel the necessity of disguising this particular incident. In such a case Rica becomes the none-too-subtle vehicle of Montesquieu's own caution.

Montesquieu is careful throughout the work to present as authentic an oriental atmosphere as possible. To this end he has drawn upon information supplied by a number of travelers to the East. M. Paul Vernière in his scholarly edition of the *Lettres persanes* (Paris 1960) has compiled the most complete list of Montesquieu's sources (pp.xix-xxv) and mlle Marie Louise Dufrenoy[16] has commented that 'Montesquieu a suivi fidèlement ses sources.' Yet Montesquieu is not content to situate his letters in an exotic novelistic framework nor does he inform the reader arbitrarily or gratuitously about the facts of the harem. He does, of course, exploit the oriental vogue of his day by utilizing certain accepted traits of eastern behaviour such as jealous and cruelty. These had

---

[16] Marie Louise Dufrenoy, *L'Orient romanesque en France 1704-1789* (Montreal 1946), p.103.

been described some time before by such authors as Chardin and Tavernier in their travel accounts and by Galland in his 1704 translation of the *Arabian nights*. The use of this source material reveals Montesquieu's concern for authentic detail and his efforts to give a genuine oriental flavour to his work.

The exchange of letters between Rica and Usbek offers another example of Montesquieu's efforts at planned realism. Montesquieu realized that while his two heroes were together in Paris it would not be realistic for them to write to one another. Therefore, certain excuses were necessary to make such a correspondence possible. In all cases the letters carry an address, and at no time are both characters in Paris when they correspond. Since all the letters in that series but one are from Rica to Usbek, they are addressed from Paris to Usbek who is frequently in the unnamed province of ***. In letter 45, the first between Usbek and Rica, Montesquieu is careful to justify its necessity: 'Adieu, mon cher Usbek. J'irai te voir demain, et, si tu veux, nous reviendrons ensemble à Paris' (p.193). In all such cases Montesquieu consciously emphasizes that the two characters are separated and that a letter is indeed needed: 'Je crois que tu veux passer ta vie à la campagne: je ne te perdois au commencement que pour deux ou trois jours, et en voilà quinze que je ne t'ai vu' (p.222). This same type of textual illusion is repeated in letters 126, 141 and 144. Yet the fact that Montesquieu does not consistently justify this correspondence within the text of each of the letters is no indication that he has approached the problem in a haphazard fashion. He establishes a pattern for this particular illusion of reality in the first letter between Rica and Usbek, repeats the process from time to time, and expects the reader to carry on the pattern where it is not explicitly stated.

The most consistent efforts of Montesquieu to create an authentic framework for the letters can be found in the various time elements of the novel. First of all, there is the care with which historical events are made to coincide with the actual dates of certain letters. For example in letter 91 we find a discussion of a visit of the Persian ambassador to Paris in 1715 while in letter 129, which is written five years later, there is a description of the abdication of queen Ulric-Eleanor of Sweden in 1720.

Secondly Montesquieu has been meticulous in respecting the travelling time from Ispahan to Paris. M. Vernière (p.11) has pointed out that: 'L'itinéraire de nos Persanes est, en sens inverse, celui que Tavernier suivit deux fois, lors de son deuxième voyage et lors du sixième en 1664'. Tavernier counted twenty-four days by caravan between Tauris and Ispahan, Chardin, twenty-eight, and Usbek, twenty-five. In letters 6, 19 and 23 Montesquieu stresses the reality of travelling time by faithfully following Tavernier's indications.

It is amusing, though, to see Montesquieu attempting to maintain the illusion that he is transcribing authentic material while at the same time betraying himself as author. We might give as example the dating device within the text of the letters. Each letter is dated according to both the Christian and Islamic lunar calendars. The Christian solar year is used instead of the complicated Islamic years of the hegira to preserve a sense of actuality in the letters whereas the Islamic lunar months are employed to convey the exotic flavour of the east. On the one hand, Montesquieu is careful not to destroy a sense of time for the western reader by preserving the Christian solar year, and on the other hand, he is anxious to preserve the exotic, authentic atmosphere of the orient through use of the Islamic lunar months. While it is easy to see the hand of the author behind this double dating device, Montesquieu uses it in a rather sophisticated fashion to preserve a sense of passing time[17]. Thus, a letter takes from five to six months to go from Persia to Paris. Letters 41 and 42 are both dated 'le 7 de la lune de Maharram, 1713' (7 March 1713) and are answered by Usbek 'le 25 de la lune de Rhegeb, 1713' (25 September 1713); letter 147 which is dated 'le premier de la lune de

[17] for a complete discussion of Montesquieu's efforts to present a realistic time sequence in the Lettres persanes see Robert Shackleton, 'The Moslem chronology of the Lettres persanes', French Studies (1954), viii.17-27.

Rhegeb, 1717' (1 September 1717) is answered 'le 11 de la lune de Zilhagé, 1718' (11 February 1718).

In the last few letters Montesquieu preserves realism while succeeding in creating dramatic vividness. Roxane's betrayal is the culmination of a series of fourteen letters exchanged by Usbek and members of the harem and written over a period of three years (1717-1720). Montesquieu presents these letters as a unit in order to give a greater dramatic impact to the harem intrigue and the ending of the novel than would have been possible had they been dispersed chronologically throughout the work. His concern for chronological time caused him to antedate these letters so that the final letter from Roxane, 1 May 1720, would arrive in Paris just as Usbek was sending his final letter, 22 October 1720, to Rhédi. Thus by adjusting the dates, Montesquieu was able to make chronological time coincide with fictional time.

It is surprising to find before Richardson an author so sensitive to the demands and possibilities of the epistolary form. Montesquieu was conscious of the multiple devices for creating realism which are at the epistolary novelist's disposal and employed them intelligently and effectively. When he does violate realism or betray the conventions of the epistolary form, and these moments are few, he does it knowingly and with a clear purpose in mind.

III. Problems of the epistolary method

I have discussed so far only surface realism in the *Lettres persanes*. In this section I hope to prove that Montesquieu was fully aware of the intricacies of the first-person narrative and was successful in handling such problems as exposition, variety, and credible and consistent characterization.

Responding to his own requirements for realism and verisimilitude, Montesquieu fashioned characters with particular manners of expression or styles which are indicative of their personalities and which coincide with the seriousness or frivolity

THE *LETTRES PERSANES*

of the subject under discussion. For example, he was careful to differentiate stylistically and thematically between his two main characters. Usbek is older than Rica and is of a more serious philosophic bent than his young travelling companion. Rica enters the mainstream of social life and observes the human comedy of Parisian society unfolding before him. Rica's first letter, letter 26, comes at at a strategic moment and determines his role in the novel. It is the earliest letter written from Paris and defines Rica's role as the chief commentator of the contemporary Parisian scene. The tone of the letter is refreshing after the unrelieved seriousness of Usbek's correspondence. Rica's pen moves swiftly and vivaciously from subject to subject in a charmingly ingenuous fashion. And speaking of Rica in letter 25, Usbek confirms what is readily apparent from the style and content of Rica's first letter: 'La vivacité de son esprit fait qu'il saisit tout avec promptitude. Pour moi, qui pense plus lentement, je ne suis en état de te rien dire' (p.168).

Typical of Rica's youthfulness and his sense of humour is letter 52 in which he uses irony most effectively, while posing as an innocent observer of Parisian society. This letter exemplifies Rica's occasionally flippant tone and the somewhat frivolous subjects he chooses to discuss. While the vain coquette had been painted by La Bruyère ('Des femmes'), Montesquieu's portrait is fuller and more entertaining than La Bruyère's rather dry narrative.

The artistry and charm of Montesquieu's treatment of an age-old theme rests in the sprightly dialogue between Rica and his aging beauties and in Rica's insinuating asides to the reader. In order to mock the efforts of these women to appear young and to amuse himself and the reader at the expense of silly vain women, Rica wears the mask of an innocent bystander, and he gleefully disguises his criticism in the form of a compliment: 'Madame, vous vous ressemblez si fort, cette dame à qui je viens de parler et vous, qu'il me semble que vous soyez deux sœurs, et je vous crois à peu près du même âge' (p.207). In a letter of this sort Rica becomes the creator, the *metteur en scène*, of an amusing episode and guides the reader's critical reaction of a particular scene.

In most cases, however, Rica is only the objective reporter of events in which people unconsciously reveal themselves as ridiculous. For instance, in letter 45 on alchemists, the external description of the action and the suspended conclusion are characteristic. The *récit* moves in a staccato manner. A few brief traits sketch the portrait: 'son habillement étoit beaucoup plus que modeste; sa perruque de travers n'avoit pas même été peignée; il n'avoit pas eu le temps de faire recoudre son pourpoint noir, et il avoit renoncé, pour ce jour-là, aux sages précautions avec lesquelles, il avoit coutume de déguiser le délabrement de son équipage' (p.192). Rapidly successive orders stimulate the reader's curiosity and imagination: ' "Levez-vous, me dit-il; j'ai besoin de vous tout aujourd'hui: j'ai mille emplettes à faire, et je serai bien aise que ce soit avec vous." Dès que je fus habillé, ou peu s'en falloit, mon homme me fit précipitamment descendre. "Commençons, dit-il, par acheter un carrosse, et établissons l'équipage" ' (pp.192-193). An economical explanation reveals the motives for the frenzied behaviour and appearance of the alchemist: ' "Voyez-vous cette liqueur vermeille? Elle a à présent toutes les qualités que les philosophes demandent pour faire la transmutation des métaux. J'en ai tiré ces grains que vous voyez, qui sont de vrai or par leur couleur, quoiqu'un peu imparfaits par leur pesanteur" ' (p.193). The scene ends quickly with several incisive gestures which express better than words Rica's exaspération: 'Je sortis et je descendis, ou plutôt je me précipitai par cet escalier, transporté de colère, et laissai cet homme si riche dans son hôpital' (p.193).

Usbek's style, by contrast, reveals the gravity and the maturity of his mind. He often inclines towards an aphoristic or pedagogical style. His philosophical notions and concepts are supported by illustrative examples. In letter 50, for example, Mirza quotes Usbek as having stated that 'les hommes étoient nés pour être vertueux, et que la justice est une qualité qui leur est aussi propre que l'existence' (p.145). This letter provides a pretext for Usbek's digression on the Troglodytes. The parable illustrates Usbek's philosophical concept with such epigrammatic statements as 'l'intérêt des particuliers se trouve toujours dans l'intérêt commun' (p.149). Again in letter 112 there is a similar pattern of composition. Rhédi's comments on the decrease of world population in areas which flourished formerly are supported by examples which Usbek chooses from different spots around the globe.

But occasionally this pattern is reversed and the concrete gives rise to the philosophical. In letter 33 Usbek begins with a brief comparison between east and west on wine usage. He goes on to discuss the metaphysical question of evil and the benefits of exhilarating drinks to help man cope with the cruel state of the human condition. Again letter 44 begins with Usbek's remarks on the rivalry existing between the different *états* in France. It procedes to the generalization that all men have an exaggerated sense of their own importance.

In his presentation of Usbek, Montesquieu is careful to mould the reader's opinion of his hero gradually. In the early letters of the novel Usbek appears as a mature, thinking individual whose philosophical notions of justice and natural law are based on an enlightened world view. But that is not the whole personage. In an expository flashback in letter 8 Montesquieu reveals the true reasons for Usbek's departure from the orient. The desire to instruct himself in the sciences of the west, suggested in Usbek's first letter, was only secondary to a desire to escape from his enemies: 'Je restois toujours exposé à la malice de mes ennemis, et je m'étois presque ôté les moyens de m'en garantir. Quelques avis secrets me firent penser à moi sérieusement. Je résolus de m'exiler de ma patrie, et ma retraite même de la Cour m'en fournit un prétexte plausible. J'allai au Roi; je lui marquois l'envie que j'avois de m'instruire dans les sciences de l'Occident; je lui insinuai qu'il pourroit tirer de l'utilité de mes voyages. Je trouvai grâce devant ses yeux; je partis, et je dérobai une victime à mes ennemis. Voilà, Rustan, le véritable motif de mon voyage' (p.141).

Usbek, then, is a voluntary exile who yearns for his native land. His approach to western civilization is intellectual while his heart and soul, his emotions, remain oriental. Letters 6, 27 and 155 to Nessir stress the theme of Usbek's loneliness and solitude in a strange and foreign land: 'Je vis dans un climat barbare, présent à tout ce qui m'importune, absent de tout ce qui m'intéresse.... Je ne puis plus, Nessir, rester dans cet affreux exil.... Je vais rapporter ma tête à mes ennemis' (pp.367-368).

Montesquieu makes a careful contrast between Usbek's well-ordered, philosophical world and the brutal oriental aspect of his personality, his savagely jealous behaviour. Usbek's treatment of wives and eunuchs reveals this side of his character. His attitude towards the *beau sexe* is disclosed first through his choice of vocabulary. In letter 2 he refers to his wives as merchandise; they form a 'dépôt' which needs a 'gardien' armed with 'clefs'. Letter 6 to Nessir reinforces this attitude. The availability of women in numerous harems has allowed Usbek to anticipate each new experience with a certain jaded objectivity. His passion is not that of a man in love but rather that of a man who is guarding a possession jealously. In effect Usbek's fears and distrust indicate Montesquieu's implicit condemnation of the injustice of the harem system, point out its instability, and foreshadow the eventual disorders within the *sérail*: 'Je vois une troupe de femmes laissées presque à elles-mêmes; je n'ai que des âmes lâches qui m'en répondent. J'aurois peine à être en sûreté, si mes esclaves étoient fidèles. Que sera-ce s'ils ne le sont pas? Quelles tristes nouvelles peuvent m'en venir dans les pays éloignés que je vais parcourir' (p.138)?

The tone of Usbek's letters becomes violent and menacing as suspiciousness emerges as an active ingredient of his character. The style changes accordingly. As early as letter 20 he is depicted as a cruel tyrant who rules through fear. Having learned of Zachi's conduct with a white eunuch, Usbek reproaches her

THE *LETTRES PERSANES*

violently for betraying his trust and sounds the death sentence of the guilty eunuch. His anger is not the wrath of the reasonable man which he pretends to be but that of a man who sees a pattern of life he believes in threatened. The letter foreshadows Usbek's violent measures as the end of the novel and demonstrates his conviction of god-given power in the harem. He treats the white eunuch as an object which he can dispose of at will: 'Et qui êtes-vous, que de vils instruments que je puis briser à ma fantaisie; qui n'existez qu'autant que vous savez obéir; qui n'êtes dans le monde que pour vivre sous mes lois ou pour mourir dès que je l'ordonne; qui ne respirez qu'autant que mon bonheur, mon amour, ma jalousie même, ont besoin de votre bassesse; et enfin, qui ne pouvez avoir d'autre partage que la soumission, d'autre âme que mes volontés, d'autre espérance que ma félicité' (p.162)? Usbek's despotic character and oriental nature emerge most strongly in the final letters. Following letter 147 in which he learns of the growing disorders in the harem, he grants full power to the chief eunuch and recommends strict discipline and rigorous punishments. The terseness of his language reveals better that his overt threats the violent measures he is prepared to take if his wives do not conform to his wishes: 'Puisse cette lettre être comme la foudre qui tombe au milieu des éclairs et des tempêtes! Solim est votre premier eunuque, non pas pour vous garder, mais pour vous punir. Que tout le sérail s'abaisse devant lui! Il doit juger vos actions passées, et, pour l'avenir, il vous fera vivre sous un joug si rigoureux que vous regretterez votre liberté, si vous ne regrettez pas votre vertu' (p.367).

Yet is should be kept in mind at this point, and this will be brought out more clearly in the following part, that Montesquieu is also seeking to show the destructive force of absolute power on Usbek as well as on the harem. Usbek is not a free agent, and therefore he remains true to his heritage. He is not a complete tyrant and does not lack a sense of justice, as is witnessed by the paternal protection he offers the black slave Pharan in letter 43. Montesquieu purposely undercuts our negative impression of

Usbek's dealings with the harem. Thus he points out that in fact Usbek has the compassion of a human being but unfortunately has been led astray and corrupted by the very tyranny of which he is an example.

Let us turn now to Montesquieu's treatment of the harem and his description of Usbek's wives and eunuchs. The intrigue in the seraglio is invented for two reasons primarily. It is employed as a literary device to maintain reader's suspense and interest until the end of the work, and it is a means of 'going behind', as Henry James called it, to reveal the true workings of Usbek's heart and mind and to penetrate the psychology of eunuchs and the women they guard.

It is enlightening, first of all, to glance at Montesquieu's chief source of information for various oriental practices and to examine the way in which the artist weaves these factual details into the fabric of a fiction. We know that the largest single source of information for the *Lettres persanes* was Chardin's *Voyages en Perse* which Montesquieu possessed in a 1687 edition. Montesquieu used Chardin as one would use an encyclopedia; yet he added a sympathetic understanding to the bare facts of harem life. This is especially true in the presentation and creation of the character of the chief eunuch. For instance, in letter 9 we can analyze and measure the nature and extent of Montesquieu's borrowings. Chardin, the historian, had described succinctly the state of hatred which existed between women and eunuchs: 'Ce que je puis dire de certain, c'est qu'on assure généralement en Orient que les femmes haïssent les eunuques à la mort, comme des argus qui veillent sur toutes leurs actions'[18]. By rewriting Chardin's observations and by placing them in the mouth of the chief eunuch, Montesquieu was able to create an atmosphere of realism and actuality and to give Chardin's statement a poignancy which it does not otherwise possess.

---

[18] *Collection choisie des voyages autour du monde*, ed. William Smith (Paris [n.d.]), p.381. Hereafter referred to as Chardin.

THE *LETTRES PERSANES*

On the one hand, Montesquieu gives an objective appraisal of the eunuch's unfortunate condition. He creates a sympathetic collusion between the narrator of the letter and the reader, by revealing the insecurity which exists between eunuchs and harem wives. The constant see-saw battle for favour in the eyes of the master results in a highly tense situation between wives and eunuchs. The kingdom of one becomes the prison of the other.

On the other hand, Montesquieu explores on the subjective level the effects of harem life on a human being and the psychological reasons for the chief eunuch's harshness and for the perverse enjoyment he derives from his cruelty. Chardin (p.381) had said: 'Quelques gens assurent qu'il y a des eunuques qui ressentent la passion de l'amour et qui recherchent le commerce des femmes'. Montesquieu borrowed these simple observations and transformed them into psychological reflectors which mirror the eunuch's innermost psyche. In this way Montesquieu penetrates the eunuch's own objective presentation of reality and observes subjective phenomena and a more fundamental reality. Thus, letter 9 demonstrates the idea that castration does not kill sexual desires necessarily but rather increases the frustration of being physically unable to release or satisfy sexual passion. This condition of being constantly surrounded by desirable objects and the ever-present image of the sexually contented master have profound psychological effects on the aging eunuch who approaches women with personal venom. From these few comparisons we see that Chardin merely supplied the raw material and that Montesquieu's creative optic transformed dry fact into a revealing and compelling tale.

In his treatment of Usbek's wives Montesquieu has done little to characterize them in depth. Yet he gives us enough information about them to define their function in the work. In the early letters from the harem Montesquieu amuses himself and his readers with the rather naked desires of Usbek's women and foreshadows their eventual infidelity. Zachi and Fatmé speak as one, their complaints and frustrations being similar. The petulant ardour of these wives forms a sharp contrast with Usbek's calm and almost placid indifference to them as sexual objects. In letter 3 Montesquieu reveals Zachi's frustration through a voluptuous scene. In the turbulence of erotic memories Zachi conjures up fantasies and images which reveal graphically her frantic mental condition. Fatmé writes in the same vein in letter 7. She provides an early warning for Usbek when she speaks of the 'violence de son amour' and says 'qu'une femme est malheureuse d'avoir des désirs si violents, lorsqu'elle est privée de celui qui peut seul les satisfaire' (p.139).

Roxane and Zélis are more clearly defined. From the tone of her letters Zélis seems the most perceptive and most mature of Usbek's wives. In letter 62 she is depicted as a subtle critic of the confinement of women. Her lucidity is an insinuating threat to Usbek's position as lord and master. She raises the question of the unnatural state of women in the *sérail* by pointing out that duty and inclination are not enough to guarantee fidelity, while adding that restraint is necessary to squelch natural passions and to support women 'dans ce temps critique où les passions commencent à naître et à encourager à l'indépendance' (p.221). The fact that Usbek has created a prison for himself through his jealousies and suspicions and that Zélis realizes it not only does Zélis honour but provides her revenge: 'Dans la prison même où tu me retiens, je suis plus libre que toi: tu ne saurois redoubler tes attentions pour me faire garder, que je ne jouisse de tes inquiétudes; et tes soupçons, ta jalousie, tes chagrins sont autant de marques de ta dépendance' (p.222). It is not surprising that this letter causes Usbek to suspect Zélis later of instigating many of the harem troubles (p.363) and shifts his suspicions away from the other wives, especially Roxane: 'tu soupçonnois Zélis, et tu avois pour Roxane une sécurité entière. Mais sa vertu farouche étoit une cruelle imposture' (p.371).

Two views of Roxane's character emerge from the *Lettres persanes*. First of all, we see her through the rose-coloured glasses of the man who loves her, and secondly, we see her as she

THE *LETTRES PERSANES*

reveals herself in the final pages of the novel. She does not love Usbek and never has. The reader's view of Roxane, which is Usbek's at first, is completed when Montesquieu lets us into the secret of her deception. Thus, in retrospect Usbek's attachment to her appears somewhat pathetic, certainly misguided, and rather ironic.

Montesquieu purposely distorts our impression of Roxane through a series of indirect reports about her character in order to give a greater surprise impact to the final letter of the work. The first mention of Roxane occurs in letter 20 in which Usbek appears as the unwitting dupe of her virtue: 'Roxane n'a d'autre avantage que celui que la vertu peut ajouter à la beauté' (p.162). Letter 26 continues a series of false interpretations of Roxane's character and her behaviour, as Usbek describes Roxane's initial resistance to his overtures of love as a struggle between love and virtue: 'Deux mois se passèrent dans ce combat de l'Amour et de la Vertu' (p.169). The extent to which appearance belies reality is revealed in Usbek's interpretation of Roxane's words and gestures: 'quand je vous vois rougir modestement; que vos regards cherchent les miens; que vous vous insinuez dans mon cœur par des parolles douces et flatteuses: je ne saurois, Roxane, douter de votre amour' (p.170). Again in letter 151 Roxane is depicted as a model of virtue and fidelity, being the only wife who has remained true to Usbek. Montesquieu involves us in Roxane's successful deception by not divulging the true nature of her attitude towards Usbek until the end of the work where her revenge through infidelity and suicide surprise and shock not only Usbek but the reader as well.

Eighteenth-century writers often interpolated stories into the texts of their fictions in order to provide variety and amusement. Often these tales were digressions which had little to do with the major intrigue. Montesquieu was a victim of this tradition. The stories of Aphéridon, Astarté and Ibrahim are on the surface rather frivolous, light, and sentimental narratives which Montesquieu has highly ornamented to let a little air between the pages of his novel. Sometimes lewd in nature, these stories demonstrate Montesquieu's wish to satisfy the sentimental and oriental tastes of his day with stories which are eastern in ornamentation. It is perhaps useful to point out that the 'Histoire d'Aphéridon et d'Astarté' and the 'Histoire d'Ibrahim' indicate Montesquieu's adroitness with the *conte philosophique*, a genre which he exploits with some success in *Arsace et Isménie*.

However, it is an added tribute to Montesquieu's skill that these episodes illustrate basic themes of the *Lettres persanes* and contribute to the overall flow of the novel. The Guèbre episode with its theme of incest illuminates the relativity of social customs. By creating sympathetic characters, caught in a web of circumstance, not of their own doing, Montesquieu succeeded in arousing indulgence for a subject normally repugnant to western readers.

The 'Histoire d'Ibrahim', or the story of Anaïs, is more in keeping with the tradition of the oriental romance. There is the barbaric cruelty of harem life with all its outrages, voluptuous scenes of sensual pleasure, and the dazzling brilliance of paradisiacal splendors. The story is an interesting inversion of the situation between Usbek and his wives. In Anaïs's paradise women have the upper hand, and men are placed in subservience. Justice which is denied women in the *sérail* is finally achieved in an imaginary land. The story is a well-constructed, cleverly narrated tale within a tale. Montesquieu titillates his reader by presenting a vivid and carefully gradated picture of Anaïs's sensual pleasures. After having engaged the reader's attention and interest vicariously, Montesquieu procedes to point out the moral. Emphasis on the sensual fades as the ideological content of the tale emerges in a strong light, reflecting the change in Anaïs's own attitude. Gradually she comes to realize the value of tranquil, reflective moments 'où l'âme se rend, pour ainsi dire, compte à elle-même et s'écoute dans le silence des passions' (p.345). The need to enrich her purely sensual life with a philosophical one turns Anaïs's thoughts back to the *sérail*. She succeeds in balancing

THE *LETTRES PERSANES*

sensual pleasures with philosophical considerations by distributing poetic justice to her earthly husband.

These charming tales as well as letters from Usbek, Rica, and the harem demonstrate that Montesquieu was aware of the technical problems of the epistolary method and that he was successful in overcoming effectively the difficulties of exposition, characterization and variety. Exposition is handled rapidly and succinctly in the early letters. The oriental drama is solidly established and cuts across the philosophical concerns of the novel revealing the duality in Usbek's personality and providing an exotic oriental flavour for the novel. Characterization is treated effectively through distinctive thematic content and individualized styles. The problem of monotony is overcome by alternating the humorous with the serious, through a charmingly discursive style and through oriental romances inserted into the text. Yet the full impact of Montesquieu's skill in the *Lettres persanes* can only be appreciated through a study of how these several parts relate to the whole and form a unified structure.

IV. Structure

In his 'Quelques réflexions' Montesquieu stated that he had attempted to produce 'une espèce de roman' in which he had sought to add 'de la philosophie, de la politique et de la morale, à un roman'. From this statement we have a suggestion of the limitations which Montesquieu himself imposed upon his work and an intimation of his overall plan. Montesquieu indicated, though he did it cautiously, that the *Lettres persanes* contained more than a novel. In the 'Quelques réflexions' he was not satisfied with a simple literary justification of the letters. He insisted that his satirical intentions be known. Slyly he invited the intelligent reader to discover the *substantifique moëlle* in the letters with this equivocal comment: 'Certainement la nature et le dessein des *Lettres Persanes* sont si à découvert qu'elles ne tromperont que ceux qui voudront se tromper eux-mêmes' (pp.130-131).

It would appear from the 'Quelques réflexions' that Montesquieu had intentionally planned to combine two distinct aspects of the epistolary novel in the composition of the *Lettres persanes*. On the one hand he was using the letter technique to create an interesting fiction, while, on the other hand, he employed the epistolary method for satirical purposes. In effect Montesquieu's work remains a unique achievement in that it joins philosophical, political and social questions to a 'roman'. No follower of Montesquieu succeeded in unifying, as he had, 'le tout par une chaîne secrète'.

When Montesquieu referred to the 'roman' of the *Lettres persanes*, he undoubtedly meant the harem intrigue which reappears throughout the work. This point may seem too obvious to warrant repeating. However, this 'roman' is more than an ornament for the satirical elements of the book, and it is more than an attempt to satisfy the exotic tastes of the time. From the author's own statement, we learn that these letters from the harem are a crucial contribution to the unity of the work. Indeed, through juxtaposition with letters treating philosophy, politics, and social mores, the oriental letters form a novelistic counterpoint which provides the fundamental architecture of the work. In the light of this recurring oriental motif the planned complexity of Usbek's character is illuminated.

Montesquieu presents Usbek from three different angles. There is first of all Usbek's attachment to an oriental tradition to which he is devoted. This might be called the emotional point of view. Secondly there is Usbek's understanding of western ways and his ability to formulate philosophical concepts when it is not a personal question. This is the intellectual point of view. A third perspective emerges from Usbek's inability to confront and to merge his intellectual and emotional lives. And this is the ironic point of view of an implied author. While the letters present a certain thematic and stylistic unity and consistency in the characterization of both Usbek and Rica, the 'chaîne secrète' of the novel appears to rest in the literary device of dramatic irony.

THE *LETTRES PERSANES*

In this section I will explore this technique in order to determine the extent of the work's structural unity.

Through the juxtaposition of characters and themes, irony reveals the disparities between appearances and realities. Montesquieu tears back the masks behind which individuals and societies hide. Thus through dramatic irony the author reveals the inconsistency between Usbek's enlightened philosophy and his traditional behaviour. Usbek unwittingly condemns himself by revealing the contradictions in his own character without perceiving or correcting them. Thus Montesquieu allows the reader a clairvoyance which the main character lacks. The reader assumes a position of superiority and sees things from the point of view of the omniscient author. Montesquieu's light hand as a writer enables us to discover his ironic intent only progressively, beginning with the amused perceptions of the first letters to the tragic cry of Roxane's revolt at the end.

The structure of the *Lettres persanes* reminds one of the musical form of theme and variations. In both cases the statement of the main theme provides the fundamental structure of the work, while the variations exploit and release all the implicit meaning in the basic theme or melody. This musical form is a loose rather then rigid structure. In the *Lettres persanes* the main theme or melody is the *décalage* between Usbek's ideals and his actions. This basic theme remains constant throughout the novel and is continually re-emphasized and reinforced in various letters which treat philosophy, religion, society and harem life.

The discussion of the Troglodytes points out Usbek's main philosophical interests, *i. e.*, questions relating to justice and the nature of governments. This apparent digression is strategically placed in the novel and furnishes the first and perhaps most fundamental link in the structure of the letters. The Troglodyte chapters fall between letters 9 and 15, both of which are from the chief eunuch. The injustices of the harem revealed in these two letters form a striking contrast with the principle of justice which rules implicitly in the Troglodyte society. The disparity between

Usbek's philosophy and his actions is clearly thrown into focus when we read in letter 10 that 'la justice est une qualité qui est aussi propre que l'existence' (p.145). In terms of the novel's structure it is important to realize that letter 15 was an addition to the 1754 edition of the *Lettres persanes*[19]. The letter illustrates Montesquieu's conviction that eunuchs do possess a heart and are capable of deep feeling even though they are treated as emotionless automata and are reduced to second class human beings by the barbarous practices of the harem. Letter 15 reveals poignantly the injustice of the oriental attitude towards eunuchs. The insertion clearly indicates the author's desire to emphasize the basic theme of the novel, Usbek's paradoxal nature, by vigorously underlining the discrepancy between Usbek's principles of justice in the Troglodyte chapters with the injustices of the eunuch's condition.

The largest number of letters which Usbek receives are from the harem, totalling twenty-two in all, eleven from wives, five from the chief eunuch, and the remaining six from various harem flunkeys. Although our impressions of the harem are established in the early letters, the harem intrigue recurs as a leitmotif reminding us of the work's underlying ironies. The essential subject of this body of correspondence is the anti-nature theme, the artificiality of harem life. Connected with this main theme and reinforcing it are such supporting topics as sexual frustration, perversity, unnatural desires, severity, savage cruelty, and sadism.

In the letters dealing with eunuchs Montesquieu was interested in pointing out the abuses of a system which transformed ordinary men into near monsters. As was pointed out earlier, letter 9 reveals the warped psychology of the chief eunuch with respect to women. Elsewhere Montesquieu varies the process and

---

[19] Montesquieu called for the insertion in these terms: ' "Cette lettre doit être mise à la page 64, t.1. Elle sera la quinzième et celle qui était la quinzième sera la seizième; ainsi de suite" ' (Barckhausen, ii.13; cited by Vernière, p.38).

THE *LETTRES PERSANES*

provides explicit proof of the distorted mentality of the chief eunuch who seeks a vengeance on the objects of unsatisfied desires[20]. In letter 96, for example, the chief eunuch pursues his personal vendetta against women by demonstrating the rather sadistic pleasure he derives from admitting a new girl into the harem and by inflicting grief on the other wives.

The number of precautions and restrictions which the harem system imposes on individual liberty suggests the inherent weaknesses latent in this artificial society. In letter 47, for example, Zachi describes an excursion taken by Usbek's wives and the vigilance which is used to defend the honour of the master and the virtue of his women. The letter reveals the savageness with which the 'courouc' is enforced and the blind devotion of the eunuch to his master's honour: 'Un curieux, qui s'approcha trop près du lieu où nous étions enfermés, reçut un coup mortel, qui lui ôta pour jamais la lumière du jour; un autre, qu'on trouva se baignant tout nu sur le rivage, eut le même sort; et tes fidèles eunuques sacrifièrent à ton honneur et au nôtre ces deux infortunés' (p.196).

While the anti-nature theme of the *Lettres persanes* is mirrored in the twisted psychology of the chief eunuch and in the discontent of Usbek's wives, it is also illustrated in several letters dealing with sexual aberration and deviation. Letters 4 and 147 mention lesbianism as an extreme to which Usbek's wives are driven to release pent up sexual drives. The theme of the vain sexual desires of eunuchs initiated in letter 9 recurs in letters 20 and 53. In letter 9, as we have already seen, the chief eunuch relates the story of his youth and his frustrated sexual desires. In letters 20 and 53 Montesquieu provides an actual demonstration of a eunuch's passions when describing the cruel necessity to which Usbek's wives and eunuchs are forced as they seek a futile sexual release from one another.

The final letter from Roxane, Usbek's favourite and most trusted wife, supplies the final link in the ironic 'chaîne' which circumscribes the work. Usbek's defense of suicide in letter 76

---

[20] Montesquieu continues the theme of the eunuch's cruelly inhuman treatment of women in letter 64 (p.224) and letter 79 (p.251).

and Roxane's actual death form powerful parallels and are grotesquely ironic. Together, these two letters form a defense of suicide. Montesquieu has placed the theoretical defense in Usbek's mouth and the actual manifestation and justification of suicide in Roxane's death. In letter 76 Usbek says: 'Il me paroît Ibben, que ces lois sont bien injustes. Quand je suis accablé de douleur, de misère, de mépris, pourquoi veut-on m'empêcher de mettre fin à mes peines, et me priver cruellement d'un remède qui est en mes mains' (p.246)? Roxane's suicide becomes her only recourse. It is justified by the conditions under which she is forced to live and by her unwillingness to submit to the whims of a man she does not love. Her suicide is a final manifestation of freedom. Thus the death of Roxane becomes a symbol of the unfairness and artificiality of harem life. As such, the suicide underlines vigorously the basic contradictions in Usbek, the man who speculates fruitlessly on justice while condoning tyranny: 'J'ai pu vivre dans la servitude, mais j'ai toujours été libre: j'ai réformé tes lois sur celles de la Nature, et mon esprit s'est toujours tenu dans l'indépendance.... Tu étois étonné de ne point trouver en moi les transports de l'amour. Si tu m'avois bien connue, tu y aurois trouvé toute la violence de la haine' (pp.372-373).

In all the letters which delve behind the locked doors of the harem, our criticism falls, not on the victims of the harem, but, on Usbek, the tyrant, who holds individuals in an unnatural state and who is ultimately responsible for the disorders of the society which he helps to perpetuate. In letter 158 Zélis points out the true source of the disorders within the harem: 'C'est le tyran qui m'outrage, et non pas celui qui exerce la tyrannie' (p.370).

It is only when these harem letters are juxtaposed to other letters which treat such varied topics as natural law, government, religion, philosophy, and even population that they become ironic and make, by implication, an ironic figure of Usbek. In some cases Usbek is guilty of contradiction only by inference and association. At other times he is patently critical of his own civilization though pathetically unable to change his ways. He perceives intellectually though he does not accept emotionally.

In the letters dealing with government and legislators, Usbek exhalts the beneficent and paternal role of the legislator in society despite his own role as chief bully in the harem. As early as the Troglodyte chapters the family structure is portrayed as the microcosm of a larger social complex. The family is represented as the natural core of society and supplies the harmonious cohesion of social parts in time of peace as well as war. The notion of a patriarchal society based on natural law is further developed by Usbek in letters 94 and 104, and in letter 129 the legislator is deified and compared to the creator of the universe: 'les pères sont l'image du Créateur de l'Univers' (p.323). The legislator derives his authority from natural law. Paradoxically Usbek maintains the traditional laws of his country. He keeps slaves, treats eunuchs scornfully, and imprisons women while professing that justice is a quality inherent in all men and derived from natural law.

Even Montesquieu's apparent digression on depopulation serves to strengthen our ironic view of Usbek. Despite the fact that he perpetuates an artificial society in the harem, Usbek deplores the artificial, unnatural practices of various societies as detrimental to the propagation of the human race. In ten letters to Rhédi, Usbek condemns certain societies for having altered natural law. He maintains that it is contrary to and inconsistent with nature to 'fixer le cœur, c'est-à-dire ce qu'il y a de plus inconstant dans la nature' (p.303), although this is exactly what he attempts to do in the harem.

The character of Rica supplies an important link in the structure of the letters. Rica is in certain respects a foil for Montesquieu's criticism of Usbek. Actually the letters from Rica have a triple function. They allow us to see Parisian society from a perspective which Usbek does not possess. They form a humorous respite from the serious tone of Usbek's letters. And thirdly, they are implicitly critical of Usbek's way of life and heighten our ironic view of Usbek. Rica's emancipated view of women arises from his social contact with them whereas Usbek's blindless arises partly from his hesitancy to accept western social mores.

In contrast to Usbek, Rica undergoes development and change, gradually shedding his Persian skin and becoming more and more westernized. He discards his oriental costume in favour of western clothing and prompts the famous observation: 'Comment peut-on être Persan?' (p.177). By letter 38 Rica has begun to doubt the wisdom of his own civilization and entertains questions concerning the rights and privileges of women, a question which bears directly on the intrigue of the harem and Usbek. Rica introduces a 'philosophe galant' who maintains that nature has never dictated a law submitting females to males and further points out the injustice of the stronger sex tyrannizing the weaker. Rica pursues the thought of his 'philosophe' and mentions several highly civilized cultures in which women played an important role. It is not until letter 63 that Rica emerges as an ardent critic of the Orient and speaks out against certain oriental abuses such as slavery, rule by fear, and the need for dissimulation to disguise one's true feelings. He deplores a culture in which natural law is submerged under artificial conventions. He enjoys the free interchange between the sexes which he has encountered in France, and he emphasizes clearly the different approaches to life which the two men have (p.222):

Je crois que tu veux passer ta vie à la campagne: je ne te perdois au commencement que pour deux ou trois jours, et en voilà quinze que je ne t'ai vu. Il est vrai que tu es dans une maison charmante, que tu y trouves une société qui te convient, que tu y raisonnes tout à ton aise: il n'en faut pas davantage pour te faire oublier tout l'Univers.

Pour moi, je mène à peu près la même vie que tu m'as vu mener: je me répands dans le monde, et je cherche à le connaître. Mon esprit perd insensiblement tout ce qui lui reste d'asiatique, et se plie sans effort aux mœurs européennes.

In the letters which I have discussed the ironic view of Usbek is uniquely moulded by inference or by association through

THE *LETTRES PERSANES*

juxtaposition of letters. This ironic perspective is diminished somewhat in those letters where Usbek is directly critical of certain oriental practices. In these letters which reveal the inefficacy of Usbek's philosophy when opposed to tradition, the extent to which he is a tragic prisoner of eastern traditions becomes painfully clear. In this light Usbek himself appears as a rather pathetic example of the dangers of tyranny and of the difficulties involved in changing established laws, even though these laws are recognized as harmful.

Usbek directly criticizes the oriental practice of polygamy, religion, the administration of government and the distribution of punishments. On a purely realistic level it appears somewhat incredible that Usbek can still remain rigidly cemented in oriental tradition in view of his criticisms. In fact, the voice of an implicit author is more in evidence in these letters than anywhere else in the novel. Montesquieu no longer circumvents his criticism of despotism with dramatic irony but allows Usbek to speak out directly against certain oriental abuses.

For example, in several letters on government Montesquieu allows Usbek to criticize despotic governments explicitly. In letter 89 the orient comes under attack by Usbek and by an 'homme de bon sens' whose opinion Usbek obviously respects since they are both in agreement. Usbek's own statement: 'la gloire n'est jamais compagne de la servitude' (p.264) points out the impossibility of honour and 'gloire' existing in Persia and is an implicit criticism of despotic government and of Usbek himself who maintains in theory that 'le désir de la gloire n'est point différent de cet instinct que toutes les créatures ont pour leur conservation' (p.263).

This same pattern of self-criticism is continued in letters 102 and 103 on crimes and punishments wherein Usbek deplores the arbitrary distribution of punishments in the orient and contrasts this practice with the magnanimity of occidental rulers (pp.282-283). Also, in letters on religion Usbek is willing to question oriental tradition and to praise religious tolerance, but nevertheless, he remains a loyal Moslem since this religion sanctions harem practices. There is no difficulty in understanding this apparent contradiction since for Usbek to reject Mohammedanism would imply a refection of the harem institution.

At other times Usbek shifts to a deistic point of view and affects a certain indifference to religion provided that a man fulfills the duties of a citizen in the state. Religion is viewed from a social angle, as a cohesive force in society. In letter 46 he recommends that religion be stripped of its ceremonial trappings and reduced to certain elementals. The love of god, he maintains, is best demonstrated by a love of man and of humanity: 'Je voudrois vous plaire et employer à cela la vie que je tiens de vous. Je ne sais si je me trompe; mais je crois que le meilleur moyen pour y parvenir est de vivre en bon citoyen dans la société où vous m'avez fait naître, et en bon père dans la famille que vous m'avez donnée' (p.194). This prayer, like many of Usbek's philosophical statements, remains theoretical, and he is unable to follow his deistic point of view to its logical conclusions and to effect the changes in the harem which his love of humanity would imply.

This literary device of tragic or dramatic irony which unifies the various aspects of the *Lettres persanes* to the 'roman' is similar in nature to the Greek use of irony. If Usbek is a tragic figure as some critics have suggested, we might compare him to Œdipus in that he perpetuates a way of life which becomes his own undoing. Unlike Greek tragedy where fate and destiny are placed in the hands of inexorable gods, Usbek is master of his own fate but only within limits. Usbek's destiny issues from his oriental background. His ethnic roots, firmly grounded in the orient, explain his jealous, possessive, and tyrannic nature. Yet while we may recognize the reasons for his blindness and ineffectiveness, we cannot forgive him. He professes a knowledge of men and a love of humanity and he approves of a form of government based on the brotherhood of mankind. It is the crowning achievement of Montesquieu's ironic intent that these fundamental truths of justice and love remain dormant and are not sustained or propagated in Usbek's administration of the harem, a society to which he remains attached emotionally but which runs counter to his deeper philosophical beliefs. It is Usbek's character which gives movement to the novel, and from the earliest letters the novel is headed towards an end to which he remains blind. In Greek tragedy the *perepeteia* or reversal of fortune marked the mocking intent of the gods. In the *Lettres persanes* an implicit author replaces the gods of Greek tragedy. It is the final letter from Roxane which announces the *perepeteia* of the work and the tragic defeat of its hero.

V. Conclusion

A word remains to be said about the literary importance of the *Lettres persanes* and its role in the development of epistolary fiction in France. This subject has been treated by F. C. Green and M. L. Dufrenoy but only in terms of Montesquieu's influence on epistolary polemic literature. In addition to his role as polemicist I have pointed out that Montesquieu was an accomplished technician and artist. He was keenly aware of the logical demands imposed by the epistolary novel and was successful in meeting them. He took great care to create an illusion of reality. He was sensitive to the possibilities of the letter-form and exploited such techniques as characterization through style, double and triple exposures of the same event, ironic contrasts, and sophisticated chronological patterns. Such later writers as Richardson, Rousseau and Laclos had at hand in the *Lettres persanes* a highly polished example of epistolary style and may have learned from a master.

Through this examination of various literary devices in the *Lettres persanes*, we come closer to Montesquieu's motivating idea, and we can achieve a clearer insight into the general meaning of the letters.

By juxtaposing two civilizations, that of the orient and the occident, and by vigorously criticizing both, Montesquieu attempted to detach his potential reader from the text. This reader would have to be an extraordinary person, someone who could stand outside his own time and space and view objectively only that which is universal and permanent in life. Jean Paul Sartre[21] summed up this rather unique position enjoyed by eighteenth-century writers when he stated: 'Comme il s'est fait universel, il ne peut avoir que des lecteurs universels et ce qu'il réclame de la liberté de ses contemporains, c'est qu'ils brisent leurs attaches historiques pour le rejoindre dans l'universalité'. Needless to say the task of judging the letters objectively is much easier for a twentieth-century reader that for Montesquieu's contemporaries to whom the social, religious, and political problems under discussion were of vital concern.

Thus in the final analysis the contest is not between east and west or to discover who is right or who is wrong in the *Lettres persanes* but to uncover a basic instinct for justice in men. And this principle is the concept of justice as it appears in letter 83. It is no coincidence that this letter appears at the mid-point of the novel. This principle of justice transcends national boundaries and forms an ideological crossroads between east and west and between all men. It is a concept which guarantees the inalienable rights of each individual: 'Quel repos pour nous de savoir qu'il y a dans le cœur de tous ces hommes un principe intérieur qui combat en notre faveur et nous met à couvert de leurs entreprises' (p.257). This passage contains Montesquieu's most explicit humanistic message: 'Quand il n'y auroit pas de Dieu, nous devrions toujours aimer la Justice; c'est-à-dire faire nos efforts pour ressembler à cet être dont nous avons une si belle idée, et qui, s'il existoit, seroit nécessairement juste. Libres que nous serions du joug de la religion, nous ne devrions pas l'être de celui de l'équité' (p.256).

In a sense Sartre's remarks are an over-simplification of the situation which confronts us in the *Lettres persanes*. Nor does

[21] *Qu'est-ce que la littérature?* (Paris 1948), p.133.

THE *LETTRES PERSANES*

this inner sense of justice satisfy or resolve the predicament facing Usbek. The optimism of Montesquieu was carefully hedged, and he employed Usbek as the vehicle to modify this optimism. The novel is polarized between two opposing though unequal concepts embodied in the personage of Usbek. At one extreme, there are his abstract considerations on justice and natural law based on theory. At the other extreme, we find concrete examples of injustice and traditional laws, caused by Usbek's emotional attachment to oriental traditions. Montesquieu was an acute enough psychologist to realize that the emotional life of a man is often stronger than intellectual and theoretical principles and that man clings to established traditions, even though he realizes those traditions to be flawed. If the question should be raised as to why Usbek is unable to change and to live according to his notion of universal justice, the letters provide a warning in the disturbingly human answer that it is easier to live with the old and imperfect than to give up everything and strike out on untested ground. Montesquieu's Usbek is another illustration of what Paul Hazard called 'la crise de la conscience européenne'. Usbek's story may be taken to apply to the predicament facing a whole generation as well as an individual. When the old institutions began to crumble, and the process of decay and change was already well underway by the end of the seventeenth century, men were faced with the task of rebuilding and reorienting their thinking. Usbek was unsuccessful because his philosophical concept of justice lacked the flesh and blood meaning which his disgruntled wives and homeland provided for him. In view of this, Usbek's final remarks take on symbolic meaning and become the bewildered cry of the *déraciné* or of the society confined to a type of limbo as the old order changeth and new horizons remain obscured, undefined and frightening: 'Malheureux que je suis! je souhaite de revoir ma patrie, peut-être pour devenir plus malheureux encore' (p.368).

Destiny, sentiment and time in the Confessions of Jean Jacques Rousseau

by M. L. Perkins

Whether considering the ideas on education, the novel, or some aspect of the moral, political, and economic theory, the student of Rousseau in forming an approach soon feels the need for returning to the *Confessions* for more intimate knowledge of the man, his thought processes, values, his strengths and weaknesses. The present article continues the renewed search for the meaning of Rousseau. Giving particular attention to his own definitions and distinctions, it affords an account of the following topics closely related to his art of autobiography in the *Confessions*: verisimilitude and uniqueness; types of conflict and Rousseau's means of expressing them; the themes of affection, character, citizenship, and career.

I

The body of criticism dealing with the *Confessions* has passed through several stages. In the nineteenth century and early part of the twentieth, a polemic flared over the question of whether Rousseau was a good or bad man[1]. Later, more attention was given to his accuracy. Critics sought to discredit his story or at least began to look at his statements with somewhat 'l'œil du juge d'instruction' (Pléiade, vol.i, p.xxxviii). More recently, the art of the *Confessions* has been made the issue, particularly with respect to verisimilitude. Underlying many of the studies in all

[1] see Albert Schinz, *La Pensée de Jean-Jacques Rousseau* (1929), for a summary of attitudes expressed in the controversy.

three categories is the common-sense notion that Rousseau's main object was to make the disclosures about his life convincing. He therefore aimed to communicate with the reader through a wealth of experiences everyone has shared[2]. Evidence, to be sure, can be found to support this view. The scenes Rousseau gives of his early youth, of his efforts to find himself as a young man, of his loves, of his friendships, of the conspiracy against him relate certainly in part to elements in every man's life. Some of his temporal dimensions correspond to our own awareness of objective or psychological time. Devices he uses to uphold his veracity fit well within the verisimilar framework. He often seeks to increase his authority by the utility motive: 'La grande leçon qu'on peut tirer d'un exemple aussi commun que funeste me fait résoudre à le donner' (i.14). He moves toward the reader by supplying information about family background, environment, the quality of his character and emotions. He associates himself with behaviour and values usually considered desirable, warmth of attitude toward father, aunt, friends, sense of shame or pride because of certain acts, love of truth, hatred of injustice, slander, lying, of inhumanity of any sort. Rousseau is definitely by his intentions a member of the world of integrity and good faith men usually claim to favour.

But to insist too much on the 'shared experience' aspect of the *Confessions* means ignoring Rousseau's own words. He makes it clear that the subject-matter is his uniqueness, that any resemblance between his life and the reader's exists at a superficial level only. From the first page on, the reader is bombarded by statements announcing and recalling that Rousseau is 'autre', different

---

[2] in a very useful article, 'Art and love in the *Confessions* of Jean-Jacques Rousseau', Mark Temmer reflects this point of view when he refers to Rousseau's efforts to make 'credible and convincing the story of his life' or speaks of his method as 'an orderly succession of images drawn from a fund of experiences shared by all' (*PMLA*, June 1958, lxxiii.215-220). For other studies which stress the literary and artistic side of the *Confessions*, see Richard A. Brooks, *A Critical bibliography of French literature*, iv (supplement), pp.154-156.

from other men, 'Je ne suis fait comme aucun de ceux que j'ai vus' (i.5). In the last book he is proud in his belief that the reader has been forced to see 'dans tout le cours de ma vie mille affections internes qui ne ressemblaient point aux leurs' (i.645). To make the point so persistently and then offer the reader experiences known by all, to embrace the reader's world, could have but one effect, a reaction of boredom and disappointment. The fact is that Rousseau's claim to being different seems justified. He has opened up hidden channels of personality. The purpose of his repeated allusions to uniqueness has been no doubt to move the reader closer to the author, to make him ready for the new, the incredible: 'Voici encore un de ces aveux sur lesquels je suis sûr d'avance de l'incrédulité des lecteurs, obstinés à juger toujours de moi par eux-mêmes' (i.644). This anticipation can still be seen as part of the verisimilar technique, although it departs from the concept of universally known experience expressed in the definition already given. By announcing the improbable, then living up to expectations, the author has forestalled objections arising from the limitations of insight any reader must inevitably have with respect to the intimate experiences of an exceptional person.

But to insist too much on this diminished form of verisimilitude raises in turn serious difficulties. Knowledge that the author has been objective enough to recognize dissimilarity between himself and the reader can build very little confidence if objectivity in describing Rousseau's uniqueness is itself open to question. The reader has been forewarned of surprise, his expectation has been satisfied, but then he is left wondering if the episode he has witnessed has not been interwoven with fictional threads. Many readers of Rousseau take this path, rather indefensibly if they are bothered by minor errors in fact, more excusably if they are reacting to his subjective control of the evidence. It is clearly part of Rousseau's technique that he spurns any pretext of being impartial, of putting distance between himself as hero and as author. His motive for veracity, that his name will live in history, that he therefore wants a real being to exist with his name, is substantial, but hardly reduces his involvement, for he is writing for posterity under pressure and with the aim of setting the record straight, revealing himself 'tel qu'il fut réellement, et non tel que d'injustes ennemis travaillent sans relâche à le peindre' (i.277, 400). If he points out that truthfulness has psychological rewards, is good therapy, that unburdening his conscience 'en quelque sorte a beaucoup contribué à la résolution que j'ai prise d'écrire mes confessions' (i.86), this kind of guarantee has more often than not been taken to indicate a mood of self-justification, of excusing guilt in the name of intention or the pressures of the moment. The presence of the author in all of the confession scenes, explaining, controlling the effect of a deed by self-accusation, regret, or mitigating humour, prevents for the most part the reader's belief in Rousseau's objectivity in matters which seriously involve the emotions. The entire weight of his argument is in fact in support of his need to be one with the hero. His memoirs deal mainly not with exterior facts, but with an interior world of feeling which only he can know: 'je ne puis me tromper sur ce que j'ai senti, ni sur ce que mes sentiments m'ont fait faire; et voilà de quoi principalement il s'agit' (i.278). As he writes, his style must vibrate sympathetically to his emotional state at the time of the deed and at the time of its rediscovery: 'mon style inégal et naturel, tantôt rapide et tantôt diffus, tantôt sage et tantôt fou, tantôt grave et tantôt gai fera lui-même partie de mon histoire' (i.1154; *Ebauches*). Rather than remain aloof, the author is totally to immerse himself in the hero's personal sentiments.

Rousseau is not for the most part using the framework of verisimilitude. He is never trying to make his world convincing at the expense of either uniqueness or subjectivity. The aim, to the contrary, is to identify intimate feelings in spite of society's standardizing effect: 'Il est impossible qu'un homme incessament répandu dans la société et sans cesse occupé à se contrefaire avec les autres, ne se contrefasse pas un peu avec lui-même et quand il aurait le temps de s'étudier il lui serait presque impossible de se connaître' (i.1121; *Mon portrait*). His purpose is to free himself from typical attitudes and sentiments. When he says the reader will find certain behaviour incredible, he can because of his frankness literally mean it. His betrayal of Marion, his abandonment of Lemaître, his fascination into impotence by Julietta's deformed breast, his desire to be imprisoned on the Isle de Saint-Pierre are all beyond his own comprehension. The conspiracy against him, the 'storm' which has engulfed him, is a mystery: 'J'ignore si ce mystère qui en est encore un pour moi s'éclaircira dans la suite aux yeux des lecteurs' (i.406). He wants the reader to take his side, not Grimm's, but he cannot be sure of this result. He is filled with self-doubt, used to having listeners greet the reading of his memoirs with silence: 'Madame d'Egmont fut la seule qui me parut émue; elle tressaillit visiblement; mais elle se remit bien vite, et garda le silence ainsi que toute la compagnie' (i.656). Except for moments of happiness found in reveries, he is obsessed by the darkness which has enveloped his existence, by the need to prove to himself that his personality can survive the barrier of hostility and indifference which seems to deny the validity of his being.

To remedy these two circumstances, the author's lack of objectivity, his inability to penetrate the significance of his uniqueness, the reader, according to Rousseau, must supply objectivity and establish meaning. The author is to tell everything and avoid the superficial consistency that characterizes the lives of great men, of portraits which impose so-called likenesses of the originals: 'On saisit les traits saillants d'un caractère, on les lie par des traits d'invention, et pourvu que le tout fasse une physionomie, qu'importe qu'elle ressemble?' (i.1149; *Ebauches*). He supplies information about the adverse opinion which upsets him, the relief he gains from confession, the importance of feeling in his scale of values. In the course of the book he also reveals frankly the limits of his memory, the gaps in his documentation, his ability to recall happy memories, his trouble in dredging up unhappy associations, the laborious nature and method of his composition. He tells where and in what kind of mood he was while writing the first part and contrasts this setting and state with the less fortunate circumstances influencing his composition of the second part. With a kind of perverse pride in being a hostile witness to himself, he uses a revealing vocabulary to describe his most intimate deeds and thoughts: 'dépravation' (i.16); 'concours impayable d'effronterie et de bêtise' (i.38); 'sot plaisir' (i.89); 'mon stupide aveuglement' (i.100); his plans 'les plus bizarres, les plus enfantins, les plus foux' (i.101); 'ma tête... hors de son diapason' (i.129); 'mon air gauche et mes lourdes phrases' (i.519); 'mon imagination ... occupée à me tracer des fantômes' (i.566). In part these are self-excusing comments, but through them the reader gets closer to Rousseau's mind, experiences him directly shuddering over the recall of certain events, senses the extent of his pain and joy. Intentionally, Rousseau has made himself the patient, the informant, and has made the reader the doctor, the judge: 'Je suis observateur et non moraliste. Je suis le Botaniste qui décrit la plante. C'est au médecin qu'il appartient d'en régler l'usage' (i.1121; *Mon portrait*). The reader is to listen to the data Rousseau offers, listen to the tale of an emotionally involved person, and then himself decide what the meaning is. Rousseau's outburst at the close of book XII that he has told the truth, that anyone who still believes him 'un malhonnête homme' is himself 'un homme à étouffer', only strengthens the impression given by earlier statements that the validity of the account lies less in the author's control of the material in order to give a convincing explanation than in an outpouring of authentic detail which the reader must interpret: 'Si je me chargeais du résultat et que je lui disse; tel est mon caractère, il pourrait croire, sinon que je le trompe, au moins que je me trompe'. Rousseau's fear must be, not 'de trop dire ou de dire des mensonges; mais c'est de ne pas tout dire et de taire des vérités' (i.175). He is well enough known so that the exterior facts can be verified, and 'mon livre s'élève contre moi si je mens' (i.1121; *Mon portrait*). The author is to do no more than literally turn himself into a document for study, become the 'première pièce de comparaison pour l'étude des hommes' (i [3].1120). The reader must judge the importance of the facts, 'je les dois tous dire, et lui laisser le soin de choisir' (i.175), but the important facts, it must be remembered, are the non-verifiable sentiments which only Rousseau can know, the 'succession d'affections et d'idées' (i.174). The reader, as co-creator, finds their sense: 'C'est à lui d'assembler ces éléments et de déterminer l'être qu'ils composent; le résultat doit être son ouvrage, et s'il se trompe alors, toute l'erreur sera de son fait' (i.175). The logic of his concept of the subservient author leads to this conclusion.

Rousseau's approach to the reader is not one of verisimilitude in any of the usual senses. He expects his audience to judge him independently of any conventional code of what is probable or proper. The idea of experiences which everyone has shared is similarly not to the point. Recognizable descriptions of places or certain apt simulations of time may excite the audience's desire for identification, but images are mainly important for Rousseau to the extent they carry his personal feelings. The reader must be observant for what is new. If he is stirred by the belief he has shared an experience, he may be reacting to a non-essential element outside Rousseau's uniqueness. The reader may also be misled by a logic the author may seem to have deliberately given to the sequence of his feelings. Again he is in error, for the significance of personal feelings is beyond the grasp of the individual having them. Rousseau writing about himself has purposefully avoided attributing to them any meaning in terms of a whole: 'Quand j'écris, je ne songe point à cet ensemble, je ne songe qu'à dire ce que je sais et c'est de là que resulte l'ensemble et la ressemblance du tout à son original' (i.1122; *Mon portrait*).

Since Rousseau's representation of life is no more than unique feelings, uncurbed by adherence to a code, by the need to find shared impressions, or by a logical meaning he has imposed, it follows that he alone decides when expression is in accord with inner feeling: 'Je prends donc mon parti sur le style comme sur les choses ... j'aurai toujours celui qui me viendra' (i.1154; *Ebauches*). It seems certain that verisimilitude, then, in its first legitimate sense is style, the word itself, emanating from the writer's dedication to his feelings, to capturing them accurately through his art, finding the accent of truth, of sincerity, which may then sound in his words: 'si elle n'y porte pas témoignage d'elle-même, il faut croire qu'elle n'y est pas' (i.1123; *Mon portrait*). To these data, the reader must make a contribution, analysis to principle, then synthesis to recreate the man of whom the author himself is unaware. The artist's task is not to convince the reader of meaning. The reader is to convince himself by fashioning Rousseau's feelings into significance. Verisimilitude, then, in addition to truthful style, has a second legitimate meaning, the author relinquishing to the reader all evaluation leading to definition of the author's uniqueness.

If this doctrine seems mainly negative, it is far from empty. It gives appropriate emphasis to differences within individuals, the basic source for any investigation of human nature: 'Sa manière d'être intérieure ... n'est connue que de lui' (i.1149; *Ebauche*). This priority given to the concept of uniqueness underlies also his notion that there was in his day no known human nature in any positive sense, only in the negative sense of the second *Discours*, man as amoral, innocent, free of pressures, his potential for character not defined: 'Jusqu'ici nul mortel n'a connu que lui-même, si toutefois quelqu'un s'est bien connu lui-même et ce n'est pas assez pour juger ni de son espèce ni du rang qu'on y tient dans l'ordre moral' (i.1158). Consistent with this turning to the unique and this awareness of man's current opacity to man is the imposition of total responsibility on each individual reader. The reader, unique himself, must on his own find in Rousseau a sense meaningful in terms of his own interior vision, 'je veux tâcher de faire ... que chacun puisse connoitre soi et un autre et cet autre ce sera moi' (i.1158). The object of art is no longer the known and a convincing restatement of its significance in terms of resemblances between author and reader.

To the contrary, differences are underlined. Through differences between informant and reader, the latter moves toward the unknown, possibly a new vision of mankind.

II

Rousseau's uniqueness can first perhaps best be introduced in terms of conflict at three different levels: within himself, between self and environment, between destiny and art. Internal conflict appears in the areas of the affections and of conscience. His expansive emotionality is intense, but so curbed by self-inhibiting timidity that he is filled with the absurdity of his amorous ambitions. As a result, the air of comedy or of the grotesque attaches to the role of fool or victim his hero in love must usually play: 'cet état ridicule et délicieux' in which on his knees he remains for precious moments before Madame Basile (i.76); his waiting eight days for what are to become in his mind the incestuous favours of mme de Warens, 'redoutant ce que je désirois, jusqu'à chercher quelquefois tout de bon dans ma tête quelque honnête moyen d'eviter d'être heureux' (i.194); in his passion for mme d'Houdetot 'le ridicule enfin de bruler à mon age de la passion la plus extravagante' (i.441). There is extreme inner discord, too, in his moral activities. His conscience, lucid in seeing right, makes him aspire to right, yet is housed in a machine so pitifully weak that he is repeatedly subjected to humiliating defeats. The lie against Marion, the abandonment of Lemaître, of his children, near disloyalty to Saint-Lambert are only a few instances of his submission to pressures which thwart his intentions and scar the soul. If weakness for Rousseau is a means of self-justification, as so many have said, it brings little relief from guilt: 'Ce souvenir cruel... me bouleverse au point de voir dans mes insomnies cette pauvre fille venir me reprocher mon crime comme s'il n'était commis que d'hier' (i.85-86). What is inconceivable, monstrous almost for him, is the incongruity of his purity of intention, his utter helplessness in carrying out certain acts, the torment that pursues him in spite of his apparent irresponsibility.

Two other areas, one related to the nation, the other to personal philosophy, set him against himself and also against his times. In an age of civic callousness, he yearns to be part of a *patrie*, or at least of a *pays*, but has a concept of the citizen so totally uncompromising in its defense of individual right that he renounces his own citizenship and is cast out by the two governments he had counted on most for shelter. After decrees by Paris and Geneva, his writings for no cause apparent to him seem to have turned his fellow intellectuals into madmen: 'En cherchant vainement la cause de cette unanime animosité, je fus prêt à croire que tout le monde était devenu fou' (i.590-591). As for his personal philosophy, almost overnight because of a new vision received in middle age, he has renounced forever a life of calm to attach himself with total dedication to a controversial concept of truth. The transformation in his character is in itself beyond comprehension: 'Qu'on cherche l'état du monde le plus contraire à mon naturel; on trouvera celui-là' (i.417). The results, conspiracy, odium, censure, defamation, represent a second revolution, 'époque terrible et fatale d'un sort qui n'a point d'exemple chez les mortels' (i.418).

In his presentation of affection, conscience, concept of citizen, of truth, Rousseau's uniqueness first means the appearance within himself of deep forces which set him at odds with himself and the world around him. He seems a person with too many senses, with insights which humiliate him in his own eyes and alienate him from other men. This theme of his originality as division and rupture has a definite evolution. Internal dissension, namely, expansiveness with timidity and sane conscience with great weakness, gradually finds its resolution in a certain self-mastery, but at the same time there is aggravation of the more external dispute, liberty and truth opposed to conventional citizenship and opinion. The relatively light atmosphere surrounding Jean Jacques, timid yet desiring to expand into a world of adventure and hope at the beginning of book II, of the boy pure in intention yet weak in deed at the end of that book, has become by book XII, because of strong personal conviction and gradually mounting social pressure, Rousseau beset and depressed by mystery and darkness.

The shift in emphasis from inward to outward struggle has been prepared by a more fundamental context, antagonism between destiny and art, introduced at the close of the first book in the contrasting views of the hero in youth, led by fate, blinded by his desires and fears, leaving the Geneva of Bossey and Ducommun, and of the hero in old age, who sees in art's perspective the Geneva of his youth as paradise lost: 'J'aurais passé [à Genève] ... une vie paisible et douce.... Au lieu de cela quel tableau vais-je faire?' (i.43-44).

A climate of helplessness and suffering is attached to Rousseau's conflicts, the apparent side of his uniqueness, by regular and frequent use of the words destiny, fate, fatality, which represent all of the influences which have led him from the course hindsight tells him should have been into, instead, the life that had to be. These forces recur under three different forms. The first are the accidents of nature, the physical circumstances which have controlled him, like temperament of father and mother, his physique at birth, early conditionings of many kinds, the impact on his emotions of a cruel master, the spell cast by the first glimpse of mme de Warens, the chance arrival of Bâcle, the intervention of other agents, Vitali, mme de Larnage, Vintzenried, Grimm. His style often creates for such events a mood of foreboding. With reference to the raising of the bridge, which announces his departure from Geneva, he says, 'je frémis en voyant en l'air ces cornes terribles, sinistre et fatal augure du sort inévitable que ce moment commençait pour moi' (i.42). By fatality he is to his later sorrow 'rejetté sans y songer dans la litterature dont je me croyais sorti pour toujours' (i.416). The unexpected interest taken in him by the *maréchal* de Luxembourg fatefully turns him from his intention to retire, 'le ciel qui me préparait une autre destinée me jetta dans un nouveau tourbillon' (i.517). The sense of the pressure of events, of his being submerged by powers beyond his control, is expressed even more strongly in the first page of book XII. Since he is unable to see the hand which guides the plot against him, his misfortunes appear to originate spontaneously: 'L'opprobre et les malheurs tombent sur moi comme d'eux-mêmes' (i.589).

A second element of destiny submerging Rousseau is social in nature. In spite of his distrust of the behaviour and ethics of his day, he shows at times a strong inclination to bow to them. In Paris, he adopts the attitudes of the 'gens très aimables' who frequented the establishment of mme Selle: 'je formai ma façon de penser sur celle que je voyais en règne' (i.344). He is excessively affected by the presence of other people, by the signs and symbols of society, money, status, judgments about his abilities, intrigue, all of them for him forms of intimidation. Invited to appear before the Consistory, he forgets the speech he had been preparing for three weeks: 'je fis dans cette conférence le rolle du plus sot écolier' (i.393).

The third kind of force binding his will operates through the automatic reactions within him, passions, delirium, revery, presentiment. Under the influence of passion he knows no restraint, no shame, responds to no threat of danger, knows no sense of respect, of *bienséance*. His passions are 'ardentes, et tandis qu'elles m'agitent rien n'égale mon impétuosité'. But this may last only a minute, and then he falls back into an equally uncontrollable state, 'l'indolence et la timidité même: tout m'effarouche, tout me rebute, une mouche en volant me fait peur' (i.36). Revery of the kind which permits foresight, for example, of his happiness with Maman, is brought on by external conditions. Mme de Warens is absent, at vespers. His heart is filled with her. The sound of bells, the chirping of birds, the beauty and calm of the day induce in him a trance-like state (i.107-108). Revery can also be the recreation of idealized images of his past life, like the dream states into which he escapes on the Isle de Saint-Pierre when he is influenced by the appearance of the lake water (i.642). Another form of reflex-like response to external stimuli is presentiment: 'Depuis quelques temps des sourds et tristes pressentiments me troublaient sans que je susse à propos de quoi' (i.564). Finally, delirium, triggered automatically as were the other states, is best defined as an emotional condition which allows Rousseau to see himself momentarily, his situation, the world around him, in a completely new context. As he leaves Geneva, delirium promises a new life in which he will be free: 'Libre et maitre de moi . . . le vaste espace du monde . . . mon mérite allait le remplir' (i.45). Later, delirium provides for him the vision of a new social order, first described in the first *Discours*: 'j'étais dans une agitation qui tenait du délire' (i.351-352).

Physical circumstance, social pressure, and his own automatic reactions seem to push Rousseau further and further toward a destiny he does not want, toward a certain fame, toward isolation. No damaging event can be explained for him except 'par l'aveugle fatalité qui m'entrainait à ma perte' (i.525). In the last book he finds that 'le sort qui m'a toujours mis en même temps trop haut et trop bas, continuait à me baloter d'une extrémité à l'autre' (i.629). Although this sense of submergence is strong, it is not total. Against destiny's mystifying weight, which he repeatedly admits, he is in fact by his attitudes constantly in revolt. Weakness under pressure can be a justification for the shameful deeds he must confess. He reacts, however, with feelings of guilt, insists in other words on acting as if free. A philosophy of necessity would permit him to discard unpopular views of liberty and truth, seek success, make his fortune. He makes adherence to his own views a question of choice: 'J'aurais pu me jetter tout à fait du côté le plus lucratif. . . . Mais je sentais qu'écrire pour avoir du pain eut bientôt etouffé mon génie et tué mon talent qui était moins dans ma plume que dans mon cœur' (i.402). Illogical guilt and dedication to truth may also no doubt be seen as compulsions, part of his submergence, but the tacit belief in free choice on which they rest indicates the will to be free. Revery, whether its content is future or past happiness, his states of delirium with visions of a new world, and his presentiments of disaster are further indication of his desire to escape from necessity.

Strict verisimilitude or what convinces the ordinary man did not suit Rousseau. By this frame of reference, his person and works had already been condemned. He required a reader who would think objectively and creatively, follow him into his unconvincing world of conflict, contradiction, incongruity, strange behaviour, not judge him by conformist codes which seemed also to be a facet of destiny. In part, his memoirs are the story of his submergence by forces greater than he, forces which in his opinion drove most of the men of his day. But, more important, his originality also is to admit and deny at the same time this fatalistic creator, a denial which amounts to the will to use his faculties in order to liberate himself and his possible meaning from destiny's course. Accidents of nature, heredity, environment, people exerting influence, social institutions, laws, codes of taste and behaviour, emotional urges, automatic reactions, their effects are observable phenomena in the exterior world. One may have the sense of controlling them or being controlled by them in greater or lesser degree. Rousseau was their pathetic victim. This he felt deeply. But memory holds other feelings reducing the importance of destiny, many of them opposed to submergence. To the prosaic observer, Rousseau unable to take the initiative with mme Basile is just a victim of the conditionings of his youth, hopelessly submerged. Rousseau conveys this sentiment. Yet in terms of feeling there is also for him another dimension to the scene, for in his suspended desire he finds an eternity of emotion, a satisfying experience transcending ordinary opinion's reality and permitting him to be completely himself. The entire range of sentiment, his feelings of emergence as well as of submergence, are reality for Rousseau. An essential theme of the *Confessions* is Rousseau's struggle to put his destiny into perspective, through his art to complete the world of daily action, success, and failure by this interior life of sentiment, by his own temporality.

For Rousseau, the basic validity of feeling as a medium in artistic communication can be understood by what happens in music. When the musician recreates in sound alone what he may have received through many senses, he is dealing ultimately in sentiment: 'Que toute la nature soit endormie, celui qui la contemple ne dort pas; et l'art du musicien consiste à substituer à l'image insensible de l'objet celle des mouvements que sa présence excite dans l'esprit du spectateur; il ne représente pas directement la chose, mais il reveille dans notre âme le même sentiment qu'on éprouve en la voyant'. If feeling is the substance of art, it follows that the strength of impression in the artist's rendering through one sense what he has known through others suggests a gradation among the arts. The force needed for this transference depends on 'cette succession d'idées et d'impressions qui échauffe l'âme par degrés'. Painting by this standard is inferior in its imitation, 'toujours froide', since it lacks the succession needed to build the emotionality of the observer, since unlike music it says everything 'au premier coup d'œil'[3]. The characteristics of music, primacy of its appeal to sentiment and reliance on the principle of succession, apply directly with some variance to Rousseau's art in the *Confessions*. Through sound, the musician evokes sentiments which correspond to those aroused in him and in other spectators by an event or object in nature. The autobiographer, too, is to deal primarily in feeling, but through his words he is to reproduce sentiments not inspired by any universally observable event or object in nature. He is to 'faire connoitre exactement mon intérieur' (i.278), to present his soul as object to be known by the reader for the first time, object hidden or incomplete as part of necessity, visible only through art, but capable of arousing in the reader new emotions like those raised by a natural object seen for the first time. Love, for example, must be defined, not in traditional terms, but is to be Rousseau's very personal experience of it, the effects it produced in him, a completely new phenomenon. Certain feelings without name must be imparted to the reader, sentiments somewhat beyond the grasp of the one who has

[3] *Œuvres complètes*, ed. Musset-Pathay (1823-1826), xiii.50-51.

experienced them, which can be only suggested, for example, a feeling not love, as Rousseau knows it, 'un autre sentiment, moins impétueux peut-être, mais plus délicieux mille fois', but not friendship either, 'plus voluptueux, plus tendre' than that, which cannot be clearly defined, can be painted only in terms of its effects, 'les sentiments ne se décrivent bien que par leurs effets' (i.104). Everyone has no doubt known a countryside similar to Les Charmettes, but Rousseau is concerned not at all with the generalities of experience. He must record his very personal involvement with the setting, 'mais comment dire ce qui n'était ni dit, ni fait, ni pensé même, mais goûté, mais senti' (i.225). To succeed in the task, style must in theory trace feeling directly without outside influence: 'je dirai chaque chose comme je la sens, comme je la vois, sans recherche, sans gêne, sans m'embarrasser de la bigarrure' (i.1154; *Ebauches*).

As for force through a moving succession of ideas and impressions, natural endowment permits Rousseau to give his memoirs this attribute. Basic to his theory of art is the conviction that he is memory more than action oriented, 'les objects font moins d'impression sur moi que leurs souvenirs' (i.174-175). His point is that for an action guided person each subsequent involvement with an event partially erases the memory of a previous involvement. In spite of the passage of time, enrichment of the inner being is prevented. Recounting his life at an advanced age, a man of this type would have few sentimental roots extending to the near past and even fewer to the remote past. For the memory oriented person, like Rousseau, the situation is very different. After a first involvement has occurred and passed into memory, that memory is more vivid than any subsequent action, so that memory of the subsequent action must always combine with a framework of memories already formed: 'les premiers traits ... sont demeurés ... ceux ... empreints dans la suite se sont plustot combinés avec eux qu'ils ne les ont effacés'. Since he is also image oriented, 'toutes mes idées sont en images', recalling in detail rather than abstractly, he has the concreteness of expression needed for the

THE *CONFESSIONS*

effective reproduction of feeling. The task of the artist, then, is to sort and sift his memories of feeling in order to find the most basic combinations, trace the deepening of these by subsequent layers, offer the entire evolution of his affective life in a valid hierarchy and sequence (i.174-175). His soul may thus be made transparent by 'la chaîne des sentiments qui ont marqué la succession de mon être' (i.278). Since the feelings of operational life are identical, for Rousseau, to the feelings memory's image carries, they can be the same as art's recreation of them, the same as the feelings the reader may experience vicariously if he can be induced to relive Rousseau creatively. Only in this sense is communication significant. Life and history, without an art of sentiment to interpret them, are truly the tale of an idiot, the deeds of men submitted blindly to events, who do not truly know themselves or their neighbours: 'la plupart des caractères et des portraits qu'on trouve dans les historiens ne sont que des chimères qu'avec de l'esprit un auteur rend aisément vraisemblable' (i.1121; *Mon portrait*).

If feeling is reality, time is largely psychological, dependent on the priority Rousseau gives some events over others as he brings to the surface the sentiments constituting his soul. Two main temporal elements control the materials. The first, basic to his theory and practice of art in the *Confessions*, is the unit of all feeling sequences, the ineffaceable moment, which endures, he believes, without loss and can thus be reproduced through art. An example is the injustice done him by the Lamberciers because of the broken comb: 'Je sens en écrivant ceci que mon pouls s'élève encore; ces moments me seront toujours présents quand je vivrais cent mille ans' (i.20). Although such identical recall of feeling is no doubt scientifically invalid, repeated allusion to the phenomenon imparts a quality of permanence to Rousseau's kind of reality, counteracts the traditional view of the fleeting, unstable nature of sentiment.

The complementing aspect of time is perspective, Rousseau's personal ordering, spacing, and accentuation of sentimental moments. An illustration is his summary of the miss Vulson affair in several lines (i.29-30). In this relationship he describes a series of separated moments, each indelibly imprinted in memory, but each replaced by a subsequent state: his immediate emptiness because of her departures; the tone of his letters a little later, which reveal 'un pathétique à faire fendre les rochers'; his naive exaltation because of her return to Geneva, ostensibly to see him, 'elle n'y put plus tenir'; his depression when she leaves again, 'je fis longtemps retentir l'air de mes cris'; his rage upon learning of her marriage, her trip to Geneva having been for a wedding gown; his self-possession twenty years later when he sees her in the distance on the lake, 'Je tressaillis à ce nom presque oublié', but has the boatmen alter course in his resolve not to renew a quarrel 'de vingt ans avec une femme de quarante'; finally, the feeling of humour which envelopes the entire summary and indicates the author's emergence from necessity into time as perspective. Time in this sense, given in epitome in the Vulson episode, controls in the *Confessions* all of Rousseau's ineffaceable moments, except that Rousseau is not always so clearly emergent. His perspective often indicates, as in book XII, an inability to rise decisively above his materials. The struggle between feelings of emergence and of submergence is then in close balance. Only his will to tell his story, to defeat his enemies with the truth, furnishes a limited sense of perspective, keeps him emergent.

Contributing to time as perspective are other emphases. The sense of time as present is often strong, without relief except in imagination, because past time is only regret and longing, youth in Geneva, Les Charmettes, to whose conditions there is no real return, and future time is rarely hope, is usually fear, the present continued, particularly in part II, fear of conspiracy, his enemies. The present itself is oppressive, Rousseau trapped at San Spirito, obsessed with the enemies persecuting him after book VIII. Attrition in time or time as change appears in the wear and tear of sentiments, Rousseau's feelings toward Maman during his first meeting when she is youthful, his despair at her later indifference,

THE *CONFESSIONS*

his regret at having neglected her, his sorrow upon receiving news of her death. Like present time, attritional time gives perspective an accent of submergence. Recurrence or perseveration in time appears in the operational continuance of sentiments from early to late in life, his devotion to Maman, his dedication to liberty. Suspended time characterizes his periods of complete freedom from pressure, episodes which have a timeless quality, life at Bossey, the day at Thône spent with mlle Graffenried and mlle Galley, his moments of revery with escape to the past on the Isle de Saint Pierre. Both time as recurrence and suspended time express emergence.

Objective, measured time is not completely ignored. The memoirs run from birth in 1712 to the year 1765. Rousseau mentions departures from this chronological order. The effect is to call attention to chronology even more. But the time grid serves principally to remind the reader that the events did have time and place coordinates. Subjective time in fact reigns within this apparent framework of objectivity. Rousseau influences the order of his feelings by omission or inclusion, which means books have different tempos. For example, all books of part I are of roughly equal length in pages, but book I covers sixteen years, book II nine months, III and IV eighteen months each, books V and VI roughly twelve years together. Parts of books receive emphasis by their slow tempo. The first book has a relatively fast tempo, but there are two slow parts, one highlighting the gentle life with the Lamberciers, the other the tormented life with Ducommun.

Perspective, assisted by pseudo-chronology, tempo, oppressive present, attrition, recurrence, by time as suspension, imposes on the ineffaceable moments of Rousseau's life an intimate psychological time.

III

The themes which best illustrate Rousseau's use of sentiment and time in the *Confessions* can be divided into four major categories: affections, character or virtue, the citizen theme, the career or artist theme, areas already briefly mentioned in terms of the conflicts representing Rousseau's uniqueness. The theme of affection includes these elements: expansiveness, the enemy, sexuality, friendship, love.

Expansiveness is originally the individual's need to uncover his heart, reveal his most secret thoughts: 'Mon cœur aimait à s'épancher pourvu qu'il sentit que c'était dans un autre' (i.81-82). This feeling permeates the *Confessions*, the history in one sense of Rousseau's successes and failures in removing barriers of constraint between himself and others.

The enemy for Rousseau means the inhibitory forces curbing expansiveness. It is natural shyness and even more the behavioural patterns of other people. It is insensitivity in Rousseau's father at times, in the Lamberciers, in Diderot's responding coldly to Rousseau's embrace. Some of Rousseau's most intimate friends and loves fail him momentarily and become the enemy, Maman, m. de Luxembourg, and others. The trait has completely pervaded character and established a fixed robot-like behaviour in Ducommun, Vintzenried, m. de Montagu, the mob that stones him. In its most nocuous form, the enemy is treachery, Vitali, Montmollin, especially Grimm raising 'un édifice de ténèbres qu'il me fut impossible de percer' (i.492-493).

Sexuality, too, usually appears as a curb to expansiveness. From childhood Rousseau has regarded such union 'sous une image odieuse et dégoutante', associates it with 'les filles publiques', 'la débauche', with the holes near 'petit Sacconex' in which he had been told 'ces gens-là faisaient leurs accouplemens' (i.16). His experience with the so-called Moor at the hospice of Turin makes him view all male sexual behaviour as loathesome and believe women must have 'les yeux bien fascinés pour ne pas nous prendre en horreur' (i.67). Sex with Maman is incestuous, with mme de Larnage uninhibited pleasure, but a purely physical attachment which he soon renounces. Vintzenried's excesses revolt him (i.265). His visit to the Padoana brings fear and disgust (i.317). The experience with Kupfel's 'pauvre petite' shames him (i.355).

With Thérèse sex is for Rousseau without love and a burden to health (i.414, 595). It is hideous in Gauffecour, aged, gouty, and impotent, making lewd advances (i.390). Rousseau tries not to dishonour the divine image of mme d'Houdetot with any thought of conquest (i.444). He is offended by the sordid indiscretions of Sauttershaim (i.618). Onanism accompanied by fancy is apparently his most lasting adjustment, permits him to find a perverted kind of expansiveness, in imagination to 'disposer pour ainsi dire... de tout le sexe' (i.109, 166, 316, 595, 1569).

The enemy compromises Rousseau's friendships. Sexuality is a threat or at least an obstacle to his loves. Yet the inclination to expansiveness is not thwarted. Four great friendships enhance his life, then end abruptly, the relationships with cousin Bernard in early youth, closing with the departure from Geneva (book I), with Altuna in Italy and in Paris, ended by Altuna's marriage, then death (book VII), with m. de Luxembourg at the Hermitage (book X), broken by conspiracy, flight, then death, with milord Keith before the period of violence and persecution at Neuchâtel (book XII) and closing with the departure of Keith and Rousseau's belief that traitors had taken advantage of their separation to 'me défigurer à ses yeux' (i.596). Other associations respond to a need of the moment, show Rousseau reaching out to an individual who seems to personify one of his own aspirations or urges: the *abbé* Gaime, Bâcle, Venture, Simon, the archimandrite, Klupfel, Diderot, Sauttershaim.

The most important of the sub-themes of affection, Rousseau in love, is too broad a subject to be treated in any detail here. It is sufficient to recall briefly the wealth of feelings involved: a child's love for his aunt; love as subservience and sexual excitement during the chastisement afflicted by mlle Lambercier; vanity in his rivalry for the favours of mlle Vulson; passion teased and tormented with mlle Goton; suspended desire with mme Basile; longing for the proud, disdainful, noble mistress he might worship in mlle de Breil; the triangular balancing of desires which characterizes the day at Thône; the mother-son-lover union provided by mme de Warens, which yields at Les Charmettes the rare relationship he calls more delicious than love; the physically satiating experience offered by mme de Larnage; his impotence in the presence of the demanding beauty of Julietta, who required a conqueror; the sheltering affection he offers Thérèse; his love as the real thing with mme d'Houdetot, an idealization combining and fulfilling aspirations potential in his other partial loves and responding to book IX's desperate plaint that he has not found the perfect companion: 'Dévoré du besoin d'aimer sans jamais l'avoir pu bien satisfaire, je me voyais atteindre aux portes de la vieillesse, et mourir sans avoir vécu' (i.426).

Rousseau's presentation of his affective life is carefully controlled by temporal devices. Tempo is slowed during the descriptions of his great friendships. Episodes during which time seems suspended occur regularly for the love theme from book I through the mme d'Houdetot affair of book IX. Becoming stronger in book VII, the enemy motif increases steadily to peaks at the ends of books IX, XI, and becomes the mystery of book XII, 'l'œuvre de ténèbres dans lequel depuis huit ans je me trouve enseveli' (i.589). For these periods very often time is involvement in the present. During the night and day of crisis over *Emile*, just before the flight to Geneva, tempo is slowed to an almost hour by hour description of events. The relief from this movement offered by the Luxembourg circle is weakened by Rousseau's feeling that the relationship has contributed to his downfall. The Keith friendship is insufficient to lighten the mood of book XII. The climactic close of the affection theme as something positive, as expansiveness, occurs in fact in book IX with the mme d'Houdetot episode, during which a turning away from life to art appears. Rousseau's desire to find a love object is transformed into revery, then into artistic efforts, the preliminary setting forth of the characters of the *Nouvelle Héloïse*. Gradually, mme d'Houdetot comes to represent Julie, 'ce ne fut qu'après son départ que, voulant penser à Julie je fus frappé de ne pouvoir plus penser qu'à Madame d'Houdetot'. Art has assumed living form, but this form, mme d'Houdetot, is also more essentially art's form, for she has been first remodeled by art: 'je ne vis plus que Madame d'Houdetot, mais revêtue de toutes les perfections dont je venois d'orner l'idole de mon cœur' (i.440). Expansiveness in the *Confessions* has thus come to mean basically discontent, the rejection of existing affection in search of an inner ideal, out of reach of sexuality, of the enemy in any form. In spite of the periods of suspended time, of time as recurrence in the persisting search for a higher expression of friendship and love, the perspective is one of emergence through truth only, rather than through emotional happiness, and the truth is basically the turning from life to art and destruction of even art's ideal by opinion, slander, and the enemy.

The second category of sentiments, those related to character in its moral aspects, has a series of internally contrasting sub-themes: guilt and innocence; weakness and strength; virtue and vice.

Guilt is present in all of the confessions no matter how insignificant: the early readings with the father, precocious sexual feelings, compulsive stealing. The Marion episode represents a climax and is underlined by time as submergence in the present, indicated by pressure from superiors, the other servants, by being in the spotlight. Confession continues with exhibitionism, ingratitude toward the Gouvons, abandonment of Lemaître, his trying to pass for a music-master in Lausanne, then incest with Maman, another moment stressed by the use of time as entrappment in the present and by reduced tempo. Other high points of guilt are the abandonment of his children and the affair with mme d'Houdetot. These negative feelings alternate regularly with aspirations toward timeless innocence: Bossey; protection by Maman; the day with mlle Galley and mlle Graffenried; vagabonding through the countryside; references to the sensuality of certain religious people enjoying flowers and animals; life at Les Charmettes; calm moments spent with Thérèse; his days on the Isle de Saint Pierre. Innocence is not just a part of happiness.

Happiness, to the contrary, is much restricted and is always defined for this theme of morality within the limits of innocence, with the result that the tension between guilt and innocence is never obscured. The movement of the books is toward ascendency through personal innocence. His control in the Houdetot affair, which leaves him innocent in fact in spite of guilty passion and gossip, his regaining of equilibrium at Montlouis (book x), his departure for Switzerland with calm heart in spite of the hate surrounding him (end of book xi) are steps in his self-redemption.

This personal mastery is tied closely to the weakness-strength theme, which brings increasing intellectual awareness of the problem of character; first, in terms of the maxim that situations should be avoided which place self-interest and duty in opposition (i.56); second, in terms of the forces operating within and upon man: 'Les climats, les saisons, les sons . . . tout agit sur notre machine et sur notre âme . . . tout nous offre mille prises . . . pour gouverner dans leur origine les sentiments' (i.409). According to this framework, strength of character or virtue is knowledge of right, of its means and the will to practice right. Weakness is knowledge of right, will to do right, but ignorance of the means, therefore failure in practice, followed by feelings of guilt. Vicious character is knowledge of right and of the means, but the will to do wrong. Rousseau, weak at the beginning, attains strength. Grimm is vicious.

The third sub-theme, virtue and vice, is the struggle between Rousseau and the enemy, not in terms of the affections, expansiveness opposed to simple hate, but in moral terms, virtue against an enemy aware of right, of the means to control hate, but choosing vice. Personal innocence is not enough. Strength implies the ability to conquer vice in others. This is the goal of Rousseau's reform after the first *Discours*, to challenge vice and its mass voice, opinion (i.416-417). A climax is reached in book ix after the Houdetot affair in the confrontation of Rousseau and Grimm. The supremacy of vice is evident in this moment: 'j'allai chez M. Grimm comme un autre George Dandin lui faire excuses des offenses qu'il m'avait faites . . . combien souvent l'audace et la fierté sont du côté du coupable, la honte et l'embarras du côté de l'innocent. . . . Aussi pris-je le parti d'endurer tout et de ne dire plus rien' (i.472-473). Across the books the movement has been from guilt to personal innocence, from weakness to personal strength, but also from personal conviction to a kind of defeat, because there has been withdrawal from the field of battle. From life as relationship of man and neighbour, in which vice and opinion are in ascendency, he retreats to the world of art, in which virtue in isolation may find adequate expression. Rousseau says that in the *Lettre à d'Alembert* (book x), in the 'ton singulier qui règne dans cet ouvrage', its gentleness, he has expressed, as death seemed to approach, his regret at leaving his fellow men 'sans qu'ils sentissent tout ce que je valais' (i.496). After the catastrophe over *Emile* and during the flight to Switzerland (end of book xi), the emphasis is again on resignation, on innocence isolated and at bay. His enemies should remember that his inclination in the midst of these disasters was to write *Le Lévite d'Ephraim*, evidence of a 'cœur sans fiel qui . . . s'en console avec lui-même' (i.586-587). The perspective is in part one of moral emergence through his persisting goals of innocence, strength, and conviction, the equivalent of time as recurrence, and through the calm at Montlouis and during the flight to Geneva, periods of suspended time. But this ascent is always within a broader framework of submergence by the present in the form of pressure from false opinion and vice, submergence by the attrition felt in the ever-narrowing circle of his person to person contacts and of his everyday moral influence on other men.

The third category of themes represents Rousseau's efforts to become a useful member of the community, ultimately the good citizen. His recurring pursuit of this goal happens within a framework of time as attrition, since sub-themes, shelter, exposure, and flight, follow one another with continual variation and degeneration in relation to his civic purpose. Shelter is either a rustic or highly sophisticated setting, provided there is innocence, equilibrium, absence of pressure, time as suspension among the members of the group involved. Exposure is either of these settings accompanied by disruptive friction, time as submergence in the present. In spite of incest, Les Charmettes is for the most part shelter, until exposure begins with the death of Anet and is completed by Maman's infatuation with Vintzenried. Flight is the ending of one existence, whether exposure or shelter, and the search for new shelter, which may prove to be exposure, for example, flight from Les Charmettes to Paris.

The alternation of shelter, exposure, and flight is persistent through the books, the paradise of Bossey, the exposure to Ducommun, departure from Geneva, Maman's fleeting guidance in book II, the exposure of San Spirito, the warmth of mme Basile, the shelter of the Roque household, which because of Marion becomes in turn exposure, flight with Bâcle from the sheltering promise of a career with the Gouvons, return to Maman, and so on. More serious efforts to be useful within a community begin in book VII's Venice episode, relative shelter ending in exposure. Shelter or success among the *philosophes* comes to mean loss of friends, envy, the hate of rivals, the watchful eye of the French and Genevan governments. An incompatibility of image steadily develops between on the one hand the citizen as part of the status quo, befriending the poor in the neighbourhood of Montmorency, doing simple chores, guarding mme d'Epinay's fruit trees, copying music, supporting Thérèse and her mother, later becoming the friend of the Luxembourgs, the star of their literary circle, and on the other hand the citizen as scrupulous defender of liberty, the lawgiver of the *Contrat social*, who in the eyes of the powerful, Choiseul, *parlement*, mme de Pompadour, spurred on according to the *Confessions* possibly by Grimm and Alembert (i.586), changes from simple subject to dangerous critic, a revolutionary in conflict with the status quo and with a prime minister antagonized, Rousseau believes, by his very efforts at praise (i.554-557). Flight to Switzerland, renunciation of citizenship are the result, and threats in spite of Keith's sheltering protection are made by the government of Geneva and the people of Neuchâtel. After the lapidation, in order to return to shelter within the status quo, Rousseau wants to renounce his role of defender of liberty, seek imprisonment on the Isle de Saint Pierre, try to pass again as ordinary citizen: 'Je me souviens qu'un Bernois . . . m'étant venu voir, me trouva perché sur un grand arbre, un sac attaché autour de ma ceinture . . . plein de pommes. Je ne fus pas fâché de cette rencontre et de quelques autres pareilles' (i.644). His stay under any condition is denied by the authorities of Berne. Continuing his flight, he takes up again the burden of his role as lawgiver. Under pressure from governments of his day, especially Choiseul's (i.653), he comes to believe that his destiny is associated with that of an entire people, the Corsicans, whom the same minister has crushed: 'Il est tems de rapporter l'anecdote fatale qui a mis le comble à mes desastres et qui a entraîné dans ma ruine un peuple infortuné dont les naissantes vertus promettoient déjà d'égaler un jour celles de Sparte et de Rome' (i.648). Rather than finding the life of an ordinary citizen sheltered within an existing nation, time as suspension, he has almost unwittingly lived the future envisioned by his art, with liberty the criterion, time as recurrence, with constant exposure and flight the rewards, time as present and as attrition. The outcome re-echoes the moods created by the affection and virtue themes. The impression the reader has of Rousseau's perspective or emotional state is partial emergence through his civic purpose, but in the shadow of a broader framework of submergence by benighted political regimes.

It has been Rousseau's destiny to test by his uniqueness the existing state of affections, morality, and politics. The final theme, which relates to Rousseau's career as writer, traces the formation and tests the validity of art's response to the challenge offered Rousseau by destiny. The question is whether or not he can believe in his power to create an art truly independent of opinion and capable of carrying the uniqueness of his struggle, whether its emergent truth can be communicated to a reader, made as real as or more real than the life, the destiny almost universally accepted by his fellow men.

The first phase of the career theme, predominant in books I to VI, includes all of the allusions to his psychological and emotional roots, to the environmental factors conditioning his attitudes, to the probings by others, the Gouvons, numerous priests, who intend to help him find a trade or profession. The second, culminating in book VIII, shows Rousseau groping toward an artistic career: his reading on his own, his study under numerous masters, and his association with men who helped form his literary judgment. There are allusions to his literary preferences, to events affecting his attitudes toward liberty, justice, religion. In a third and final stage, Rousseau has become the artist. He is aware of his own powers and limitations with reference to memory, imagination, and composition. During the performance of the *Devin du village*, he experiences through art a sentimental involvement with the audience: 'la volupté du sexe y entrait beaucoup plus que la vanité d'auteur ... dévoré, comme je l'étais sans cesse du désir de recueillir de mes lèvres les délicieuses larmes que je faisais couler' (i.379). From book VIII on, liberation of self is linked to the origin, writing, and fate of his literary works. The first *Discours* meant a new vision, 'je vis un autre univers'. As a result, 'toutes mes petites passions furent étouffées', his character is transformed, 'cette effervescence se soutint ... plus de quatre ou cinq ans' (i.351). With the second *Discours* he has discovered a standard with which to free himself and mankind, 'comparant l'homme de l'homme avec l'homme naturel.... Mon âme ... s'élevait auprès de la divinité' (i.388). With the *Lettre à d'Alembert*, Rousseau transforms real places and persons by art's perspective. Grimm, Paris, the theatre are vice. Rousseau, Geneva, the people of that country are virtue. With the first two discourses the revolutionary person had expressed new insights. The *Lettre* provides a new emergence, the understanding that he is alone even among friends who were supposed to know and share his vision. He has been 'trompé par ceux qu'il avait cru de sa trempe... forcé de se retirer au dedans de lui' (i.495).

From indignant protest against man's servitude, discovery of a standard, experience of his utter isolation, Rousseau passes to the final stage of liberation, becomes the creator offering a life which transforms the old order, for the affections the *Nouvelle Héloïse*, 'on était loin de concevoir à quel point je puis m'enflammer pour des êtres imaginaires' (i.548); in the domain of character and virtue the image of Emile, the model of strength, living among friends and loved ones who respect his worth (*Emile*, Garnier, p.606), for polity the *Social contract*, destined to 'former un peuple, le plus vertueux, le plus éclairé, le plus sage' (i.405); for the artistic temperament the *Confessions*, the attempt to reveal the uniqueness of Rousseau's inner self.

Belief in the power of art is expressed by the time techniques. Attrition characterizes the early abortive parts of the career theme, but after book VIII recurrence appears in the will to express the sentiments of freedom, justice, and truth engendered by his opposition to existing institutions. Suspended time emphasizes important moments in his career, for example, his mention of the trance-like states relating to his production of the first and second *Discours* and of the *Nouvelle Héloïse*. The tempo is slowed during the description of his studies at Les Charmettes (book VI), his moment of glory as the composer of the *Devin du village* (book VIII), the description of his literary projects in books IX, X, XI, his persecution during much of book XII, the artist, alone and abused, yet not wavering in his will to make known his truth. The perspective, determination, yet doubt of his power to communicate, is expressed in the words of defiance, beginning 'J'ai dit la vérité', which bring the *Confessions* to a close (i.656).

IV

In describing Rousseau's art of autobiography, it is necessary to point out four principal stages through which the reader must pass. The first removes him from the traditional verisimilar framework. He next enters a domain of rather mystifying idiosyncrasy and faces the challenge of understanding and explaining conflict rather than standing in judgment of it. He then follows the author's sentiments across a pattern of themes controlled by temporal devices and style. During and after this initiation, he is asked as a final step to find significance objectively himself. Sympathy or dislike would distort his vision, obscure the goal, Rousseau as he was. Art has presented no clear meaning known to the author. It gives no more than subjectively authentic clues to the content and fabric of his being. In view of the emotional nature of the materials, the author's demands on the reader are at an almost unattainable level, since identification between them, if detection of uniqueness is to occur, must rest only on a common search for meaning, for one's place, implicit in every human life, 'démeler dans son propre cœur ce qui est de l'espèce et ce qui est de l'individu' (i.1158; *Ebauches*).

Three principal themes have run simultaneously through the *Confessions*. First, uniqueness is defined in terms of conflict, enigma, mystery. Second, destiny, representing all of necessity's forces, restates uniqueness deterministically. At the most definitive level, expressing the data of sentiment and time, is the theme of art with its complementing theme, the objective, creative reader, and its illustrating themes, affection, climaxing in book ix (Houdetot affair); character, with peaks in x *(Lettre à d'Alembert)* and in xi *(Lévite d'Ephraim)*; the citizen, climaxing in book xii with the lapidation; the artist, exposing his being from preface to final page. Rousseau's awareness of conflict, expansiveness with timidity, knowledge of right, yet devasting weakness, love of country and liberty, met by persecution, love of truth, met by disbelief and rejection, confirms a taste for solitude which in the opinion of his enemies, he complains, has passed for viciousness. Feelings of submergence by forces greater than his will, such as heredity, environment, his own automatic reactions, cause him repeatedly to interpret this movement of his life toward isolation as fatality. Destiny has created, moulded, and led him.

THE *CONFESSIONS*

Yet within him, too, there is rebellion in the form of feelings of guilt, of efforts to escape through memory and imagination into timeless revery, in the form of a turning to art in his affective, moral, and civic life. Destiny is submergence by necessity, but with the possibility of emergence through art based on inner sentiment and temporality. His memoirs are the test of this new reality, of his power to transmit it.

Rousseau's isolation is less basically in space, Montlouis, the Isle de Saint Pierre, the thesis of those who stress his clear intellectual ties with the *philosophes*, in history, longing for Sparta and Rome, the emphasis of those who underline his role of reformer, than in his artistic vision, his awareness of a non-verisimilar, yet authentic inner self. Art in the service of the unique personality in theory at least means art's flexibility, the uninhibited use of theme, time, and style in order to express the feelings of innovating genius. Under the demands of this task, art has become a very subtle device for exploring, identifying, communicating the part of personality which in all men resists incorporation into society, the essentially artistic side. If the reader applies the judgments of his day, finds Rousseau merely 'un malhonnête homme', destiny with its connotations of insensitivity, corrupt opinion, oppressive status quo has won, self-liberation has been thwarted. In the *Confessions*, liberty is ultimately art. Tension is less between nature and culture than between destiny or necessity on the one hand and the individual, the artist, on the other. Before the *Confessions*, the self for the most part had been defined negatively. Nature, pre-social man's freedom from pressure, was the standard utilized to measure society and its history. In his memoirs Rousseau moves inside the self, defines it in terms of private values, of idiosyncrasy. The overwhelming reality and obsession are necessity, the inevitable flow of events, forming, controlling, destroying society, its institutions, peoples, compromising and crushing personality. Resisting necessity, but constantly threatened by reabsorption into it, is Rousseau's feeling of emergence through an inner, almost uncommunicable self, the matrix for new concepts of nature, society, and the individual. The intuition, not given explicitly, but arising from the developing themes, is that his free primitive nature, his just contractual society, his own uniqueness may exist only within the artist, have no substance without his will, vanish back into necessity if his art, failing to involve the reader creatively in their formulation, does not attract him to the problems and the values of uniqueness.

Jean Jacques Rousseau and madame de Warens: some recently recovered documents

by R. A. Leigh

When, on the 29th of July 1762, mme de Warens died, in extreme poverty and squalor, lonely, ill and forgotten, in the shabby little apartment in Chambéry in which she had vegetated since the final collapse of all her dreams, something rather curious happened. On the instructions of the *intendant-général* of Savoy, her room was locked, 'à toutes bonnes fins', and all her papers sealed[1]. On the 3rd of September a detailed inventory was ordered, and was undoubtedly drawn up. Indeed, at various times, for different official purposes, several copies were made: strangely enough, they have all disappeared. Having made the inventory, the authorities then sat tight. In vain did her factotum, Jean Danel[2], the last

---

[1] many of the documents from which this account was compiled were first published by Albert Metzger in *Les dernières années de mme de Warens* (Lyon [1891]), pp.206s [Metzger 4].

[2] Jean Danel, born 17 June 1702, in Geneva, died 12 May 1776 at Chambéry. He was the son of Etienne Danel and Etienne (or Etienna) Birre. The Danel family were settled at Jussy before the Reformation, and although among the first citizens of the new republic, were Catholics at heart for a long time and accepted Calvinism with great reluctance. Jean Danel abjured Protestantism on 24 July 1728. He did not become mme de Warens's secretary until 1756, on the death of his predecessor Pierre Michal (1726?-1756). See my *Correspondance complète de Jean Jacques Rousseau* (Geneva 1965), [Leigh] iv.433, A177, note c. The last letter of Danel's name was sometimes misread as 't'. Thence it was an easy step to identify this 'Danet' or 'd'Anet' with the Claude Anet of the *Confessions*, and to assert that the latter had not really died in 1734, as stated by Rousseau, but had lingered on, in suffering and

of a whole series of apostate hangers-on from Geneva or the pays de Vaud which had included Jean Jacques himself, appeal for permission to sell his late employer's effects in order to recover his salary, unpaid for years[3]. 'Mes gages! mes gages!' The heartfelt cry of this latter-day Sganarelle was countered by the argument that mme de Warens's possessions were too insignificant to bother with and would barely raise enough to cover her debts[4]. In fact, no attempt was made to sell her effects to pay her debts: on the contrary, everything was kept under lock and key. However, once the papers had been inventoried, the *intendant-général* did appointed Danel as custodian *(gardiateur)* of her property, on the express condition that he should keep it intact for inspection whenever required to do so[5]. In the event, it was not until fourteen years later, in 1776, that the embargo was finally lifted.

What is puzzling about this affair is not, of course, the sequestration or the sealing in themselves, but the length of time which elapsed before the papers were finally released. Official anxiety about any documents retained by the former secret agent of Victor Amadeus II was only natural: but in this case it does seem that the inordinate delay was occasioned as much by incompetence, procrastination or incuria as by caution. Some diffidence, of course, was understandable. Geneva and Sardinia had finally recognised each other's existence only as recently as 1754, and there was a long history of mutual mistrust between them. But

---

humiliation, etc. etc. There were even apocryphal *Mémoires* published, attributed to Claude Anet, and embodying this myth.

[3] undated, received in Turin 16 August 1762: Turin, State archives, Section I, Lettere di particolari, C.18. The petition was drawn up free of charge by two Chambéry notaries. It was first published by Luigi Foscolo Benedetto, *Madame de Warens d'après de nouveaux documents* (Paris 1914), pp.288-289 [Benedetto 2].

[4] Joseph Capris de Castellamont (*intendant-général* of Savoy) to Giambattista Bonifacio de Mazé (principal officer of the Ministry of internal affairs, Turin); letter of 28 August 1762 (original in Turin state archives, copy in departmental archives of Savoy: cp. Metzger 4, p.206-207, printed from the copy).

[5] cp. Metzger 4, p.227.

if Victor Amadeus's ambitions to recover the lost lands of the duchy of Savoy had been an open secret, it was equally well-known that, under his son and successor, they had long since been abandoned. Any disclosures about plans, going back to the 1730s, to foment uprisings in Geneva or the pays de Vaud[6] would have been more embarrassing than compromising in the changed atmosphere of the 1760s. However, there was certainly no point in looking for trouble.

Mme de Warens's house and papers, then, were not decontrolled until 1776. Meanwhile, in 1768, there had been a comic interlude. The authorities had overlooked that, in shutting up the house, they had amputated the income of the owner, one Claude Crépine, an elderly Chambéry notary who had acquired the property about 1761 from mme de Warens's previous landlord. This man of law, chafing at the delay, and concerned about the deterioration of his investment, made repeated representations on the subject, and finally petitioned the crown, asking that his house should be cleared so that it could be repaired and relet. In the face of total silence from Turin, the *intendant-général* of Savoy took it upon himself in July 1768 to remove all the sequestered effects and have them deposited at the *intendance*[7]. However, when the *greffier*'s representative and his party arrived at the house, they found that the cupboard, if not exactly bare, was not quite so well-stocked as it ought to have been. Jean Danel, who had gone on living there, blandly informed the surprised officials that, in spite of the express condition laid on him as custodian, he had sold off some of mme de Warens's meagre possessions for the sum of 120 livres in order to provide for his sustenance, a minor matter to which no one apparently had devoted any thought when he was appointed custodian. To justify his action, he produced an account embracing both his arrears of wages and the funeral expenses of mme de Warens, and even counter-claimed for the balance not covered by the proceeds of his

[6] cp. Leigh i.297 s.
[7] Metzger 4, pp.226-228; order dated 22 July 1768 (Chambéry, departmental archives of Savoy).

surreptitious sales[8]. In view of his known indigence, no action was taken against Danel, notwithstanding the penalties prescribed in his terms of appointment[9]. The main thing was that the two cupboards and three chests or boxes containing mme de Warens's papers still bore, unbroken, the seals which had been affixed to them in 1762. The seals were broken, and the contents found to be in accordance with the inventory. Apart from these articles of furniture, and one or two other pieces so miserable that even Danel had been unable to turn them into cash, all the house contained was a lot of old junk, the relics of mme de Warens's dreams and schemes: decaying minerals in one room, decomposing chemicals in another described euphemistically as a laboratory, and a quantity of unfired and unglazed earthenware, the remnants of the stock of one of mme de Warens's factories. The minerals and chemicals were promptly thrown out into the street[10]: but the earthenware, which occupied a whole room, was, to Crépine's dismay, left on the premises. The furniture containing the documents, together with one or two other pieces, was taken to the *intendance*; and the proceedings of the day came to an end with Crépine's claim for loss of rent (885 livres, 6 sols, 8 deniers). It was not until June 1776 that he was finally able to extract from Turin an indemnity of 400 livres[11]. Meanwhile, the remainder of mme de Warens's effects had been put up for sale, but had found no takers, and were handed over to Crépine in 1776 with two of the cupboards at the same time as he was paid. It was then that the documents came to light, some wrapped in towels or table napkins. This is the 'heureux hazard' coyly referred to by Boubers in the statement quoted below. During the eight years that the papers had been deposited with the *intendance*, there had, of course, been ample opportunity to prune them discreetly. Whether anything was removed, and if so, how much, will now

[8] Metzger 4, pp.230-231: report dated 27 July 1768 (Chambéry, departmental archives of Savoy).
[9] Metzger 4, p.247: report dated 2 December 1772 (Chambéry, departmental archives of Savoy).
[10] Metzger 4, p.231, 233.
[11] Metzger 4, p.253.

never be known. Certainly, even allowing for the presence of a good deal of rubbish, since discarded, what has since come to light of the impounded papers would not have filled anything like two cupboards and three chests or boxes[12].

This story would be of only anecdotal interest today, were it not for the fact that the papers in question included two large packets of documents relating to Rousseau. The first of these consisted simply of the letters 'Petit' had written to 'Maman'. She had kept most of them, but they are not yet all accounted for: at least a dozen known to exist in 1776 are still missing and may still turn up. The second was a parcel of papers deposited with mme de Warens in 1742 by Jean Jacques when he left Chambéry for good (as we now know), and which he never claimed, having evidently forgotten all about them. This second parcel included notebooks used by him as far back as 1730, when he was only eighteen, and containing, amongst other material of interest, his earliest literary sketches. There were also a number of drafts of letters, a printed copy of *Le Verger de madame la baronne de Warens* (1739), the only one known, together with a manuscript copy of the same poem, early excursions into the drama like *La Découverte du nouveau monde* and parts of *Iphis*, and a certain amount of occasional verse, of which the most substantial pieces were the *Epîtres* to Parisot and Borde. Some of this material had evidently been intended for publication in a miscellany, for there was also a titlepage—*La Muse allobroge: ou les Œuvres du petit poucet*, dated 1742.

---

[12] they may not, of course, have been full. The documents quoted by Metzger, however, reveal one interesting fact. The extremely circumstantial *greffier*'s report of September 1768 specifically mentions as containing documents, and still bearing unbroken seals, two 'garderobbes', one 'bahu', one 'coffre' and one 'cassette'. A 1772 document mentioning the effects to be restored to Crépine speaks only of two 'vieux garde robes' (Metgzer 4, p.247). Had the *bahut*, the *coffre* and the *cassette* already disappeared, or was this simply an oversight? It may be added that about 1860 bundles of mme de Warens's business papers were discovered in a Chambéry bookshop and were bought for the Archives départementales, where they may still be consulted.

Unfortunately, both these lots were split up almost immediately. The notebooks, for instance, with some other papers of little interest, were acquired by Horace Bénédict de Saussure (1740-1799), professor at the Academy of Geneva. He lent them to Moultou and Du Peyrou in time for them to be used in the *Supplément* to the Geneva edition of Rousseau's works (1782 [1780]-1789)[13], and his heirs lent them again some thirty years later to Musset-Pathay. They are now on deposit with the Société J.J. Rousseau, Geneva.

The fate of the packet of letters was regrettably typical, many of them being disposed of separately. For instance, according to a probably apocryphal story (but one, at least, of the letters was real enough) three were in the possession of mme de Warens's last maidservant, and were taken to Spain. Towards 1790, two were in the interesting Rousseau collection built up by François Coindet, the reluctant bank-clerk whose cult of the great man was so ill-rewarded in the *Confessions*, which, to his mortification, he survived long enough to read. Another was acquired by Du Peyrou, Rousseau's principal literary executor, again about 1790, and is now at Neuchâtel. A few, in 1858, were in the hands of the marquis de Flers (unfortunately, he kept only one)[14]. The lion's share of the letters, however, together with a good slice of the second parcel (including *La Muse allobroge*) fell to J. L. Boubers, a Brussels bookseller who at that time was busy producing a handsome quarto edition of Rousseau's works with the spurious imprint 'Londres'[15]. Boubers inserted the text of the Rousseau papers he had just acquired into the volume then going through the press, the eighth, where they are separated from the *Lettres de*

---

[13] *Supplément à la collection des Œuvres de J.J. Rousseau* (Genève 1782) (vol.ii of the [first] supplement, vol.xxvi of the *Œuvres*, p.395-458). There were three formats: my reference is to the 8° edition.

[14] for the details given here, see Leigh i and ii.

[15] *Collection complette des Œuvres de J.J. Rousseau* (Londres 1774-1783, 12 vols). This edition has some fine engravings by Moreau *le jeune*. Boubers had for long been a fairly close business associate of Rey.

la montagne by some thirty pages of oddments. This eighth volume is dated 1776, but it must have been published some time in 1777[16].

This previously unpublished material is introduced by a laconic note (p.[265]): 'Toutes les pièces suivantes n'ont jamais été imprimées, un heureux hazard nous les a procuré & nous les donnons au public, d'après les originaux, la plupart écrites de la main même de l'auteur. Ces productions de sa jeunesse sont sans doute inférieures à celles qui lui ont acquis une si grande célébrité; mais telles qu'elles sont on les lira avec plaisir, puisqu'on y verra quelle étoit dans sa jeunesse la manière de voir & de sentir de leur auteur; & que peut-être il en sortira quelques traits de lumières, qui feront connoître au lecteur le vrai caractère de cet homme devenu depuis si intéressant pour le public'.

The manuscripts used by Boubers thereupon disappeared into his files, and the texts published by him remained the only authority for these early letters of Jean Jacques. Gradually, however, the originals themselves began to filter back into public view. Boubers himself apparently gave one to a m. Masson Régnier, a teacher at the Lycée de Bruxelles, and this finished up in the municipal library at Beaune. Another, written by Jean Jacques to a third party, and passed on to mme de Warens, is now in the University library, Amsterdam. Boubers's heirs sent some of the manuscripts to the Paris sale-rooms in 1867 and again in 1886. Most of these (but not *La Muse allobroge*, which went to Geneva) were snapped up by Alfred Morrison, and were acquired at the sale of his collection in 1919 by the Geneva library. But the originals of many of the letters published by Boubers were still unknown in 1965, when the first volume of my edition of the correspondence was published: and the appearance of no less

---

[16] this is the date of the fleuron on the titlepage, which reads: 'Œuvres/ mêlées/de/Mʳ. Rousseau,/de Genève./ Nouvelle édition./Revue, corrigée & augmentée de plusieurs morceaux qui/ n'ont pas encore paru./avec figures/ tome quatrième/' [i. e. of the *Œuvres mêlées*].

than five of them at a sale[17] in Paris in May 1968, together with a completely unknown letter and a *Virelai* by Jean Jacques (also first printed by Boubers) was something of an event.

This little collection, bound in boards about 1840[18], presents several interesting features (three of them unique) and raises an intriguing problem. In the first place, the originals enable us to correct many minor misreadings and in one instance to rectify an inaccurate date. In another instance, however, the original confirms the date printed in 1777, and so finally sets a long-standing controversy about the year of Rousseau's first trip to Besançon. This particular manuscript is at present the earliest extant holograph of a Rousseau letter.

The hitherto unprinted letter is the only known holograph of a letter from Jean Jacques to his father, Isaac Rousseau, though a few others are known through drafts. Though not very significant in itself, it does help to establish the date of Rousseau's return from Montpellier in 1738. It also shows that the correspondence between Jean Jacques and his father must have been much more active than the *Confessions* would lead us to suppose. There had certainly been exchanges in 1731 and 1735, and most likely in 1737, 1738, 1740 and 1742 also. In fact, after the first chilly contacts of 1731 had been forgotten, the correspondence between them must have been fairly continuous. But how did this solitary letter come into the possession of the nineteenth-century collector who had it bound with the others, which all came from the Boubers manuscripts? The obvious answer is that it must have originated, indirectly, from Nyon. In view of the

---

[17] Collection d'autographes littéraires, Paris, Hôtel Drouet, 29 May 1968 (Librairie Andrieux), item no. 100. The sale actually took place the next day, owing to the 'événements'.

[18] the catalogue suggests 1820, but the blank paper added when the *cahier* was bound bears a watermark dated 1838. These documents are now in the possession of a London collector who desires to remain anonymous. I should like to thank him for permission to see and study them, and also mr Besterman, through whose good offices they were acquired. The *cahier* was formerly in the possession of the Everard family, Brussels, and was acquired by a French collector, in Paris, in March 1928.

total disappearance of the originals of Jean Jacques's letters to his father, it was natural to suppose, before this one came to light, that they must have all been lost or destroyed at Isaac Rousseau's death in 1747 (if, indeed, it could be assumed that they had survived for so long), or at the very latest at the death of his second wife, Jean Jacques's stepmother, a few years later. The unexpected appearance of this letter, however, raises the hope, admittedly slender, that others might one day emerge.

Another of the newly discovered originals also presents a unique feature: it is the only private letter of Rousseau's, as far as I know, which is not in his writing. Though signed by Jean Jacques, it is in a hand which I identify as that of the *abbé* de Binis. We know little of the *abbé*. He arrived in Venice as one of the secretaries of Montaigu, the French ambassador to the republic, a few months before Jean Jacques (say in July 1743), and stayed there a little longer (he seems to have left before the end of October 1744)[19]. There was little enough inducement for him to stay. Quite apart from anything else, the pittance he was paid was a miserable one if indeed he was paid anything at all, which, with an ambassador forced by Versailles to live off his own fat and reduced to darning his own stockings, seems somewhat unlikely[20]. When engaged, he was offered only 300 livres per annum, which the ambassador's brother made up to a total of 600 livres from his own pocket[21]; but how much he received, and when, is problematic. His desperate financial situation might well account for his succumbing to the temptation to supplement his resources by a little smuggling, if (as I am rather inclined to suspect) he was the unnamed secretary whom Montaigu accused of this peccadillo in a letter to the ministry, and who has been assumed by some,

---

[19] this is the date of the last document at the quai d'Orsay in his hand.
[20] Rousseau's own salary remained unpaid for several years after his return. It is true that in his case there were special circumstances, but even before these circumstances arose, his salary was unpaid. All he received was an advance of 330 livres (Leigh i.190, no.55).
[21] Leigh ii.37, no.115, note *a*.

rather hastily, to be Jean Jacques himself[22]. The papers preserved for so long at La Bretesche, home of the Montaigu family, and now, most of them, at the Bibliothèque nationale in Paris, confirm that Binis often worked under Jean Jacques's direction. In his *Confessions*, Rousseau tells us that he passed on a few pickings to his subordinate, and their relations seem, at the time, to have been quite good: 'S'il était complaisant envers moi, je n'étais pas moins honnête envers lui, et nous avons toujours bien vécu ensemble' (Pléiade i.299). But between the composition of book vii of the *Confessions* and that of the sixth *Promenade* of the *Rêveries*, something had occurred to displease Jean Jacques, who at that time suspected everyone of ingratitude and treachery, and he went out of his way to make an acid reference to the *abbé*: 'C'est ainsi que l'abbé de Binis que j'avois pour sous secretaire à Venise, et qui me marquoit toujours l'attachement et l'estime que ma conduite lui dut naturellement inspirer, changeant de langage et d'allure à propos pour son interest a su gagner de bons bénéfices aux dépends de sa conscience et de la vérité' (*ibid.* i.1056).

On turning over the pages of Boubers's eighth volume, it is impossible not to think of what Jean Jacques's reactions would have been if he had been able to do the same. He certainly knew of the edition, for he denounced it on general grounds in his *Dialogues* as part of a campaign to falsify his work (*ibid.* i.959). Apparently, however, he never actually saw it. If he had, he would have undergone, a year before his death, and only a few months before the composition of the unfinished tenth *Promenade* of the *Rêveries*, a poignant confrontation with the reality of a period in his past which, in some of the best-known pages of the *Confessions*, he had already tried to resurrect, but poetically transfigured and moulded nearer to his heart's desire. The idyll of Les Charmettes, followed by two melancholy years in the empty places

[22] Leigh i.239, no.91, notes explicatives.

haunted by past happiness, is recalled in a minor key in the tenth *Promenade*: 'Ah! si j'avois suffi à son cœur comme elle suffisoit au mien! Quels paisibles et délicieux jours nous eussions coulés ensemble! Nous en avons passé de tels mais qu'ils ont été courts et rapides, et quel destin les a suivis!'

The man who, at the age of sixty-five, was about to pen, for the eyes of posterity only, those elegiac lines, heavy with longing but free from the sharp jab of immediate pain, was fortunately spared the paralysing shock of reading in cold print, advertised to the contemporary world he so mistrusted and despised, what he had written in anguish at the age of twenty-five: 'Au nom de Dieu, rangez les choses de sorte que je ne meure pas de désespoir.... Ah! ma chère Maman, n'êtes-vous donc plus ma chère maman? ai-je vécu quelques mois de trop?'

TEXTS

6*

Rousseau à Françoise-Louise-Eléonore de La Tour, baronne de Warens

Madame. [le 29 juin 1732][1]

J'ai l'honneur de vous écrire des le lendemain de mon arrivée a Besançon, j'y ai trouvé bien des nouvelles auxquelles je ne m'étois pas attendu, et qui m'ont fait plaisir en quelque façon, je suis allé ce matin faire la[2] révérence a M[r] l'Abbé Blanchard qui nous a donné a diner a Monsieur le Comte de St Rieux et a moi. Il m'a dit qu'il partiroit dans un mois Pour Paris ou il va remplir le quartier de Mr Campra qui est malade, et come il est fort âgé, Mr Blanchard se flatte de lui succéder en la Charge d'Intendant, premier maître de Cartier de la musique de la chambre du Roy, et conseiller de S:M: en ses conseils; il m'a donné sa parole d'honneur qu'au cas que ce projet lui reussisse, il me procurera un apointement dans la chapelle ou dans la Chambre du Roy, au bout du terme de deux ans le plus tard; Ce sont la des postes brillans et lucratifs qu'on ne peut assez menager, aussi l'ai-je trés fort[3] remercié avec assurance que je n'epargnerai rien pour m'avancer de plus en plus dans la composition, pour laquelle il m'a trouvé un talent merveilleux. Je lui rens a souper ce soir avec deux ou trois officiers du Regiment du roi avec qui j'ai fait connoissance au concert; Monsieur l'Abbé Blanchard m'a [p][4]rié d'y chanter un recit de basse-taille, que ces messieurs [ont eu][4] la complaisance d'aplaudir aussi bien qu'un Duo, [de Pyr][4]ame et Thisbé que j'ai chanté avec Mr Duroncel, fameux haute contre de l'ancien Opera de Lion; c'est beaucoup faire, pour un lendemain d'arrivée.

---

* these numbers are those of my edition of Rousseau's correspondence.

J'ai donc resolu de retourner dans quelques jours a Chambery ou je m'amuseray a enseigner pendant le terme de ces[5] deux années, ce qui m'aidera toujours a me fortifier, ne voulant pas m'arreter icÿ ni ÿ[6] passer pour un simple musicien, ce qui me feroit quelque jour un tort considerable. Ayez la bonté de m'écrire Madame si j'y seray receu avec Plaisir, et si l'on m'y donnera des écoliers, je me suis fournÿ de quantité de papiers et de piéces nouvelles d'un gout charmant et qui sûrement [7]n'est pas connu[7] a Chambery, mais je vous avouë que je ne me soucie guères de partir que je ne sache au vrai si l'on se rejouïra de m'avoir, j'ai trop de delicatesse pour y aller autrement. Ce seroit un tresor et en méme tems un miracle de voir un bon[6] musicien en Savoie, je n'ose ni ne puis me flatter d'étre de ce nombre; mais en ce cas je me vante toujours de produire en autrui ce que je ne suis pas moi-méme, d'ailleurs tous ceux qui se serviront de mes principes auront lieu de s'en louër, et vous en particulier Madame, si vous voulez bien encore prendre la peine de les pratiquer quelquefois. Faites moi l'honneur De me repondre par [le][4] premier ordinaire, et au cas que vous voiÿez[8] qu'il n'y ait pas de [débouché][9] pour moi a Chambery, vous aurez s'il vous plait la bonté de me [le marquer][4], et come il me reste encore deux partis a choisir, je prendrai la liberté de consulter le secours de vos sages avis sur l'option d'aller a Paris en droiture avec l'abbé Blanchard, ou a Soleure auprès de Mr l'ambassadeur, cependant comme ce sont la des[10] coups de partie qu'il n'est pas bon de précipiter, je serois[11] bien aise de ne rien presser[12] encore.

Tout bien examiné, je ne me repens point d'avoir fait ce petit voiage qui pourra dans la suitte m'étre d'une grande utilité. J'attens, Madame, avec soumission, l'honneur de vos ordres et suis avec une respectueuse consideration
  Madame,
    [5]Votre tres humble et tres obeissant serviteur et filieul[5]

                             JJRousseau

a Besançon le 29. Juin *1732*

⁵A Madame / Madame la Baronne / de Warens de la Tour / A Chamberï⁵

MANUSCRIPT

* London, private collection: 4 p., the address on p.4: red-wax seal (a coat of arms): holograph.

FIRST PRINTED

Boubers viii (1776, *sc.* 1777).357-358.

TEXTUAL NOTES

In the upper right-hand corner of p.1 of the ms., an xviiith-century hand has written: 'Lettres à Mᵈ. La baronne/ De Warens de La Tour / à Chamberi'.

¹ [for a comment on the date, see below, explanatory notes] ² Boubers: ma ³ Dufour-Plan: fortement ⁴ [hole made by the seal] ⁵[omitted, Boubers] ⁶ [omitted, DP] ⁷ Boubers: ne sont pas connus ⁸ Boubers: voyez ⁹ [this word, lost in the hole made by the seal, is conjectural: it was printed in italics by Boubers, but this does not, of course, convey any emphasis] ¹⁰ Boubers: de ces ¹¹ Boubers: serai ¹² ⟨précipiter⟩

EXPLANATORY NOTES

For detailed explanatory notes on this letter, see Leigh i.17-19. A point worth elaborating here is the question of the date. Boubers printed it correctly, but Musset-Pathay, convinced that Rousseau had remained at the *cadastre* until 1735, shifted the letter to that year (cp. *Œuvres complètes de J.-J. Rousseau*, 1820, xviii.18). Courtois adopted '1734', though 'sans enthousiasme' (*Considérations sur la chronologie . . . de J.-J. Rousseau*, 1922, p.159), but his argument is based also on an erroneous estimate of the time JJ spent at the *cadastre*). Mugnier had preferred '1733' (*Madame de Warens et J.-J. Rousseau*, 1890, p.142-143). This was partly owing to a mistake, as he thought that Boubers had printed '1733'. However, he went on to support this date on other grounds. Dufour-Plan reverted silently to Boubers's date, but without giving any reasons, whilst the Pléiade (i.1319-1320) supported Mugnier. In my edition (i.17-18), I argued strongly for 1732, and this in fact turns out to be the date given by the holograph.

This manuscript is at present the earliest known original of a Rousseau letter.

20 bis

Rousseau à Isaac Rousseau

Chambéri 28ᵉ Février 1738.

Monsieur mon trés [cher]¹ Pére

Je vous prie de vouloir donner cours a l'incluseᵃ aussitôt aprés la reception de la présente.

Il est inutile de vous rien dire ici sur l'état de ma santé, qui va toujours trainant, et achevant de se détruire de plus en plus: Accordés moi, la grace, Mon trés cher Pére, de continuer a me donner des nouvelles de la vôtre, et de celle de ma chére Mére[b] pour le rétablissement de laquel[le][2] je fais les voeux les plus sincéres.

Je vous envoie 6. tablettes de chocolat adressées à M[r] Patron suivant votre ordre[3]. Je souhait[e][2] que ma chére mére le trouve de son gout. Je Suis avec le plus tendre respect, Monsieur Mon trés cher Pêre, Vôtre trés humble et trés obeissant serviteur et fils

JJRousseau

MANUSCRIPT

* London, private collection; 2 p., p.2 bl.; holograph.

There was originally a second (blank) leaf, of which only a scrap remains.

TEXTUAL NOTES

[1] [this word, omitted by Rousseau, is supplied by a later hand] [2][the right hand margin was trimmed too close by the binder, and a few letters have been lost] [3] ordre⟨s⟩

EXPLANATORY NOTES

Previously unpublished. This manuscript is the only known original of a letter from Rousseau to his father.

The date of this letter enables that of Rousseau's return from Montpellier to be determined rather more precisely than hitherto. Courtois in his *Chronologie critique* (*Annales J.-J. Rousseau* xv, 1923) p.29, had suggested 'janvier-février 1738', whereas the *Pléiade* edition (i.civ) had preferred 'février-mars'. The present letter shows that Rousseau had been back at Chambéry long enough for an exchange of letters between him and his father to have taken place.

a. this letter is unknown.

b. or rather his stepmother, Jeanne François, daughter of Elie François. His father had married her at Prangins on 5 March 1726. She was two and a half years older than he was, having been baptised at Nyon between the 20 February and the 14 March 1670), and survived him. According to the first version of the *Confessions*, she was a 'bonne femme, mais mielleuse et grondeuse tout à la fois'. In the final version, this was softened to 'bonne femme, un peu mielleuse'.

26

Rousseau à Françoise-Louise-Eléonore de La Tour, baronne de Warens

[le 3 mars 1739]

Ma trés chére et trés bonne Maman

Je vous envoie ci-joint, le brouillard du Mémoire[a], que vous trouverés aprés celui de la lettre a Mr Arnaud. Si j'étois capable de faire un chef d'oeuvre, Ce mémoire, a mon gout seroit le mien; non qu'il soit travaillé avec beaucoup d'art: Mais parce qu'il est écrit avec les sentimens qui conviennent a un homme que vous honorés du nom de fils. Assurément, une ridicule fierté ne me conviendroit guéres dans l'êtat ou je suis: Mais aussi j'ai toujours crû qu'on pouvoit sans[1] arrogance, et cependant sans s'avilir, conserver une certaine dignité dans la mauvaise fortune et dans les supplications, plus propre[2] a obtenir des graces d'un honnête homme, que les plus basses lachetés. Au reste, je souhaite plus que je n'espére de ce mémoire a moins que vôtre zêle et vôtre habileté ordinaire[3] ne lui donnent un puissant véhicule: Car je sai par une vielle expérience, que tous les hommes n'entendent et ne parlent pas le même langage. Je plains les âmes a qui le mien est inconnu; il y a une maman au monde qui a leur place l'entendroit tres bien: Mais me dirés-vous, pourquoi ne pas parler le leur; C'est ce que je me suis assés[4] représenté. Aprés tout, pour quatre misérables jours de vie, vaut-il la peine de se faire faquin?

Il n'y a pas tant de mal cependant, et j'espére que vous trouverés par la lecture du mémoire que je n'ai pas fait le rodomont hors de propos, et que je me suis raisonnablement humanisé. Je sais bien, Dieu merci [5]a quoi[5], sans cela, petit auroit courû grand risque de mourir [6]de faim en pareille occasion[6]; Preuve que je ne suis pas propre a ramper indignement dans les malheurs de la vie, c'est que je n'ai jamais fait le rogue ni le fendant dans la prospérité: Mais qu'est-ce que je vous lanterne-là? sans me souvenir, chére

Maman que je parle a qui me connoit mieux que moi-même. Baste; un peu d'effusion de coeur dans l'occasion ne nuit jamais a l'amitié.

Le memoire est tout dressé sur le plan que nous avons plus d'une fois digéré ensemble. Je crois[7] le tout assés lié, et propre a se soûtenir. Il y a ce maudit voiage à Besançon, dont pour mon honneur[8] j'ai jugé à propos de déguiser un peu [9]les motifs[9]. Voiage éternel et malencontreux S'il en fut au monde, et qui S'est déja présenté a moi bien des fois, et sous [10]bien des faces différentes[10]. Ce sont des images ou ma vanité ne triomphe pas. Quoiqu'il en soit j'ai mis a cela un emplâtre, Dieu sait comment! en tout cas, si l'on vient me faire subir l'interrogatoire[11] aux Charmettes, j'espére bien ne pas rester court. Comme vous n'étes pas au fait [12]des dattes[12] comme moi, il sera bon en présentant le mémoire de glisser légérement sur le détail des circonstances crainte de quiproquo, a moins que je n'aie l'honneur de vous voir avant ce tems-là.[b]

A propos de cela. Depuis que vous voila établie en ville, ne vous prend-il point fantaisie[13], ma chére maman, d'entreprendre un jour quelque petit voiage a la campagne? Si mon bon génie vous l'inspire, vous m'obligerés de me faire avertir quelques[14] trois ou quatre mois a l'avance, afin que je me prépare à vous recevoir, et a vous faire duëment les honneurs de *chés moi*.

Je prens la liberté de faire ici mes honneurs a Monsieur le Cureu, et mes amitiés a mon frére. Aiés la bonté de dire au prémier que comme Proserpine (ah la belle chose que de placer là Proserpine!

Peste! ou prend mon esprit touttes ces gentillesses?)

comme Proserpine, donc, passoit autrefois[15] six mois sur terre et six mois aux enfers, il faut de même qu'il se résolve de partager son tems entre vous et moi: Mais aussi les enfers ou les mettrons-nous? Placés-les en ville si vous le jugés a propos; Car pour ici, ne vous déplaise, *n'en voli pas gés*. J'ai l'honneur d'étre du plus profond de mon coeur, ma trés chere et trés bonne maman, [12]vôtre trés humble et trés obeissant serviteurs[14] et fils[12]   JJRousseau

Je m'aperçois que ma lettre vous pourra servir d'apologie quand il vous arrivera d'en écrire quelqu'une un peu longue: Mais. aussi il faudra que ce soit a quelque maman bien chére et bien aimée. Sans quoi la mienne ne prouve rien.

3ᵉ mars

MANUSCRIPT

* London, private collection 4 p., p.4 bl.; holograph.

FIRST PRINTED

Boubers viii (1776, *sc.* 1777).372-374.

TEXTUAL NOTES

[1] Boubers: avec [it has often been conjectured that this was a slip] [2] Boubers: propres [3] Boubers: ordinaires [4] Dufour-Plan: bien [5] [this strange sentence has puzzled the editors. Musset-Pathay amended it silently to 'à quoi, que', which does not help much: Dufour-Plan silently excised 'à quoi' and were left with Musset-Pathay's 'que' and a sentence which makes sense, but not that of the original. As it stands, the sentence is an anacoluthon. It may be amended in a number of different ways. Perhaps, as I have already suggested, Rousseau had originally intended to write something like 'Je sais, Dieu merci, à quoi m'en tenir là-dessus', or 'à quoi il faut se résigner'.] [6] [interlinear addition] [7] Boubers: vois [8] Boubers: bonheur [Musset-Pathay misprinted this as 'honneur', and this was followed by Dufour-Plan. It now turns out to be the correct reading!] [9] Boubers: ce motif: Musset-Pathay and Dufour-Plan: le motif [10] Boubers: 'sous des faces bien différentes'. [11] Dufour-Plan: un interrogatoire. [12] Boubers: [omis] [13] Dufour-Plan: la fantaisie [14] [Boubers corrects these two slips] [15] Dufour-Plan: [omitted]

EXPLANATORY NOTES

For fuller explanatory notes, see Leigh i.89-90.

a. an earlier version, now lost, of no. 28 (a petition for a pension, addressed to the governor of Savoy).

b. I have tried to show that this paragraph probably refers, not to the 1732 trip to Besançon, which seems innocent enough, but to a different, much more mysterious journey which took place in June 1735. For a summary of the argument, see Leigh i.28.

30

Rousseau à Françoise-Louise-Eléonore de La Tour, baronne de Warens

Ma trés chére Maman, [le 18 mars 1739]

J'ai receu comme je le devois le billiet que vous m'écrivîtes Dimanche dernier, et j'ai convenu sincérement avec moi-même que puisque vous trouviés que j'avois tort, il faloit que je l'eusse effectivement, ainsi sans chercher à chicaner j'ai fait mes excuses de bon ¹coeur a mon¹ frére; et je vous fais de même ici les miennes trés humbles. Je vous assure aussi que j'ai résolu de tourner toujours du bon cotê les corrections que vous jugerés à propos de me¹ faire sur quelque ton qu'il vous plaise de les tourner.

Vous m'avés fait dire qu'a l'occasion de vos Pâques vous voulés² bien me pardonner. Je n'ai garde de prendre la chose au pié de la lettre; et je suis assuré³ que quand un coeur comme le vôtre a autant aimé quelcun que je me souviens de l'avoir été de vous, il lui est impossible d'en venir jamais a un tel point d'aigreur qu'il faille des motifs de religion pour le réconcilier. Je reçois cela comme une petite mortification que vous m'imposés en me pardonnant, et dont vous savés bien qu'une parfaitte connoissance de vos vrais sentimens adoucira l'amertume.

Je vous remercie Ma très Chére Maman, de l'avis que vous m'avés fait donner d'écrire a mon Pére. Rendés-moi cependant la justice de croire que ce n'est ni par négligence ni par oubli que j'avois retardé jusqu'a présent. Je pensois qu'il auroit convenu d'attendre la réponse de M. l'Abbé Arnaud, afin que si le sujet du Mémoire*a* n'avoit eu nulle apparence de reussir; comme il est a craindre, je lui eusse passé sous silence ce projet évanouï. Cependant vous m'avés fait faire réfléxion que mon délai étoit appuyé sur une raison trop frivôle, et pour reparer la chose le plustot qu'il est possible, je vous envoie ma lettre, que je vous⁴ prie de prendre

183

la peine de lire, de fermer, et de faire partir si vous le jugés a propos.

Il n'est pas[1] necessaire, je croi, de vous assurer que je languis depuis longtems dans l'impatience de vous revoir. Songés, ma trés chére Maman, qu'il y a un mois et peut-être au delà, que je suis privé de ce bonheur. Je suis du plus profond [5]de mon[5] coeur, et avec les sentimens du fils le plus tendre Ma trés Chére Maman,

[5]Vôtre trés humble et trés obeissant serviteur et fils.

JJRousseau

Charmettes 18ᵉ mars 1739

A Madame / Madame la Baronne de Warens / A Chambéri

MANUSCRIPT
* London, private collection: 4 p., p.3 bl., the address p.4; traces of red sealing-wax; holograph.

FIRST PRINTED
Boubers viii (1776 sc. 1777).370-371.

TEXTUAL NOTES
The right-hand margin has again been trimmed too close, with the result that a letter or two has been lost here and there.

[1] [interlinear addition] [2] Boubers: voulez [3] Boubers: sûr [4] Dufour-Plan: [omitted] [5] Dufour-Plan: du

EXPLANATORY NOTES
For fuller explanatory notes, see Leigh i.99.

a. this is not the *mémoire* referred to in no. 26, but a different one, addressed to the abbé Gabriel Arnau[l]d (Leigh no. 25), in which Rousseau claimed the maternal inheritance of his brother, presumed to be dead.

59

Rousseau à François-Joseph de Conzié, comte des Charmettes

A Venize ce 21 X^{bre}[1] 1743

Je Connois Si bien, Monsieur, vôtre générosité naturelle que je ne doute point que vous ne preniez part à mon désespoir et que vous ne me fassiez la grace de me tirer de l'état affreux d'incertitude ou je Suis, je compte pour rien les infirmités qui me rendent

ROUSSEAU AND MADAME DE WARENS

mourant au prix de la douleur de n'avoir aucune nouvelle de M^{de} de Warens, quoyque je luy aye êcrit dépuis que je Suis icy par une infinité de voyes différentes*a*, vous connoissez les liens de reconnoissance et d'amour filial qui m'attachent à elle, jugez du regret que j'aurois a mourir Sans recevoir de Ses nouvelles, ce n'est pas Sans doute vous faire un grand éloge que de vous avouër, Monsieur, que je n'ay trouvé que vous Seul à Chambéri capable de rendre un Service par pure générosité, mais c'est du moins vous parler Suivant mes vrais Sentimens que de vous dire que vous êtes l'homme du monde de qui j'aimerois mieux en recevoir, rendez moy Monsieur, celuy de me donner des nouvelles de Ma pauvre Maman, ne me déguisez rien, Monsieur, je vous en Supplie, je m'attens à tout, je Souffre déja tous les maux que je peux prévoir, et la pire de touttes les nouvelles pour moy est[2] de n'en recevoir aucune. Vous aurez la bonté, Monsieur, de m'adresser votre Lettre[3] Sous le plix de quelque correspondant de Genêve, qui[4] me la fasse parvenir, car elle ne viendroit pas en droiture.

Je passay en poste à Milan, ce qui me priva du plaisir de rendre moy même votre Lettre que j'ay fait parvenir depuis: j'ay appris que votre aimable Marquise S'est remariée il y a quelque tems. Adieu, Monsieur, puisqu'il faut mourir tout de bon, c'est à présent qu'il faut être philosophe, je vous diray une autrefois quel est le genre de philosophie que je pratique. J'ay l'honneur d'être avec le plus Sincere et le plus parfait attachement, Monsieur, [5]votre tres humble et tres obeissant Serviteur.[5]   JJRousseau

faites moy la grace, Monsieur de faire parvenir Sûrement l'incluse que je confie à votre générosité.

M. le Comte des Charmettes

MANUSCRIPT
* London, private collection: 4 p., the postscript p.4, the address at the foot of p.1; original in the hand of the abbé de Binis, the signature holograph.

FIRST PRINTED
Boubers viii (1776 *sc.* 1777).412-413.

TEXTUAL NOTES
[1] [i. e., 'December': Boubers printed

'septembre'] ² Boubers: c'est ³ [interlinear addition] ⁴ Boubers: pour qu'il ⁵ Boubers: [omitted]

EXPLANATORY NOTES

This letter has been previously placed in September 1743. The correction makes Rousseau's anxiety about mme de Warens's silence more understandable.

As far as I am aware, this is the only original of a private letter of Rousseau's not written in his own hand.

a. only one of these letters seems to have reached mme de Warens (Leigh no. 62, dated 5 October 1743.) The rest probably went astray owing to the war.

144

Rousseau à Françoise-Louise-Eléonore de La Tour, baronne de Warens

A Paris le 26ᵉ Août 1748¹

Je n'espérois pas, ma très bonne Maman, d'avoir le plaisir de vous écrire: l'intervalle de ma derniére Lettre ²à celle ci² a été rempli coup sur coup de deux maladies affreuses. J'ai d'abord eu une³ Attaque⁴ de Colique Nephretique, fievre, ardeur et retention d'urine; la douleur s'est calmée à force de bains, de nitre, et d'autres diuretiques, mais la difficulté d'uriner Subsiste toujours, et la pierre qui du rein est descenduë dans la vessie, ne peut en sortir que par l'operation. mais ma Santé ni ma bourse ne me laissant pas en état d'y songer, il ne me reste plus de ce côté là que la patience et la resignation, remedes, qu'on a toujours sous la main mais qui ne guérissent pas de grand chose.

En dernier lieu je viens d'être attaqué de violentes coliques d'estomac accompagnées de vomissemens continuels et d'un flux de ventre excessif; j'ai fait mille remèdes inutiles, j'ai pris l'Emetique et en dernier lieu le Symarouba; le vomissement est calmé, mais je ne digére plus du tout. Les Alimens sortent tels que je les ai pris, il a falu renoncer même au ris qui m'avoit été prescript, et je suis réduit à me priver presque de toutte nourriture, et par dessus tout cela d'une foiblesse inconcevable.

Cependant, le besoin me chasse de la chambre, et je me propose de faire demain ma prémiére sortie, peut être que le grand air et un peu de promenade me rendront quelque chose de mes forces perduës: On m'a conseillé l'usage de l'extrait de Geniévre, mais il est ici bien moins bon et beaucoup plus cher que dans nos montagnes.

Et vous ma chére Maman, comment êtes vous a présent. Vos peines ne sont-elles point calmées; n'êtes-vous point appaisée[5], au sujet d'un malheureux fils qui n'a prévu vos peines que de trop loin sans jamais les pouvoir soulager. Vous n'avez connu ni mon coeur, ni ma Situation; permettez-moi de vous repondre [2]une fois[2] ce que vous m'avez dit si souvent, vous ne me connoitrez que quand il ne[6] sera plus temps.

M. Leonard a envoyé Savoir de mes nouvelles il y a quelque tems. Je promis de lui écrire, et je l'aurois fait si je n'étois retombé malade précisément dans ce temps-là. [Si vo][7]us jugiez à propos, nous nous écririons à l'ordi[naire pa][7]r cette voye. Ce seroit quelques ports de Lettres, quelques affranchissemens épargnés dans un tems ou cette Lesine est presque de nécessité. J'espére toujours que ce tems n'est pas pour durer éternellement. Je voudrois bien avoir quelque voye sure pour m'ouvrir à vous Sur ma véritable situation. J'aurois le plus grand besoin de vos conseils. J'use mon esprit et ma santé pour tacher[8] de me conduire avec sagesse dans des[9] circonstances difficiles, à[10] sortir S'il est possible, de cet état d'opprobre et de misère[11] et je crois m'appercevoir chaque jour que c'est le hazard seul qui régle ma destinée, et que la prudence la plus consommée n'y peut rien faire du tout. Adieu, mon aimable Maman, écrivez moi toûjours *à l'Hôtel du St Esprit*, ruë Plastriére.

MANUSCRIPT

* London, private collection: 4 p., the address p.4; fragment, of red sealing-wax; post-marks: stamp: 'PORT PAYÉ': charges: '6' (on a different fold) and '2'; note by a postal clerk: 'pr alé au pont Bauvoisin'; holograph.

FIRST PRINTED

Boubers viii (1776 sc. 1777).382-383.

TEXTUAL NOTES

[1] [the last figure of the year is written over another, illegible.] [2] Boubers:

[omitted] ³ Dufour-Plan: [omitted]
⁴ ⟨Colique⟩ ⁵ Dufour-Plan: affligée
⁶ Boubers: n'en ⁷ [hole made by the
seal] ⁸ tacher ⟨me⟩ ⁹ Boubers: ces
¹⁰ Boubers: pour

EXPLANATORY NOTES

See Leigh ii.109 for a comment on this 'colique néphrétique' and its timing, which contradicts the account given in the *Confessions* (*Pléiade* i.361).

A Madame / La Baronne de Warens

Virelai. [1738?]

Madame aprenez la nouvelle
De la prise de quatre rats
Quatre rats n'est pas bagatelle
Aussi ¹n'en badine-je¹ pas.
Et je vous mande avec grand Zêle
Ces vers qui vous diront tout bas
Madame aprenez la nouvelle
De la prise de quatre rats

A L'odeur d'un friand appas²
Rats sont sortis de leur Caselle
Mais ma trappe arrétant leurs pas
Les a ³d'une mort très cruelle³
Fait passer de vie a trépas
Madame aprenez la nouvelle
De la prise de quatre rats

Mieux que moi savez qu'icy bas
N'a pas qui veut fortune telle
C'est triomphe qu'un pareil cas.
Le fait n'est pas d'une allumelle
Ainsi donc avec grand soulas
Madame aprenez la nouvelle
De la prise de quatre rats.

JJRousseau

MANUSCRIPT

*London, private collection; 2 p.; holograph.

FIRST PRINTED

Boubers viii (1776 sc. 1777).344.

TEXTUAL NOTES

¹ *Pléiade:* ne badiné-je ² *Pléiade:* repas ³ Boubers: par une mort cruelle

EXPLANATORY NOTES

This *virelai* is difficult to date, but seems to belong to a period when JJ was at Les Charmettes and mme de Warens at Chambéry. This is the only known manuscript of the *virelai*. The *Pléiade* édition (ii.1222) follows Boubers (with two slight slips). Boubers amended the text of the second stanza.

I did not include this text in my edition of Rousseau's correspondence, because it did not appear to be a letter. The manuscript, however, shows that it is a marginal case. It is signed, has something like an address at the top of the first page, and has been folded like a letter.

Virtue on trial:
a defense of Prévost's Théophé

by Emita B. Hill

The heroine of Prévost's *Histoire d'une Grecque moderne* is presented by the narrator as an enigma: she professes to love virtue and yet seems to follow vice. 'Seems' and 'professes' are all he knows—or can know—of her real nature. Therefore, the narrator oscillates in his opinion, ready to believe her all good or all evil and unable to prove either. Most readers accept this portrayal and repeat dutifully after the narrator: Théophé is an enigma. Mlle Engel, for example, writes as follows: 'On ne sait à aucun moment si Théophé est une menteuse raffinée qui mène avec audace une intrigue secrète, ou une victime calomniée'[1].

Although explanations for her behaviour have been suggested —they are, in fact, present and articulated in the novel itself— still readers persist in disregarding them and in regarding Théophé as incompréhensible, the enigma as insoluble. In an excellent introduction to a recent edition of the novel, Robert Mauzi refers to one such interpretation—a psychological one that appears quite plausible and that is, moreover, put forward by the heroine herself[2]. But if we accept this explanation, protests Mauzi,

---

[1] Claire Eliane Engel, *Le Véritable abbé Prévost* (Monaco 1957), p.199.

[2] 'Obsédée d'expiation et de pureté, Théophé rêve d'oublier un passé dont elle a honte. Il lui est donc impossible d'aimer le narrateur, dont les procédés les plus généreux lui remettent ce passé en mémoire, et dont les exigences quelquefois l'y plongent'; *L'Histoire d'une Grecque moderne* (1965), p.xxxv. (All page references to the novel in our text will be to this edition). Théophé's 'obsession' would account both for her inability to love her protector, the narrator, and for her readiness to love a young Frenchman unacquainted with her past.

'il n'y a plus d'énigme, et n'est-ce pas tout le sens de l'œuvre qui se trouve remis en question?' The strongest argument against this solution is, apparently, that it is too simple, too reasonable, that it does indeed resolve the enigma of Théophé. Mauzi reminds us that Théophé's explanation does not satisfy the narrator nor in any way alter or clarify their relationship. 'Le récit se poursuit comme si rien n'avait été dit, comme si Théophé, soit par méconnaissance d'elle-même, soit par pure tromperie, soit par bon procédé au contraire et désir de rassurer, n'avait rien dévoilé d'essentiel' (p.xxxvi).

What is at stake is Théophé's reputation as an enigma, the mystery and complexity of her feminine personality, the very aspects that permit the reader to relate her to Prévost's most famous creation, Manon Lescaut. It is perhaps inevitable that the reader of Prévost, imbued with the story of Manon and Des Grieux, should seek in his lesser works imitations or variations on that story[3]. Thus Mauzi, while taking care to point out the discrepancies in the personalities of the two girls and also in their relationship to their respective admirers, nevertheless does suggest a strong parallel between the two works, a parallel that stresses precisely the enigmatic nature of the two girls. He suggests that in both novels the central figure is 'le personnage énigmatique que ni l'auteur[4], ni le narrateur, ni le lecteur ne voient

---

[3] Francis Pruner claims for the *Grecque moderne* equal status with *Manon*. 'Je ne parviens pas à comprendre pourquoi *l'Histoire d'une Grecque moderne* ne jouit pas auprès de mes contemporains du même prestige que *Manon Lescaut*'; 'Psychologie de la Grecque moderne', *Actes du Colloque d'Aix-en-Provence (Publications des Annales de la Faculté des lettres Aix-en-Provence)*, 1965, n.s. 50, p.146. (This volume will be designated hereafter as *Colloque-Prévost*.)

[4] Mauzi points out the similarity of Prévost's different narrators. They all display characteristics of Prévost's own personality. 'Cet homme qui dit "je", nous le reconnaissons à son exaltation, à ses faiblesses, à sa mauvaise foi, et à son inquiétude: c'est l'Homme de qualité, c'est Des Grieux, c'est Cleveland, c'est Prévost lui-même' (p.iv). But despite their common origin, despite the indisputable elements of self-portraiture or autobiography in all these works, there is no reason to conclude that Prévost's point of view is restricted to that of his narrator.

jamais de l'intérieur, mais dont ils doivent interpréter les sentiments et sonder le mystère à partir de signes désespérément ambigus' (p.v).

One can argue, however, that the central focus of *l'Histoire d'une Grecque moderne* is not Théophé herself, not the object of the narrator's love, but the nature of that love, not the 'enigmatic' personality of the woman, but the personality that creates that enigma. Clearly the narrator does not and, apparently, cannot be convinced by Théophé's self-analysis. None the less, his lack of comprehension, his stubborn disbelief, his continuing unwillingness to see her as other than enigmatic, do not constitute a statement of fact, but a statement of opinion—his own, interested opinion. Rather than adopt or assimilate his attitude, the novel invites us to question it, to ask what generates it, what prevents him from revising it, what forces this man repeatedly to disregard or to disbelieve Théophé in her attempts to explain herself to him. If Théophé remains in the shadows, it may be that her importance is in fact secondary in this novel, that, as Jean Rousset has observed: 'c'est la vérité subjective qui fait l'intérêt principal de la narration; c'est lui-même et sa passion que le narrateur révèle, par les limites ou les erreurs de sa vision déformante'[5].

Prévost has written a very different novel here from that of *Manon*, one that has modern counterparts in, for example, Robbe-Grillet's *La Jalousie* or Butor's *La Modification*, a novel in which plot and characters are subordinated to and relative to the subjectivity of the narrator, the relation or revelation of a single personality to the exclusion of all others. The mystery surrounding Théophé in the narrator's tale remains impenetrable precisely because he himself has created it. Their mutual adventures consist of a succession of events that are only ambiguous in so far as the narrator himself, through his anxiety and his pathological jealousy, has made them ambiguous. Indeed, he stubbornly

[5] 'Prévost romancier: la forme autobiographique', *Colloque-Prévost*, pp. 197-205.

refuses to comprehend them and deliberately distorts them. As in Robbe-Grillet's novel, every event is interpreted rather than related because the narrator is incapable of a simple relation, incapable of objective observation. Yet, although we see through his eyes only what he himself saw or was able to see, our knowledge and our judgment are not bounded by his. He confides in us and we learn not only the content, but the form and function of this confidence; we study his narrative, but also the narrator, in order that we may formulate independently our own judgment of the events and the personalities narrated, a judgment that may supplement or even contradict what he would have us believe.

The narrator would have us accept this as a love story—the story of his love for a woman who has scorned and betrayed him, rewarding his kindness, his generosity and his devotion with ingratitude and a series of real or imagined infidelities—that is, committed in her imagination for want of opportunity. 'Je suis un Amant rebuté, trahi même, si je dois m'en fier à des apparences... dont j'abandonnerai le jugement à mes Lecteurs' (p.3, 4). And yet one wonders whether this novel can properly be called a love story in the sense that the story of Manon and Des Grieux is a love story[6].

The narrator professes to place Théophé before the tribunal of his readers—and yet he himself has already judged her and found her guilty on the basis of the appearances. The burden of the proof is forever on her. She must prove herself innocent, or he will continue to believe her guilty. His eternal suspicions are tantamount to condemnation. His mistrust precludes the possibility of trust. Mauzi observes: 'La jalousie du narrateur n'est pas loin de prêter à la bien-aimée une nature diabolique, d'autant plus inquiétante que rien ne peut jamais être prouvé. Toute la dernière partie de la *Grecque moderne* est consacrée à l'interpré-

---

[6] 'Il s'agit de ne réduire le roman ni à la seule Manon, ni au seul Des Grieux, mais de déchiffrer cette histoire à deux qu'est toujours, bien ou mal réussie, une histoire d'amour'; Roger Laufer, *Style rococo, style des 'lumières'* (Paris 1963), p.74.

tation par la jalousie de signes ambigus qui donnent lieu à des interrogations sans réponse et à des contestations infinies' (pp.xxviii-xxix). But the 'interrogations' and 'contestations infinies' are not at all ambiguous, although the signs relating to Théophé's guilt or innocence may be. Such treatment is inconceivable except in a climate of suspicion and mistrust. Théophé is not on trial in the mind of the narrator; sentence has been passed, with little hope of reprieve. If the signs are 'ambiguous', they serve to confirm his fears; they cannot dispel them. If they appear to be in her favour, he discounts them as inconclusive, or suspects her of further deception, of skillful dissimulation of what must be her guilt'[7].

If we ask what is this guilt, what is Théophé's crime, on what grounds can she be accused of ingratitude and infidelity, we discover simply that she does not love the narrator, nor has she ever claimed to love him, which would, incidentally, absolve her

[7] Francis Pruner, rather than believe Théophé guilty or innocent, suggests that she is both—but at different times and in different geographical settings. He believes her innocent in Turkey, guilty in France, and suggests that it is not her behaviour as such that constitutes an enigma, but this inconsistent behaviour. 'Comment concilier la vertueuse indignée qui refuse la couche, illégitime puis légitime, d'un ambassadeur de France, la niaise qui, à Livourne, est la dupe du premier hâbleur venu, la dévergondée qui, à Paris, se déniaise aisément?' (p.144). He finds psychological and physiological arguments for her 'virtue' in Turkey. Her liberation from the harem is recent and her memories of it kept fresh by its geographical proximity; equally important, she is surfeited with love-making 'plus que comblée, lassée déjà par l'amour physique, à un âge où les jeunes occidentales en général l'ignorent encore (p.145). In France, the same forces become the excuse or motivation for her supposed *libertinage*. 'Mais alors, sa dégringolade finale dans un amoralisme sans remords? Disons que sa féminité longtemps assoupie, par lassitude et par piété, ne peut que s'éveiller à la longue au fur et à mesure que sa force morale flanche' (p.146). I personally find such a complete inversion of Théophé's morality and the assumption that she can pass easily and naturally from open sincerity to constant duplicity quite unbelievable and indefeasible. I hope to demonstrate by a recapitulation of some of the crucial moments in the story that her behaviour is at all times consistent with what she professes, and that her profession, her own analysis of her behaviour and its motivations, is invariable throughout.

at once of the charge of infidelity. More precisely, she does not love him as a woman loves a man, for in every other way she will gladly, at whatever cost to herself, love, honour and obey him. When he purchases her freedom from a seraglio her gratitude and her joy know no bounds. 'Son premier mouvement fut de se jetter à mes genoux, qu'elle embrassa avec un ruisseau de pleurs... elle m'adressa mille fois les noms de son Libérateur, de son Père, et de son Dieu' (pp.21, 22). She cannot love him as her equal at the same time that she worships him as her saviour, her protector, and her deliverer. He is a god-like figure to be reverenced, obeyed, even propitiated; all her attitudes are those that are incompatible with the kind of love he craves from her, that could only seem incongruous, almost incestuous, given the terms of their relationship and her total dependence on him. She regards him as her father, her confessor[8], her mentor and her judge; he is her master and she his slave, for although he claims to have purchased her freedom, he has in fact purchased her.

Théophé herself recognizes the illusory nature of her freedom. 'Hélas! qu'ai-je droit de vous refuser?... Ai-je en mon pouvoir quelque chose qui ne soit pas à vous plus qu'à moi-même?' (p.95). She must sleep with him if he demands, as his object and his possession; but as an individual, as a woman of her own free will, she cannot. The narrator naturally declines to abuse his rights and coerce Théophé into becoming his mistress. But he is confident that his pleasure is only deferred and that sooner or later she will love him and come to him willingly. His assurance is such that he deliberately eschews any expression of his love, any intimation to Théophé of his tenderness towards her, lest he thus influence her and diminish the chances of her taking the initiative: 'j'eus assez de force pour retenir le mouvement qui me portoit à l'entretenir de ma tendresse... je n'aurois pas voulu devoir la conquête

---

[8] 'Sa pruderie n'a rien d'hypocrite: elle est le réflexe normal d'une convertie qui ne souhaite plus qu'effacer si possible un honteux passé: d'où sa confession qui lui dictera désormais la conduite à tenir à l'égard de son confesseur (Pruner, p.145).

de son cœur à mes séductions; et ce que je désirois d'elle, mon bonheur auroit été qu'elle eût paru le souhaiter comme moi' (p.132).

What appears to be delicacy and a respect for Théophé's feelings can also be interpreted as arrogance or complacency, since the narrator entertains no doubts whatsoever concerning the dénouement. His respect does not extend so far as to leave her free to love whom she will, but only to allow her to choose her own time for loving him[9]. Moreover, at this time, she must make all the advances. Despite the evident sincerity of the narrator in his attempts to respect Théophé's wishes, this illusory freedom is no more nor less than that accorded by Valmont in the *Liaisons dangereuses* to his présidente; it is, in fact, no liberty at all, but the expression of his self-confidence. Valmont declared that: 'Mon projet ... est ... de ne lui accorder le bonheur de m'avoir dans ses bras, qu'après l'avoir forcée à n'en plus dissimuler le désir. Au fait, je vaux bien peu, si je ne vaux pas la peine d'être demandé' (1964 ed., p.141).

The ambassador will not 'force' Théophé; he could not conceive of the necessity of force. Nonetheless his 'project' is no less absolute than that of Valmont, and he awaits the outcome with the same certainty of success. His actual control over Théophé far exceeds that of Valmont over madame de Tourvel, who twice escapes her lover by fleeing his presence. Flight and escape are denied to Théophé, who must remain under her protector's roof while continuing to refuse him. Escape is impossible, for she has no place to go, no one to turn to but him; every other liaison is systematically undone. The narrator's hold on her is absolute and irrevocable: despite his protestations to the contrary, it remains the relationship of a master to his slave. He seems unable—or perhaps unwilling—to realize that it is this hold and this relationship

---

[9] 'Il croit qu'à force de soumission il l'obligera à prendre elle-même l'initiative des avances: ce n'est donc une fois de plus qu'un piège qu'il tend à la Grecque; il joue au platonisme pour se faire accorder librement les seules faveurs qui l'intéressent'; Pruner, p.142.

above all else that separates them and that must eternally prevent Théophé from conceiving a free or gratuitous affection for him. Understandably, he fears relinquishing this hold lest she escape from him altogether. Thus he continues to hope and to wait, unwilling to make the experiment of her freedom that might gain him her love, yet dissatisfied in the assurance of her company, without her love.

It seems inconceivable to him that she should be unable to love him. Time and again he upbraids her for ingratitude and accuses her of complicity with other lovers, the only interpretation he can find for her refusal and her resistance to his love. And yet what is this love he offers her that she should not resist? The narrator admits—even insists, as though it should be to his credit—that at first it was not love at all. At the time that he freed Théophé and encouraged her to behave with the dignity, the modesty and the self-respect of a European woman, he himself continued to regard her as little more than a prostitute and readily attributed to 'delicacy' his unexpected indifference to her charms. 'Je me dois ce témoignage, que malgré les charmes de sa figure... il ne s'étoit encore élevé dans mon cœur aucun sentiment qui fût différent de la compassion. Ma délicatesse naturelle m'avoit empêché de sentir rien de plus tendre pour une jeune personne qui sortoit des bras d'un Turc' (p.23). His indifference is to his credit in so far as it absolves him from suspicion or slander regarding his motives for purchasing Théophé from her former master. This same indifference, however, prevents him from ever penetrating her thoughts and her motives, from understanding what she is apart from what she was. He cannot accept at face value a profession of virtue from an ex-dancing girl, from the former mistress of a Turk.

Mauzi calls this scepticism 'lucidity', a lucidity that might, if preserved, remove the mystery that surrounds Théophé. 'Un tel doute pourrait servir à dissiper à la fois les chimères du narrateur et le mystère de Théophé. Mais il n'apparaît que dans l'instant d'une lucidité fragile, aussitôt occultée par la masse des illusions, le vertige de l'amour et l'exaltation des projets' (p.xxvi). On the contrary, if the narrator could set aside these doubts and sustain his belief in her conversion, if he could only treat her as the free, virtuous and responsible creature he wishes her to be, she might be able to answer his trust with her own and even with love. If it were possible for him to forget her past, she might forget it, too.

When the narrator first discovered Théophé in the midst of the other women in Cheriber's harem, she was innocent of any feelings of guilt or remorse. She was not responsible for her presence there; nor, in her natural state as the child if not of nature, then of a non-Christian, non-western society, had she experienced shame. As she explained to the narrator: 'je suis moins tombée dans le désordre que je n'y suis née. Aussi n'en ai-je jamais connu la honte ni les remords' (p.25). It is only since meeting him that she views her past and her own person with horror and loathing. With his help she has eaten of the fruit of knowledge, knowledge for which she hungered, but whose taste is bitter. She learns to see herself as he sees her—a woman raised in a harem, a vile prostitute, a creature defiled and defamed. This bitter knowledge, this shamed recognition of her status in the eyes of her liberator and protector, is always a gulf between them that neither can bridge. This knowledge determines the narrator's conduct with her, his inability to understand her, his cruel lack of respect for her. He can only interpret her initial trust in his protection, her passionate demonstrations of gratitude and adoration, as proofs of her eagerness to become his mistress, of her willingness to replace her Turkish master with a younger and more attractive French one. His scruples are for his own account; he is reluctant to approach a woman from such a shady past. As for her, he never doubts that she will be honoured to become his mistress, proud to be deemed worthy of that estate. He hesitates no longer after discovering her noble birth: 'la naissance de Théophé qui passoit pour certaine à mes yeux avoit achevé d'effacer les idées importunes qui revenoient toujours blesser ma délicatesse' (p.67). Her birth was such that the rôle of mistress was now beneath her, or would have been, were she not, happily for him, still lowered in his esteem by her past. 'Avec tant de belles qualités et la noblesse de son origine, en aurois-je voulu faire ma Maîtresse si elle n'eût rien eu à se reprocher du côté de l'honneur? Il se faisoit de ses perfections et de ses taches une compensation qui sembloit la rendre propre à l'état où je voulois l'engager' (p.67). Here, far from forgetting her past, the narrator insists on it as a necessary ingredient to their relationship, or, more precisely, to the relationship he intends to establish between them.

Théophé's flight interrupts his tranquil meditations on her merits as a future mistress and precipitates his first reactions of jealousy and fierce possessiveness that are to characterize the remainder of his long and disastrous acquaintance with this young girl. Théophé confesses that his presence shames her; his knowledge of her past humiliates her, and she longs to escape from him as from a part of herself. '... comme j'étois l'homme du monde à qui elle avoit le plus d'obligation, j'étois aussi celui pour qui elle avoit le plus d'estime, et par conséquent celui dont la présense, les discours et l'amitié renouvelloient le plus vivement la honte de ses avantures' (p.69).

Although her explanation is entirely rational and consistent with what she has told him before and will tell him again, over and over, to him it is meaningless, because irrelevant to what he intends to make of her. He interrupts her flight, accuses her of ingratitude, and, by reminding her of her vulnerability and her evident need for protection from the dangers and temptations of a world she does not know, he brings her back—ostensibly to provide that protection. He manages to convince himself that he is acting in her interest, but at the same time he is more determined than ever to make her his mistress. He quite obviously does not recognize any incompatibility in these two aims, for the simple reason that he still regards her as a courtesan, not imagining that she might regard herself differently. He assumes she will therefore welcome and approve his plans for her, assured, as his mistress, of a safe and comfortable haven from the world and its hazards.

Thus, when they arrive at this country house, he proceeds to undress in her presence, making no attempt to observe any amenities, for, as he reminds us—lest we should forget—these are unnecessary for someone with Théophé's experience! 'Ce n'étoit point avec une femme qui m'avoit raconté si ouvertement ses avantures de Patras et celles du Sérail, que je me croyois obligé de prendre les détours qui soulagent quelquefois la modestie d'une jeune personne sans expérience; et si l'on me permet une autre réfléxion, ce n'étoit pas non plus d'une femme sur qui j'avois acquis tant de droits, et qui s'étoit livrée d'ailleurs à moi si volontairement, que je devois attendre des excès de réserve et de bienséance' (p.93). When Théophé repulses him with tears of horror and shame, he is surprised and even hurt. As on every similar occasion—and there are several variations on this scene—her reactions are to him an enigma.

He should understand, for, as Théophé reiterates, he alone is responsible: 'ne vous offensez point de l'effet que vos propres leçons ont produit sur mon cœur' (p.103). His inability to understand what she affirms necessitates her frequent recapitulation of her sense of guilt and unworthiness, a recapitulation that can only become increasingly more painful. 'Ce sont vos questions mêmes... c'est la nécessité où vous me mettez de parler clairement qui cause mon chagrin' (p.102). Her punishment seems excessive. She must forever confess and forever repent without hope of absolution or pardon; she cannot be cleansed and sent on her way. Her sin must remain with her, her past be ever present. When the ambassador stopped her flight and took her back under his protection, she knew, as he could not, the cost to her of that protection. And yet she obeyed him and returned to him and to this confrontation with herself. 'Quoique vous fussiez plus redoutable pour moi que tous les hommes ensemble, parce que vous connoissiez mieux toute l'étendue de mon infortune, quoique chacun de vos regards me parût une sentence qui portoit ma condemnation, je suis rentrée avec vous dans Constantinople' (pp.102-103).

Her conviction of her own guilt compelled her to endure his presence and the burden of his condemnation. Like Cain, she tried and failed to hide from her god, from this foreigner whom she reverenced as the source of knowledge and the model of virtue. To see him apparently corrupted, contaminated by her sin, tempted to the very vice he taught her to abhor, shatters her hopes for herself and her trust in him. 'Je vous ai regardé comme mon Maître dans la vertu, et vous voulez me rentraîner vers le vice' (p.103). Rather than judge her master she condemns herself as the root of this evil, attributing his weakness to her influence. Her self-revulsion is now total. In the future when the narrator offers her his love and later still offers her marriage, she is each time overwhelmed by this revulsion and will not listen to him. 'Elle accusa la fortune de mettre le comble aux malheurs de sa vie, en la faisant servir non seulement à ruiner le repos de son père et de son bienfaiteur, mais à corrompre les principes d'un cœur dont elle prétendoit que les vertus avoient été son unique modèle' (p.206).

Like partners in a ballet they retrace their steps, repeat the familiar pattern, advance, clash and withdraw. Each time she reaffirms her initial statement; each time he is confounded, unable to reconcile her behaviour with his expectations, unable to penetrate the 'enigma' of this woman whom he can only see in his own terms; which have never evolved in the years they have lived under the same roof. 'Il me paroissoit si étonnant à moi-même que j'eusse besoin de tant de précautions pour expliquer mes sentimens à une fille que j'avois tirée des bras d'un Turc, et qui dans les premiers jours de sa liberté se seroit peut-être crue trop heureuse de passer tout d'un coup dans les miens, qu'au milieu même de la tendresse dont je prenois plaisir à m'enyvrer, je me reprochois une timidité qui ne convenoit ni à mon âge ni à mon expérience' (p.171).

In his own words she is still 'une fille que j'avois tirée des bras d'un Turc'. The only change in his attitude is in the intensity of his desire. Where he had before been indifferent to her charms, put off by his 'delicacy', he now finds those charms irresistible and craves their possession. He claims to love her, but admits that he does not truly know her, since he is incapable of understanding or evaluating her as a person apart from himself, apart from his own feelings towards her. When he resolves to marry—and it is only after the generous Selictar has honourably proposed marriage and been refused—he congratulates himself on his own generosity, quite surprised to feel no distaste at the prospect: 'je passai sans répugnance au dessein de l'épouser; et ce qui devoit être surprenant pour moi-même après avoir passé près de deux ans sans oser m'arrêter un moment à cette pensée, je me familiarisai tout d'un coup avec mon projet jusqu'à ne m'occuper que des moyens de le faire réussir'(p.202).

When Théophé once again refuses him, he finds the only explanation acceptable to his ego, namely, that Théophé is incapable of love, 'à l'épreuve de tous les efforts des hommes' (p.208). Convinced that her virtue is impregnable, that she can love no man if not himself, his jealousy and possessiveness begin to subside, only to erupt later—more violently than before—when this theory is disproved.

In Italy Théophé is courted by a young French nobleman and falls in love with him. Her sudden susceptibility is consistent with her former adamancy; her guilt and her shame had prevented her from loving any man so long as her past lay between them. But now with this stranger in a new country, she thought she had left her Turkish past behind; she believed that her release was possible, that she might begin anew: 'ne lui croyant aucune connoissance de mes misérables avantures, je me suis flattée de pouvoir rentrer avec lui dans les droits ordinaires d'une femme qui a pris l'honneur et la vertu pour son partage' (p.234).

The narrator's reactions pass from disbelief to suspicion to indignation. He makes no attempt to appreciate Théophé's situation or to understand her feelings. Nor does the possibility of her happiness enter his thoughts. For her to respond to another man is perfidy, outrage, a betrayal. When he surprises the count on his knees before Théophé, his jealousy distorts this into a vision of monstrous evil: 'La vûe d'un Serpent, qui m'auroit soufflé son poison, n'eût pas répandu plus de trouble et de consternation dans tous mes sens' (p.225). He must interpret every sign as a confirmation of her 'guilt' even when the sign itself reads in her favour. If the lovers appear modest and circumspect in their behaviour, he is convinced, not of their innocence, but of their guilt. If the count treats Théophé with respect and does not press her, he must have already satisfied his desires. Théophé must be guilty—must always have been guilty—behind her façade of innocence and her talk of virtue. 'Je rougissois même d'avoir été la dupe de ces belles maximes qui m'avoient été répétées tant de fois avec tant d'affectation, et je me reprochois moins ma bonté que ma crédulité et ma foiblesse' (p.225). The fault is hers alone; his only mistake was an excess of kindness and credulity! He casts himself as the wronged hero; Théophé is the culprit. But, once again, what is Théophé's crime? Only that she does not love him and cannot even contemplate loving him. Now that to her own surprise she has been able to love another man, now that she has allowed herself as a free individual, with a freedom the narrator himself purchased and guaranteed to her, to admit this new emotion, she sees no reason to suppress or deny its existence.

This is no crime, no falling away from virtue, unless virtue is equated with indifference, and we know how desperately the narrator sought to overcome Théophé's indifference to his love. And yet in his eyes she can only be criminal. She cannot love another man with impunity. The narrator must accuse her of total complicity with her lover, of a total reversal of her virtuous role. Appearances that are favourable to her must be deceptive. The denials of her maid he sets aside, for either she too is lying, or the lovers have succeeded in deceiving her. Totally the prey of his insane jealousy, the narrator searches Théophé's room, even measuring the imprint of her body in her unmade bed, finally covering with his kisses the empty sheets where she had slept.

A DEFENSE OF PREVOST'S THEOPHE

He can find no evidence, no witness against her except within himself. But it does not really matter whether she is innocent or guilty in her actions. To him she is irremediably guilty through her failure to love him and her willingness to love another. This alone matters. The circumstances of her behaviour are irrelevant pretexts for his anger. Her statement of her innocence further enrages him: 'l'opinion qu'elle avoit de son innocence étoit précisément ce qui causoit mon désespoir' (p.235). She should feel guilty; she should consider his feelings and not her own; she should have resisted her inclinations for his sake. 'J'étois mortellement irrité qu'elle fît si peu d'attention à mes sentimens, ou qu'elle en fût si peu touchée, qu'elle ne parût pas même occupée de la crainte de m'affliger' (p.235). Long ago, when his jealous suspicions were focussed on another man, on Synese, the Greek who was—or was not—Théophé's brother, he had warned her: 'Je me fais une violence mortelle pour vous laisser Maîtresse de votre cœur; mais si vous l'accordez à un autre, votre dureté causera ma mort' (p.121).

It is not, however, the narrator himself, but Théophé who must be made to suffer for what he calls her 'dureté'. Hurt, reproachful, self-pitying even as he accuses and torments Théophé for her 'disloyalty', thinking only of himself, he succeeds in ruining her one chance for happiness, her only opportunity to exist independently of him, for the Frenchman—significantly—suspects that Théophé is the narrator's mistress and hastily disappears. Her hopes gone, her newly awakened emotions frustrated, Théophé falls ill. Though she does not die, she undergoes a symbolic death in the loss of her beauty: 'si elle ne pût perdre la régularité de ses traits, ni la finesse de sa phisionomie, je trouvai beaucoup de diminution dans la beauté de son teint et dans la vivacité de ses yeux' (p.243).

With no further cause for jealousy the narrator discovers that he has ceased to love her. He attributes his indifference to distaste for her infidelity and impatience with her sorrow and her suffering: 'je ne pus la voir dans cette langueur pour un autre, sans éprouver que la plus vive tendresse se refroidit enfin par la dureté et l'ingratitude. Insensiblement je m'apperçus que mon cœur devenoit plus libre' (p.239). His pride will not permit him to pity her in her affliction; he could not so forget himself as to sympathize with her loss. He tells us that more than ever now he sees her merely as his own creature, as an adjunct to his own person, and that he values her primarily as the object of his attentions and the recipient of his charity'. 'C'étoient mes propres bienfaits qui sembloient m'attacher à elle comme à mon ouvrage. Il ne m'échappoit plus une expression passionnée, ni une seule plainte des tourmens que je lui voyois souffrir pour mon rival' (p.243).

He could part with her willingly now, and even goes so far as to seek a marriage for her, to effect the separation he could not contemplate before 'en la rendant la femme d'un autre' (p.243). He claims to have Théophé's interests at heart, but we have just seen how cruelly he disregarded those interest while they conflicted with his own desires. He readily admits to another motive, namely, concern lest Théophé's presence in his home in Paris prove an embarrassment and interfere with his ambitions. 'Outre son intérêt, qui étoit mon premier motif, je faisois réflexion qu'il me seroit difficile à Paris d'éviter les soupçons qui naîtroient sur mon commerce avec elle; et quoique je ne fusse point encore dans un âge où l'amour est une indécence, j'avois des vûes de fortune qui ne s'accordoient point avec des engagemens de cette nature' (p.245). But, understandably, his attempts to persuade Théophé to look with favour on this new suitor only serve to humiliate her further. Only his monumental egotism can explain the narrator's claim to seek her happiness when he obliges her to receive the visits of a man she finds distasteful after he has driven away the man she loved. Her distaste for this suitor, like her inclination to the other, appears to him wholly arbitrary and unjustified. Spitefully, he reminds her that after her adventure with the count she can no longer claim to prefer solitude and celibacy, as though her readiness to love the one should oblige her to accept all others. But the narrator only encourages this marriage; he does not attempt to force Théophé into it, for this would be an act of deliberate cruelty and his cruelty is never intentional, never overt. Such an act would destroy his complacency and force him to recognize the true nature of his conduct towards his protégée. His ego demands instead that he preserve his status as benefactor. With Theophé still dependent on him, indebted to him, he continues to address her in a complex sequence of accusations, reproaches, and endearments, calculated to engender feelings of guilt and humiliation.

One last time Théophé tries to escape from this cycle, from the disastrous pattern of this relationship which dominates her existence. She decides to enter a convent, to remove herself from all temptations and all persecution, to escape the narrator's surveillance and his jealous suspicions, at the same time sparing him any further need to survey her actions or to suspect her[10]. But even this escape is denied her. The narrator experiences once again his former passion in all its intensity, and with it his tormenting jealousy. Once again he concentrates exclusively on his emotional needs at the expense of hers. Although he is prevented by illness from desiring her physically, he resolves to monopolize her time and her affections by having her attend him in his illness and minister to his wants. When Théophé proposes instead to retire to a convent, the narrator reacts like a spoilt child, with no thought except for himself, hurt and resentful that she should contemplate leaving him at this time. He insists that she remain and abandon forever any project that might remove her from him. 'Je me sentis si mortifié de son indifférence, que n'écoutant que mon ressentiment, je lui déclarai d'un air assez chagrin que je n'approuvois point son projet, et qu'aussi long-tems qu'il lui

---

[10] Pruner says, incorrectly, that Théophé contemplated conventual life 'à l'époque de son plus parfait ascétisme, mais sa ferveur s'affaisse et la chair triomphe' (p.146). On the contrary, Théophé expresses this desire repeatedly during her stay in Paris, the period to which Pruner elsewhere refers as 'sa dégringolade finale dans un amoralisme sans remords' (cf. note 8).

resteroit quelque considération pour moi, je la priois d'en éloigner absolument l'idée' (p.261).

Only death finally delivers them both from the cruel bond that unites them. So long as she lives, the narrator continues to suspect her and to torment her and himself with his suspicions, ready to hear and to explore any accusation from whatever source. His only satisfaction comes from her presence[11], he will never let her depart, never put an end to their sad story until it ends with her death, although, oddly enough, the time and circumstances of her death are unknown to him, concealed from him over a period of several months, by his friends and his family. Once again, apparently, his feelings had subsided into indifference, after he had asserted their paramount importance in a confrontation with Théophé.

Even her death in no way alters his earlier attitudes nor enables him better to appreciate the true nature of their relationship. He maintains at the end as at the beginning that he cannot comprehend and therefore cannot judge the nature of this woman he claims to have loved. Her person, her feelings, her motivations and her actual conduct are for him forever shrouded in mystery, opaque, impenetrable.

The explanation, however, for this mystery and opacity cannot be found in Prévost's presentation of Théophé herself. On the contrary, we hope to have shown that Théophé, as she is described to us by the narrator himself in her demeanour, her behaviour and her conversation, in every external or tangible manifestation of her inner being, exhibits a consistency and a rationality that contradict the narrator's personal impressions. The source of these impressions, clearly, lies in his own personality, in his own egotism and insensitivity, in the intense subjectivity of his reactions that clouds and distorts his perceptions. Prévost's achieve-

---

[11] 'J'ai continué depuis cette étrange avanture de jouir de la vûe et du commerce de Théophé, sans en prétendre d'autre satisfaction que celle de la voir et de l'entendre' (pp.271-272).

ment in this novel is to have created a character wholly different from Des Grieux, a character whose tragedy consists in his inability and his fundamental unwillingness to see outside of himself and therefore to evolve, to learn, to perceive reality except through the distortions imposed on it by his subjectivity, and who imposes these distortions with tragic consequences on the reality of another human creature.

Thirteen additional letters of La Harpe[1]

edited by Alexander Jovicevich

After publishing a volume of La Harpe's unpublished correspondence, I had the good fortune to locate thirteen additional letters which La Harpe addressed to various people during the last thirty-six years of his existence. These letters deal with several of the most tense and crucial moments of La Harpe's life, including the affair surrounding the theft of Voltaire's manuscripts, the music war, his problems with the authorities following the uprising of the 13th Vendemiaire, an IV, and his activities under the *directoire* and the *consulat*. They deserve, therefore, to be published and brought to the attention of those who may be interested not only in La Harpe, but also in life in general during the latter part of the eighteenth century in France.

The first two letters reflect La Harpe's state of mind during his long stay at Ferney in 1767 and his feelings about three months after his return to Paris in 1768, following the scandalous affair involving the theft of Voltaire's manuscripts. The extent of La Harpe's guilt in this affair was never unquestionably proven. Certainly, it is hard to conceive, as two letters[2] of Alembert to Voltaire state, that La Harpe readily confessed, upon his returning from Ferney, his wrongdoings to Alembert while he persisted in

---

[1] I found most of these letters while doing research on La Harpe's biography as a grantee of the American philosophical society, of the Shell chemical company, through Seton Hall university, and of the National endowment for the humanities. I want to express my gratitude to all three organisations.

[2] Best.13886 (7 March 1768), 13898 (13 March); see also a letter to the marquise de Florian, 15 March 1768 (Best.13904).

denying, obstinately and rather arrogantly, the whole affair to Voltaire. And if La Harpe really stole some manuscripts which Voltaire kept under lock and key and then confessed, the act could hardly be called an 'imprudence'. Such a crime could only be termed 'malhonnêteté' and 'bassesse' or still better 'larcin'. The second letter to Pierre Michel Hennin, the then French minister in Geneva, indicates, quite to the contrary, that La Harpe had nothing whatsoever to do with his host's manuscripts. Indeed, La Harpe was on his way to build an impressive collection of his own writings which, although prized very highly by the French Academy[3], did not fare nearly as well on the booksellers' racks.

Another newly discovered letter refers to a musical quarrel and was written to Pierre Louis Ginguené during the climax of the war between the Piccinists and Gluckists. Ginguené, the champion and mainstay of the Piccinists, argued their cause in various newspapers either anonymously or under the pseudonym of 'Mélophile'. He had the unique advantage of being the only one in either camp, according to the *Biographie universelle* (xvi.475), to have any knowledge or understanding of the art he wrote about. His main opponents, the 'anonymes de Vaugirard' (Arnaud and Suard), offered solid arguments for Gluck's music in the *Journal de Paris*, but they may well have obtained help from an expert[4]. This note proves, I believe, that La Harpe made an effort, as he often did in his criticism, to be fair and impartial in a dispute where passions ran very high and one which he deplored as a divisive element in the Academy: 'Je vois avec chagrin', says he, 'que cette misérable querelle sur la musique a divisé l'académie'[5]. In his *Lycée*, La Harpe explains that, in spite of his

---

[3] for his success at the 'concours académiques' and his literary activities at Ferney see my 'An Unpublished letter of La Harpe', *Modern language notes* (May 1963), pp.304-307.

[4] Gustave Desnoiresterres, *La Musique française au XVIIIe siècle* (Paris 1872), p.153.

[5] *Œuvres diverses; Correspondance littéraire* (Paris 1826), i.481. Henceforth I shall refer to this work as *Corr. litt*. The same procedure, whenever applicable, will be adopted for all the footnotes.

indifférence to both Gluck and Piccini[6], he was drawn into the quarrel by necessity of professional duties incumbent upon a reviewer of events of entertainment: 'Marmontel et moi, nous sommes les seuls [parmi les partisans de Piccini] qui ont écrit, lui, par intérêt pour son musicien, moi, comme obligé de rendre compte des spectacles dans le *Journal de Littérature*' (*Corr. lit.* i.482).

The two letters[7] to Suard, who, as previously pointed out, was La Harpe's antagonist in the music quarrel of 1777-1778, should dispel the contention of the *Mémoires secrets* (15 October 1779; xiv.208) that La Harpe became a Piccinist because Suard discovered that La Harpe was the lover of mme Amélie Suard, and 'M. Suard n'a pas trouvé cela bon, & a expulsé l'ami de la maison. Celui-ci [La Harpe] piqué à l'occasion du chevalier Gluck, extrêmement prôné par M. l'abbé Arnaud, & conséquemment par M. Suard, son écho, a pris parti en faveur de Monsieur Marmontel à la tête des Piccinistes'. On the contrary, the two letters indicate that La Harpe and Suard were very close friends soon after the supposed incident. Surely a 'mari cocu' would not be likely to forget and forgive so quickly the violated trust of an intimate friend of the household. Moreover, the letters reveal La Harpe's personal life when he talks about some of his works. He appears to be quite contented with the public's approving reaction to his mending of the wrong he had done to the memory of Voltaire when he criticized one of the patriarch's plays, *Zulime*, in the *Mercure de France*, immediately after Voltaire's death in 1778. This conduct had evoked much criticism from La Harpe's enemies in the *Journal de Paris* appearing under the signature of the marquis de Villevieille. Looking at this affair from a distant

---

[6] *Lycée* (Paris 1825), xii.176. Subsequently I shall refer to this work as *Lycée*, indicating the edition if different from this.

[7] these two letters, as well as some other items related to La Harpe, were indicated to me by professor John Pappas, to whom I feel greatly indebted for his generosity and help.

point in history, one cannot but agree with the substance of La Harpe's criticism while questioning the timing of his remarks.

The most interesting and perhaps the most important of these letters is number seven, addressed to Merlin de Douai who at the time was minister of justice. The letter was written between April and November, most likely in May 1796, while La Harpe was under a 'mandat d'amener' issued on 14th Vendémiaire[8]. Accused of being one of the chief instigators of the uprising on the 13th Vendémiaire, an IV, La Harpe here denies, as one would expect, any involvement in the revolt. Before the uprising, however, he was elected president of the 'section de la Butte-des-Moulins'[9], where on the 23rd Fructidor he delivered a speech attacking certain manœuvres of the *convention*, particularly the proposed purge of electors. This address may be found at the Bibliothèque nationale and is entitled *Sections de Paris, prenez'y garde, discours prononcé dans la section de la Butte-des-Moulins*. La Harpe participated considerably in the events leading to the uprising of the 13th Vendémiaire, as is shown by an unpublished speech which I found several years ago and which will soon be published in the *Annales historiques de la révolution française*. This address was very likely delivered on the eve of the revolt in the same 'section de la Butte-des-Moulins'. In his speech, La Harpe criticizes again the oppressive moves of the *convention*, likens the *convention*'s policy to, and considers it even worse than, the reign of terror, and suggests some unspecified energetic measures to prevent the dangers of another oppression of that kind: 'ne pas s'occuper de les [les dangers] prévenir serait une

---

[8] Archives nationales F⁷ 7151; this is a letter from a judge Landry dated '18 Brumaire, an v', and addressed to the minister of the 'police générale'. See also a police report in the same dossier. These are both unpublished documents, as well as all subsequent documents from the Archives nationales.

[9] Archives nationales F⁷ 6311; this is an unsigned note which is in the same dossier where another note written in 1806 by a Polish comte Otockie speaks about an unpublished epic poem by La Harpe entitled *la Louisiade*.

négligence coupable, et balancer sur les mesures énergiques qu'ils nécessitent serait une pusillanimité aveugle et funeste, car s'il est une vérité que six ans de révolutions successives aient dû nous rendre familière et pour ainsi dire usuelle, c'est que de tous les moyens de salut le meilleur et le plus sûr c'est le courage'[10].

Papers seized along with the royalist agent Lemaître describe La Harpe, with Lacretelle and Sérizy, as one of the leaders of the opposition in Paris[11]. Yet it still remains to know what happened to a *mandat d'arrêt* issued on the 5th Ventôse, as this letter states, or on the 6th. If so, what happened to it and why was the arrest never made? Daunou maintains that Marie Joseph Chénier 'déchira publiquement et avec indignation un mandat d'arrêt décerné contre La Harpe'[12]. This fact was never proved, but a letter written by this same Abancourt to the comte Cochon de Lapparent indicates Chénier's intervention. At the time the note was written, Cochon was *ministre de la police générale*, and Abancourt tells him in the capacity of a *sous-directeur du dépôt général de guerre* that 'toutes les pièces d'après les sollicitations du Représentant du Peuple Chénier . . . ont été renvoyées définitivement pour y être statué . . . au Ministre de la Justice'[13]. La Harpe was acquitted in November 1796, as Aulard reported, quoting the *Courrier républicain* of 22 November 1796: 'Le citoyen La Harpe . . . depuis treize mois dans les liens d'un mandat d'arrêt . . . vient d'être acquitté par le jury d'accusation'[14].

Finally, these letters include three addressed to the *éditeur-imprimeur* Agasse which reflect generally the political climate under the *directoire*. They also reveal La Harpe's personal plight at the time and his fears of reprisal should Agasse publish precipitately the *Lycée*. Presented here, too, are two letters dealing with La Harpe's final year, 1802, under the *consulat*, when he incurred

---

[10] Darmouth College, Hanover, New Hampshire, MSS, Ticknor collection, folio 1.

[11] *Moniteur universel*, 22 Oct. 1795.

[12] *Lycée* (Paris 1826), vol.i, p.xli.

[13] Archives nationales, F⁷ 7151.

[14] *Paris pendant la réaction thermidorienne et sous le Directoire* (1898-1902), iii.114.

Napoleon's disfavour, was exiled to Corbeil and, for reason of health, was allowed to return to the capital. There is a rather curious letter written to Decroix as a note of thanks for the ode *Mort de Voltaire* which Decroix composed about the patriarch approximately two years after Voltaire's death in 1778[15]. Decroix wanted La Harpe to bring the ode to the attention of Catherine II of Russia. For the letter no.11 of the collection, I could not complete the date but dr Theodore Besterman identified the addressee as Delisle de Sales. (I want to express my gratitude to dr Besterman for his help.)

These letters appear in chronological order and their texts are copied literally. Modern spelling, however, replaces the eighteenth century mode of writing. Explanatory notes, reduced to a minimum, follow each letter wherever deemed feasible and necessary. Three periods enclosed in parentheses represent a word or words in the text which could not be deciphered.

1. to Pierre Michel Hennin

Monsieur,   Ferney le   1767

Des affaires de famille m'obligent de ramener incessamment ma femme à Paris pour le mariage d'une de ses sœurs. Elle voudrait bien aussi que moi avoir l'honneur de vous faire ses adieux. Si vous pouviez nous envoyer demain pour le midi une voiture, nous serions à vos ordres pour la journée.

J'ai l'honneur d'être très respectueusement, Monsieur, votre très humble et très obéissant serviteur.   Delaharpe

Manuscript: Bibliothèque de l'Institut de France; my copy.

---

[15] for another letter on the same subject and for a review of the ode in the *Mercure de France* see my *Correspondance inédite de Jean-François de La Harpe* (Paris 1965), pp.37-38.

LETTERS OF LA HARPE

2. to Pierre Michel Hennin

Monsieur, à Paris, ce 14 juillet [1768]

Je n'ai pas oublié que c'est environ ce temps-ci que vous devez me rendre visite à notre grande ville de Paris, que vous trouverez encore agrandie. Personne ne compte tirer plus de profit de votre voyage que moi, et je me flatte que vous voudrez bien me témoigner ici les mêmes bontés que vous aviez pour moi dans vos états de Genève. Pour commencer, je vous prierai de vouloir bien remettre ce petit billet à Mr. (...). C'est pour le faire souvenir qu'il eut la complaisance de me promettre la suite du théâtre français[16]. Vous m'obligerez beaucoup, si vous voulez vous charger des volumes qu'il voudra bien vous remettre. Tout est ici dans le plus grand engourdissement. Les spectacles ont cessé depuis quinze jours et ne rouvrent que le (...) de ce mois. Rien de nouveau en littérature que ce qu'on attend ou ce qu'on reçoit de Ferney. Vous êtes à la source. J'entretiens toujours un commerce assez exact avec le seigneur du lieu, et j'en ai lieu d'être satisfait de la manière dont il m'a défendu[17] contre la canaille littéraire[18] qui voulait absolument que je ne fisse d'autre commerce que de voler ses manuscrits et de les vendre, quoique assurément je ne vends jamais que les miens, encore assez mal. Mais ce qui m'a fait grand plaisir, c'est que tous les principaux gens de lettres et tous les honnêtes gens, qui en sont amateurs, ont paru savoir autant de gré que moi à Mr. de Voltaire, de la démarche juste qu'il a faite et des choses obligeantes qu'il y a mêlées. Le prix de l'académie sera bientôt décidé. Je ne manquerai pas de vous apprendre si la personne à qui vous vous intéressez a réussi; le marquis de Ximénès[19]. Oserai-je vous prier de me rappeler au souvenir de

---

[16] La Harpe refers here most likely to the *Théâtre français* (Genève 1767-1768).

[17] Voltaire's 'Déclaration' in the *Mercure de France* (1 April 1768), ii.148-149.

[18] in the *Gazette d'Utrecht* (18 March 1768).

[19] the marquis Augustin Louis de Ximenès, minor writer, soldier, visited Ferney, aspired to marry mme Denis. He had also once been accused of

Mr. de (...) et de Mr. Tronchin Labat[20]? J'ai dîné ici avec le jeune Mr. Tronchin[21] chez le comte de Creutz[22]. Il a bien de l'esprit.

J'ai l'honneur d'être avec autant d'attachement que de respect, Monsieur, votre très humble et très obéissant serviteur.

Delaharpe

Manuscript: Bibliothèque de l'Institut de France; my copy.

3. to Pierre Louis Ginguene

Monsieur, [end of September 1777]

C'est avec grand plaisir que j'imprimerai votre lettre, qui, d'un bout à l'autre, me paraît la raison même. Mais comme cette querelle de musique m'a déjà attiré des tracasseries et que je suis intimément lié avec ceux[23] dont vous attaquez l'opinion, je vous prie, Monsieur, pour l'acquit de ma conscience de mettre votre nom au bas de votre lettre[24]. Je n'y vois point d'inconvénient, et cela même ne peut vous faire que beaucoup d'honneur. J'attends votre aveu sur cet article. Votre lettre au surplus ne peut être que dans le N° du 5 8-bre. Le journal prochain est imprimé.

J'ai l'honneur d'être avec la considération la plus distinguée, Monsieur, votre très humble et très obéissant serviteur.

Delaharpe

[adresse:] A Monsieur / Monsieur Ginguené / à Paris.

involvement in a theft of manuscripts along with Voltaire's niece.

[20] Jean Armand Tronchin who married Jeanne Louise Labat. He was the nephew of Jean Robert Tronchin, the banker.

[21] Jacob Tronchin, counselor to the government of Geneva, resigned that position in summer 1768, came to Paris and settled there.

[22] the count Gustave Philippe de Creutz, diplomat.

[23] Arnaud and Suard.

[24] all the letters that appeared in the *Journal de politique et de littérature* up to December of 1777 dealing with that quarrel seem to be written by La Harpe himself. The first letter written by Mélophile I found in the *Journal de Paris* of February 15, 1778, in which he argues Piccini's talents 'pour la musique dramatique', against criticism to the contrary in the same newspaper of February 12, 1778.

Manuscript: Archives de l'Académie française, collection H. L. moulin; my copy.

4. to Decroix

à Paris, ce 20 août 1780

J'espère, Monsieur, que vous voudrez bien excuser le retard involontaire de ma réponse. J'ai été voir (...) à la campagne et toutes mes lettres m'attendaient à Paris. Je n'ai trouvé la vôtre qu'à mon retour. J'ai reçu avec reconnaissance les marques de votre souvenir et l'ouvrage que vous avez bien voulu m'envoyer. Je ne puis que vous féliciter de l'hommage que vous avez rendu à la mémoire du grand homme que nous aimons tous deux. Vous étiez bien fait, Monsieur, pour sentir tout ce qu'il valait, et tous ceux qui, comme vous, aiment les lettres et l'humanité doivent longtemps déplorer sa perte.

N'ayant point l'honneur d'avoir aucune relation directe avec l'Impératrice de Russie, je n'ai pu me charger de votre commission, mais j'ai fait parvenir votre ouvrage au Grand Duc, son fils, qui sans doute le lira avec plaisir, et j'ai prié Mr. le comte de Schowaloff de se charger des autres exemplaires pour la cour de Pétersbourg. Je vous prie, Monsieur, d'être bien persuadé de l'empressement que j'aurai toujours à faire ce qui pourra vous être agréable, et du sincère et respectueux attachement avec lequel je suis, Monsieur, votre très humble et très obéissant serviteur.

Delaharpe

[*adresse:*] A Monsieur / Monsieur Decroix, Secrétaire du Roi / Rue Princesse à Lille.

Manuscript: Archives de l'Académie française, collection H. L. Moulin; my copy.

5. to Jean Baptiste Suard

Voilà mon cher et aimable ami, l'*Eloge de Voltaire*[25]. Je souhaite qu'il vous fasse autant de plaisir qu'il paraît en avoir fait ici généralement[26]. Je n'ai encore rien fait qui ait eu un succès plus agréable. J'ai bien de l'impatience de vous conter tout cela, quand vous serez dans ce pays-ci. Vous verrez, qu'excepté la famille Fréron[27], avec laquelle comme de raison Voltaire et moi, nous ne serons jamais bien, tout le monde d'ailleurs s'accorde à peu près à penser, que je n'ai rien écrit de mieux en ce genre. Vous conviendrez qu'après les Muses rivales[28] et le Dytirambe[29] cela n'était pas trop maladroit. Pardonnez si je ne vous entretiens pas plus longtemps. Ma lettre est courte, mais je vous envoie un long discours. Je vous aime et vous embrasse bien cordialement.

Delaharpe

à Paris ce 9 (?) avril 1780

Manuscript: Institut et Musée Voltaire, Les Délices; my photocopy.

6. to Jean Baptiste Suard

[23 or 25 March 1781]

Vous m'inquiétez beaucoup, mon cher et aimable ami. N'auriez-vous pas reçu l'exemplaire de *Philoctète*[30] que je vous ai adressé sous contreseing, et la lettre[31] par laquelle je vous l'an-

---

[25] published in February or at the beginning of March 1780.

[26] for favourable comments see *Journal de Paris* (15 April 1780), pp.439-40; also *Mercure de France* (13 May 1780), pp.67-87.

[27] *L'Année littéraire* questioned La Harpe's eloquence, impartiality and good faith (1780), iii.5, 16.

[28] a one-act play also written in memory of Voltaire, staged in February 1779.

[29] the *Dithyrambe aux mânes de Voltaire* was given the Academy award in 1779.

[30] an adaptation of Sophocles's tragedy published in 1781. Parts of the play were read in the Academy about a year earlier. See Grimm, *Correspondance littéraire* (Paris 1878), xii.435.

[31] these texts are unknown to me.

nonçais? En ce cas mandez-le-moi au plus tôt je vous prie, car je n'ose vous envoyer *Menzicoff*[32] par la même voie, avant de savoir si elle est sûre. Je crains aussi que vous ne soyez malade. Sans cela seriez-vous si longtemps sans m'écrire? Tirez-moi d'inquiétude le plus tôt possible, je vous en conjure, et recevez les nouvelles assurances des sentiments qui m'attachent à vous pour la vie.

Delaharpe

Manuscript: Institut et Musée Voltaire, Les Délices; my photocopy.

7. to Philippe Antoine Merlin de Douai

Citoyen Ministre, [May 1796?]

Au moment où l'on me donnait communication d'une lettre[31] de vous au citoyen d'Abancourt, par laquelle vous vouliez bien m'offrir vos bons offices auprès du Directoire, j'apprends que c'est à vous-même qu'il renvoie l'examen définitif de l'affaire qui me concerne et qu'il est disposé à lever le mandat d'arrêt[31] contre moi, s'il ne se trouve à la suite ni charges ultérieures ni commencement de procédures, je ne pense pas que ni l'un ni l'autre ai pu avoir lieu. Si l'on avait cru réellement que je fusse *un des provocateurs de la journée* du 13 Vendémiaire, il n'est pas vraisemblable que l'on n'eut fait aucune espèce de poursuite contre moi pendant trois mois; et la date même du mandat d'arrêt qui est du 5 Ventôse[33] est une présomption de mon innocence. A cette même époque, il est vrai, une femme[34] dont je partageais le domicile, a été arrêtée

---

[32] it was staged 'devant Leurs Majestés sur le Théâtre de Fontainebleau au mois de novembre 1775'. The publishers are Lambert et Baudoin, 1781.

[33] Archives nationales, F7 7151. In the letter of the judge Landry, previously cited, the date of issue of a *mandat d'arrêt* is the 6 'nivose' 1795, but an unsigned letter written as an answer to Landry's report by someone in the *bureau de la police générale* and addressed to the director of the *Jury d'accusation du Canton de Paris* affirms that their search resulted only in finding that a *mandat d'amener* was issued but no *mandat d'arrêt*.

[34] Archives nationales, F7 7151. This is a certain 'citoyenne Minute or Minutte', but in Archives nationales, F7 4774[40], dossier 4, arrestation de Meat, the name is Desminus.

comme prévenue de conspirer avec moi; mais au bout de huit jours elle a été mise en liberté[31] et reconnue parfaitement innocente; c'est encore une présomption. Quant aux faits, les voici.

J'ai été opposé, il est vrai, aux Décrets de fructidor; mais ma conduite a toujours été renfermée dans les limites les plus strictement légales et bien loin de provoquer la funeste et coupable journée du 13 vendémiaire tout ce qui s'est passé à cette époque était contre mon opinion et contre mon vœu.

1º Je n'étais pas même à ma section lors qu'on y adhérait à l'arrêté de la Section Pelletier pour rendre les armes et, l'on saisit, pour faire passer cette adhésion, une des séances du matin, où je n'allais jamais et qui étaient peu nombreuses.

2º Depuis ce moment je n'ouvris pas la bouche dans l'Assemblée, si ce n'est pour improuver fortement, *comme illégale et innocente*, la démarche où l'on nous engagea le 11 par un mensonge très hardi; en nous assurant que la majorité des Secteurs se rassemblait au Théâtre français d'après le *vœu de leurs Commentants*. Envoyé par les miens à cette prétendue convocation, je reconnus l'imposture. Je m'en plaignis fortement, et revins au moment de la proclamation, avec mes collègues. A 7 heures, j'étais à la Tribune de ma section, où je parlais dans le même sens devant deux mille témoins. Je suis donc en cette circonstance, comme dans toutes les autres hors de l'inculpation, puisque je me suis conformé à la loi proclamée. Tous les faits que je rappelle ici sont publics.

3º Je défie qu'on apporte la moindre preuve ou même le moindre indice que j'aie eu jamais aucune espèce de rapport quelconque avec aucun des Membres du Comité de la Section Pelletier, ni de vive voix ni par écrit. Je n'en connaissais pas un, et n'appris leur existence que le jour où venant à ma section le soir, je trouvai tout le monde armé.

4º Je ne pus combattre cette Résolution, parce que je n'aurais pas même été écouté dans l'effervescence générale. Mais le matin du 13 je rédigeai, avec quelques-uns des meilleurs Citoyens de ma section un projet d'arrêté pour le désarmement[31], qui fut même envoyé à l'impression, mais qui ne put avoir d'effet, parce que ceux qui avaient besoin de mesures violentes en précipitèrent l'exécution.

Voilà tout ce qui regarde ma conduite en vendémiaire, l'un des motifs du mandat d'arrêt sur lesquels vous paraissez désirer que je me *disculpe*. L'arrêt porte que je suis *prévenu de conspiration contre la sureté intérieure et extérieure*. Vous n'exigerez pas sans doute, que je prouve que je ne suis pas *conspirateur*: je pourrais exiger si j'étais en jugement, qu'on prouvât que je le suis. Je crois en avoir assez dit pour vous, Citoyen Ministre, qui sans doute êtes disposé à me rendre justice, puis que vous voulez la solliciter pour moi; et je vous dois déjà des remerciements pour les offres obligeantes que contenait votre lettre, et pour la manière dont vous y exprimez l'intérêt que vous voulez bien prendre à moi.

Salut et respect Laharpe

Manuscript: Archives nationales, F^7 7151; my copy.

8. to *Agasse*

lundi 7 aoust [1797]

Vous m'avez totalement oublié, Monsieur, depuis six mois et sans doute vous n'avez pu faire autrement, car je ne puis croire que la petite difficulté, que nous avons eue à nous entendre un moment, ait pu rien diminuer de l'importance qu'un aussi honnête homme que vous attache à ses obligations. Cependant les miennes deviennent de plus en plus onéreuses par un déménagement très coûteux puis qu'il a fallu que je rachetasse des meubles, après avoir été obligé de me défaire des miens. Outre les 900^{tt} [livres] de l'arriéré les 900^{tt} de l'année courante sont échues du 1er juillet dernier. Plus vous avez agi honnêtement avec moi, moins j'ai voulu vous presser, et vous devez croire que je cède à une nécessité pressante. Vous m'avez promis de me donner 300^{tt} de mois en mois, et cet arrangement, le plus commode pour vous, me convient encore, si vous vouliez le tenir régulièrement. Dans cet instant même j'ai le pressent besoin d'argent, et je vous prie instamment de m'envoyer cent écus, si vous ne pouvez pas faire davantage[35].

La petite brochure d'Helvétius[36] n'était pas dans le cas de rendre beaucoup. Elle a produit fort peu au delà des frais. Le compte vous en sera remis dès que vous le souhaiterez.

J'ai l'honneur, Monsieur, de vous saluer de tout mon cœur.

Laharpe

[*adresse:*] A Monsieur / Monsieur Agasse / Rue de Poitevins.

Manuscript: Bibliothèque de Rouen, collection Duputel 684; copy made by the personnel of that library. Let them find here my expression of gratitude for their fine service.

9. to *Agasse*

26 janvier 1798

Quoique vous paraissiez m'oublier un peu, Monsieur, je ne vous oublie point, moi, dans ma solitude. Vous recevrez avec cette lettre deux gros cartons contenant la copie des trois volumes du *Lycée*, c'est-à-dire les trois premiers du *18ème Siècle*, formant les tomes 8, 9 et 10 de l'ouvrage entier. Tout est dans le plus bel ordre et revu avec soin, et une grande partie a été faite ici comme on s'en apercevra à tout ce qui est de ma main, car je ne suis plus à portée d'avoir de copiste. Mais l'écriture est lisible et assez nette quoique serrée, et j'espère que je recevrai les épreuves.

J'ai enfin reçu des livres et je vais travailler à la fin du troisième volume, que vous aurez sous un mois. Mais je dois présumer que vous n'êtes pas pressé de paraître, et je le conçois dans un moment où règne une inquisition si tyrannique sur toute espèce d'ouvrage.

---

[35] a receipt over La Harpe's signature and in his handwriting says: 'J'ai reçu du citoyen Agasse la somme de quatre cens livres en numéraire à compte des arriérages de la rente viagère qu'il me doit. Paris ce vingt (. .). thermidor an cinquième. Laharpe'. This then is a day or two later.

[36] *Réfutation du livre de l'esprit* (1797).

Il vaut mille fois mieux attendre des temps meilleurs que de songer même à entrer dans aucune espèce de composition avec les tyrans de la pensée, car si vous donniez jamais dans ce piège, imaginez que vous seriez sabré de manière que votre édition ne serait plus d'aucune valeur, et c'est ce dont ils s'embarrasseraient le moins; et les frais de remaniement et les cartons absorberaient tout. Je ne vous crois pas capable d'un si mauvais calcul, et j'en juge par votre prudente circonspection. Mais, Monsieur, à moins que les moyens d'imprimer ne vous manquent, qui vous empêche d'imprimer toujours à l'avance en attendant la publication? Voilà trois volumes de copie: pourquoi perdre un temps précieux? Et qui sait si je serai toujours à portée de revoir les épreuves comme aujourd'hui, ce qui n'est rien moins qu'indifférent pour le mérite de votre édition et d'un ouvrage de fonds?

Je ne vous ai point pressé dans le temps du nouvel an, parce que j'ai pensé qu'à cette époque vous deviez être surchargé, mais j'ai un pressant besoin d'argent et vous me redevez encore 300^{lt} de l'arriéré, ce qui joint aux 900^{lt} échus le premier de ce mois fait 1200^{lt}. Je vous prie instamment, Monsieur, de m'envoyer dans les décades prochaines, en deux payements successifs, la moitié de cette somme, et pour la seconde moitié, je ne vous demanderai rien d'ici à Pasques, mais obligé de payer tout comptant, je suis près d'être à court, et je compte sur vous d'autant plus que j'ai déjà éprouvé combien vous étiez empressé et de vous acquitter et même d'obliger, ce qui, je l'avoue, n'est pas commun aujourd'hui.

Adieu, Monsieur, je ne sais pourquoi vous n'avez pas répondu à ma dernière lettre, qui, je crois, n'a pas pu vous désobliger en aucune façon. J'espère que vous me ferez l'amitié de me marquer cette fois à quoi vous vous arrêtez sur l'impression, et quand vous pourrez remettre de l'argent à mon domestique, qui, sur votre réponse, que j'attends, aura de moi des quittances toutes prêtes aux époques que vous voudrez bien indiquer.

Je vous salue de tout mon cœur, en vous faisant mille compliments de bonne année, en vous la souhaitant, ainsi qu'à moi et à tous, meilleure que la dernière.

L. H.

[*adresse:*] A Monsieur / Monsieur Agasse, imprimeur-libraire / Rue de Poitevins / à Paris.

Manuscript: Bibliothèque municipale de Versailles; my copy.

10. to Agasse

Mardi [1800?]

En arrivant ici, Monsieur je me trouve au dépourvu, faute d'un payement sur lequel j'avais compté et qu'on remet indéfiniment. Vous m'aviez très obligeamment offert, en dernier lieu, quelques avances que je n'ai pas cru devoir accepter, comptant sur ces douze cents [n] qui m'auraient suffi pour le présent et surtout d'ailleurs que vous êtes vous-même quelquefois gêné. Mais, en ce moment, vous rendrez un vrai service en m'envoyant 25 louis, sans quoi je ne puis parer aux dépenses les plus urgentes.

Me voici de demeure à Paris, et nous terminerons, quand vous voudrez, notre acte nouveau chez M. Boulard[37]. Je ne saurais vous dire combien je suis touché de la noblesse de vos procédés, et vous savez d'ailleurs quels sont pour vous mes sentiments d'estime et d'amitié.

Delaharpe

[*adresse:*] A Monsieur / Monsieur Agasse.

Manuscript: Bibliothèque de l'Institut de France; my copy.

11. to Jean Baptiste Claude Isoard Delisle de Sales[38]

Les devoirs et les embarras dans ces jours m'ont empêché de remercier plus tôt l'illustre solitaire de Franconville des vers

---

[37] Antoine Marie Boulard, less known writer and bibliophile, executor of La Harpe's testament, was a long-standing friend of La Harpe and Delille. He edited La Harpe's *Triomphe de la religion* (1814).

[38] Delisle de Sales was three years younger than La Harpe and survived him for thirteen years. He corresponded also with Voltaire (see for instance Best.18808). He was a minor writer who gained notoriety when his work *Philosophie de la nature*, published in 1769, attracted the attention of a magistrate a few years later and which was condemned as containing dangerous ideas.

charmants qu'il a bien voulu m'envoyer. Le mot de son énigme n'est pas difficile, mais dans ce cas-ci, elle n'en est que meilleure. On dit que l'hermite de la vallée se porte mieux, et qu'il sera bientôt ici. Je serai bien empressé à l'aller chercher et lui renouveller l'hommage de mon respectueux attachement.   Delaharpe
19 janvier (?)

Manuscript: Bibliothèque municipale de Nantes, Mss.fr.669, 143; my photocopy.

12. to Louis Nicolas Pierre Joseph Dubois

Corbeil, 25 juillet [1802]

Recevez, Monsieur, mes justes remerciements de l'intérêt que vous avez bien voulu prendre, sans me connaître, à la situation fâcheuse où je suis. Sans doute il est instant que je sois le plus tôt possible à portée des secours de l'art qui me manquent ici, et je crois aussi que le sous préfet de Corbeil, homme fort honnête ne doutera non plus que moi de l'autorisation que vous attestez. Mais sans s'opposer à mon départ, il est en droit de me dire comme municipal qu'il ne connaît que les ordres du ministre, et je n'ai point de réponse à cela. Je préfère donc en cette occasion, comme en toute autre, de me tenir strictement dans la règle et d'autant plus que, si le ministre de la police[39] veut bien, comme il m'a promis, en dire un mot mardi au consul[40]. L'expédition qu'il peut vous remettre, Monsieur, m'arrivera le lendemain, et c'est une nouvelle obligation que je vous aurai et que je serai charmé de vous avoir.

Agréez, Monsieur, les témoignages de mon respect et de ma reconnaissance.   Delaharpe

Manuscript: Archives nationales F⁷ 6311; my copy.

[39] the count of Otrante, Joseph Fouché, member of the Convention in 1792 for Loire-Inférieure, appointed *ministre de la police générale* in July 1799 and occupied that post until September 1802; Dubois was *préfet de police*.
[40] Napoleon Bonaparte.

13. to Joseph Fouché, comte d'Otrante

Citoyen ministre,

Sur l'assurance réitérée de votre part, que je pouvais revenir à Paris, sans attendre une permission par écrit, je suis venu hier au soir me remettre entre les mains de mon médecin, et je crois de mon devoir de vous donner avis sur le champ et de vous remercier des égards que vous avez bien voulu avoir pour mon état et pour les secours qu'il exigeait.

Agréez mes très humbles respects.   Delaharpe

Paris, jeudi 29 [July 1802]

Manuscript: Archives nationales, F^7 6311; my copy.

Les Idées religieuses
de Davy de La Fautrière

par Pierre Chevallier

On sait qu'au folio 130 du volume 184 de la collection Joly de Fleury se trouve une liste de noms et d'adresses écrite par une main britannique, sans doute celle du sieur Broomett, clerc de loge. Toutes les déductions militent, malgré le doute élevé par A. Le Bihan dans son compte rendu des *Ducs sous l'acacia*[1] pour qu'il s'agisse de noms de la loge de Saint Thomas N° II dite du Louis d'Argent. Or il existe à Paris en 1737 au moins six loges, savoir celle de Saint Thomas N° I qui est celle de Derwentwater, celle de Saint Thomas N° II du Louis d'Argent, celle de Coustos-Villeroy, celle de Bussi-Aumont, celle du duc de Richmond à la fois sans doute berrichonne et parisienne et enfin celle du comte Czapski. Or aucun nom de la liste du folio 130 ne se retrouve dans ceux de la loge Saint Thomas N° I donnés par Bord, aucun non plus dans les noms donnés par le registre de la loge Coustos-Villeroy, pas davantage dans les noms relevés dans la correspondance de Bertin Du Rocheret, membre, on le sait de Bussi-Aumont, et il est peu vraisemblable qu'il s'agisse de membres de la loge du duc de Richmond ou encore de celle du comte Czapski qui devaient comprendre toutes les deux un élément étranger important, alors que la liste du folio 130 ne comprend que des noms français et comme d'autre part au folio 131 se trouve une invitation à assister à une tenue adressée au vénérable du Louis

---

[1] *Annales* (Paris mars-avril 1967), xxii.399.

d'Argent: 'à Monsieur Lebreton chez Mons. Thiéri orfèvre vieille cour du Palais à Paris', le doute élevé par A. Le Bihan sur l'appartenance des noms de cette liste à la loge du Louis d'Argent ne paraît vraiment pas devoir être retenu.

Or le deuxième nom de cette liste est celui de Louis Davy de La Fautrière (1700-1756), conseiller au Parlement, cul de sac Saint Dominique rue d'Enfer. Dans l'histoire politique et intellectuelle de son temps, ce conseiller au parlement occupe certes une place mineure, mais non négligeable. Pour commencer, il a fait partie du célèbre club de l'Entresol, qui peut être tenu pour une préfiguration de la maçonnerie du point de vue intellectuel, philosophique et même politique, et le conseiller y fit la connaissance de Ramsay. Le marquis d'Argenson par qui nous connaissons ces faits parle ainsi de La Fautrière: 'M. de la Fautrière nous a lu à différentes fois de longs et magnifiques morceaux d'une histoire des finances et du commerce, qu'il a avec raison enlevée à M. de Caraman, et dont il n'est qu'à l'introduction; essai qui vaudra bien le corps de l'ouvrage, étant rempli d'une infinité de traits et de maximes sublimes sur le droit public et la science du gouvernement'[2].

Mais le conseiller avait une activité politique qui devait lui valoir la disgrâce de la Cour un peu plus tard et dont nous entretient encore Argenson: 'Il arriva encore cet automne [1731] que M. de la Fautrière qui a beaucoup d'esprit, de savoir et de courage, ayant perdu son père, a été refusé en cour, sur une légère grâce qu'il demandait, il s'est extrêmement mutiné contre le ministère et il ne ménage rien dans son avis sur les dernières affaires. Il est à côté de l'abbé Pucelle, de sorte que cela fait chez nous un membre bien désagréable à la Cour' (i.106). La brouille entre le conseiller et la cour eût-elle une cause gratuite, ce n'est guère pensable et elle s'explique mieux, si on songe que le conseiller avait des inclinations jansénistes que le ministère n'ignorait pas. Aussi

[2] *Journal et mémoires*, éd. Rathery (1869), i.99.

LES IDEES RELIGIEUSES DE LA FAUTRIERE

Argenson désireux de maintenir l'Entresol, après les lettres adressées par Fleury à l'abbé de Saint-Pierre en avril 1731, et dans lesquelles le ministre désapprouvait que l'on traitât d'ouvrages de politique[3], nous fait part de sa décision à l'automne de 1731: 'Je me déclarai donc à la Saint-Martin pour rétablir l'Entresol, et en même temps le purger de ce qui pouvait nuire et surtout de toute indiscrétion. Nous convînmes, avec les autres, de garder un grand et inviolable secret avec les exclus, dont était certainement l'abbé de Pomponne, et de ne sonner mot dans le monde qu'il y eût un Entresol; nous changeâmes notre jour et nous le mîmes au mercredi, pour dépayser nos gens, qui pourraient être nos espions; nous convînmes de tenir l'assemblée, à tour de rôle chez les académiciens, les uns après les autres. Il s'en est tenu trois dans ce goût-là, la première chez moi, puis chez l'abbé de Bragelonne; la troisième et dernière, chez M. de La Fautrière, où je ne vins que pour dire qu'il ne fallait plus venir absolument parce qu'on nous espionnait pour le sûr; surtout étant chez M. de La Fautrière, qui venait de faire des siennes plus que jamais au Parlement, où il s'était passé grand tumulte' (i.110).

C'est en effet l'année suivante que La Fautrière fera partie d'une première charette d'exilés en septembre au plus fort des querelles entre le parlement et la Cour, et il suffit de consulter la table des *Nouvelles ecclésiastiques* à l'article 'Parlement de Paris' pour être bien renseigné sur son activité de conseiller janséniste; et son attitude d'opposition à la Cour persistera jusqu'à la fin de sa vie[4]. C'est ainsi que l'année de sa mort, en 1755, La Fautrière se prononce au parlement en faveur des droits des curés contre les évêques: 'Dans la dernière assemblée des Chambres du Parlement il se fit trois belles harangues par des Conseillers; l'on parle surtout de M. M. de La Fautrière et Titon, gens affidés à mon

---

[3] i.108-109, par deux lettres dont l'une est datée de Versailles, le 11 avril 1731.
[4] La Fautrière exilé en septembre 1732 dut se rendre à Salins (Jura).

Cf. encore, d'Argenson, vi.237 où le 29 juillet 1750, La Fautrière est soupçonné d'avoir rédigé des remontrances au parlement.

frère, ce qui marque qu'il est aujourdhui pour le système du Parlement. Ils prouvèrent que l'autorité politique doit empêcher le despotisme des évêques sur le second ordre' (viii.419; 23 janvier 1755).

Le jansénisme de La Fautrière est donc évident. Sa qualité de franc-maçon attestée par la liste d'adresses du folio 130 est encore corroborée de façon indirecte par la présence dans sa bibliothèque du recueil de Naudot les 'Chansons notées des Maçons libres'. On ne sera pas surpris d'y voir figurer, non plus, les *Voyages de Cyrus* de Ramsay, le *Repos de Cyrus* de l'abbé Pernetti et l'*Histoire de Cyrus le jeune* de l'abbé Pagi parus en 1736. Or l'abbé Pernetti figure, lui aussi, sur la liste d'adresses du folio 130 et, une fois de retour à Lyon, où il aura un rôle intellectuel notable, il paraît très probable qu'il a eu une activité maçonnique[5].

Du reste, si La Fautrière a fait partie du club de l'Entresol comme du Louis d'Argent, c'est parce qu'il y trouvait un auditoire pour entendre ses travaux d'histoire, d'économie politique, de science et de philosophie. La preuve de son activité scientifique, on la trouve dans un *Avis aux curieux* qui à la fin de décembre 1755 et au début de 1756 annonce la mise en vente à partir du mardi 24 février 1756 et jours suivants des 'machines, instrumens, outils et ustenciles de physique, astronomie, méchanique, mathématique, horlogerie, peinture, chimie, tours à tourner, etc., composant les cabinets et laboratoires de feu M. de La Fautrière'[6]. La vente de sa bibliothèque eut lieu le 10 mai 1756 toujours en sa maison du faubourg Saint-Jacques. Le catalogue imprimé à cette occasion a sous la rubrique théologie, gardé trace des préoccupations apologétiques du conseiller janséniste:

'N° 90 La Friponnerie laïque des prétendus Esprits Forts, traduit de l'anglais, Amsterdam, 1738, in-12°.

N° 91, Lettres sur la religion essentielle à l'Homme, Londres, 1739, 4 part. en 2 vol. In-12°.

---

[5] cf. *Ducs sous l'Acacia*, pp.52, 56.
[6] Bibliothèque d'Epernay, coll. Bertin Du Rocheret, ms.142 non folioté. Cf. *Annales de l'est* (1966), p.144.

N° 92. Préservatif contre le précédent ouvrage par Fr. de Rocher, Genève, 1740, 2 vol. in-12 . . .'[7]

Or c'est justement en 1738 et 1739 que le conseiller prend la plume pour défendre, ainsi qu'on va le voir plus loin, l'orthodoxie religieuse contre le spinosisme panthéiste et le système de Newton. Le catalogue des imprimés de la Bibliothèque nationale contient l'indication de quatre poèmes et opuscules de La Fautrière: une *Epitre Newtonienne sur le genre de philosophie propre à rendre heureux; Examen du vuide ou espace newtonien relativement à l'idée de dieu* (1739); *L'idée du vuide, ode métaphysique* (1738); *Lettre de l'auteur de l'Examen du vuide ou espace newtonien relativement à l'idée de dieu* (1739).

De ces quatre pièces, les plus intéressantes pour notre propos sont les trois dernières, et ce sont celles justement qui ont reçu le permis d'imprimer. *L'Idée du vuide* obtient le permis d'imprimer le 25 octobre 1738, signé par m. Hérault, lieutenant de police. *L'Examen du vuide* a non seulement le permis d'imprimer, mais une approbation (p.23). Voici ce qu'écrit Hérault au révérend père Castel, jésuite: 'Vous trouverez, ci joint, mon très Révérend Père, un Manuscrit qui peut intéresser la Religion. Je vous prie de l'examiner, et de vouloir bien ensuite me mander, si vous pensés que je puisse en permettre l'impression'. Castel répondit (p.24): 'J'ai lu par votre ordre, l'écrit intitulé Examen du vuide ou Espace newtonien, relativement à l'idée de Dieu, et je le trouve extrêmement utile pour empêcher le progrès d'une espèce de spinosisme spirituel qui commence à s'introduire par l'abus qu'on fait du nom du célèbre Newton, de même que le spinosisme matériel s'est introduit par l'abus qu'on a fait du nom du célèbre Descartes. Ces deux spinosismes sont au fond le même: l'un divinisant la matière, l'autre matérialisant la Divinité. . . . à Paris ce 25 février 1739'. En conséquence de l'approbation du père Castel, Hérault signait le permis d'imprimer le 26 février 1739. Enfin le

---

[7] cf. *Annales de l'est*, Nouvelles recherches sur les f.m. parisiens et lorrains (1966), ff.144-145. L'auteur du *Préservatif* est le pasteur genevois François de Roches.

17 avril 1739 le père Castel donnait encore son approbation à la *Lettre de l'auteur de l'Examen du vuide* (p.15) en ces termes: 'J'ai lu la présente lettre de l'auteur de l'Examen etc...; et je l'ai trouvée polie, comme il convient aux gens de lettres et pleine de respect pour la Divinité, comme il convient à un philosophe chrétien' et dès le lendemain 18 avril 1739 Hérault signait le permis d'imprimer.

On comprend que le lieutenant de police qui avait fait saisir en juillet 1737 les documents contenus dans le volume 184 de la collection Joly de Fleury, et qui avait pu voir le nom du conseiller sur la liste d'adresses du folio 130, ait préféré obtenir l'approbation du père Castel. Hérault avait eu un frère dans la Compagnie, et il ne pouvait courir le risque de se faire désavouer par le cardinal Fleury. Mais il est curieux que les opuscules du conseiller janséniste franc-maçon reçoivent la bénédiction conjointe d'un membre de la Compagnie de Jésus et du lieutenant de police, qui ne pouvait ignorer aucune des qualités de l'auteur. Comme dit le psalmiste, quelquefois, ex inimicis nostris salus.

Examinons maintenant les textes de notre auteur. Le premier, l'*Epitre newtonienne*, est d'une versification aimable et facile, non dépourvue de lyrisme d'ailleurs et elle roule sur les thèmes alors à la mode, de la raison, de l'éloignement du luxe, de la vertu, de tout ce que l'on appelait alors la philosophie. Elle est adressée à madame de *** nommée, bien entendu, Uranie. Le poète se transporte dans un 'séjour enchanté' qui 'par sa noble simplicité, fait honte au luxe asiatique'. C'est là que la nuit venue, il est amené à contempler le ciel et à chercher les raisons du mouvement des corps célestes (p.5):

> Sur ces faits qui des Cieux l'ordre immuable annonce
> J'interroge Newton et telle est sa réponse:
> Sur un centre donné que tout pèse à la fois,
> D'une attraction mutuelle
> Que tout corps éprouve les loix.
> Voilà la cause universelle;

LES IDEES RELIGIEUSES DE LA FAUTRIERE

> Nul mobile dans l'Univers
> N'échappe à ces loix générales.
> Du combat des forces centrales
> Naissent les mouvemens divers.

Satisfait d'une leçon qu'il estime si claire, le philosophe se pose aussitôt la question de la finalité des corps célestes et il conclut trop précipitamment que l'univers a été fait pour la seule fin et la seule utilité de l'espèce humaine. Enivré par la puissance humaine, il dépasse en esprit Saturne, perd la terre de vue et au moment où il croit (p.7):

> Toucher à ce fatal instant
> Où la matière inanimée
> Doit retomber dans le néant.

L'auteur de la nature s'adresse alors à lui, dans un passage qui explique peut-être que l'*Epitre* ne soit pas revêtue de l'approbation du père Castel et de m. Hérault (p.8):

> Vois ces soleils sans nombre au foyer de leurs mondes,
> Mobiles sur leur axe, et traînant après eux
> De leurs planettes vagabondes
> Le cortège majestueux;
> A cette grandeur sans limite
> Compare, si tu peux, le globe où l'homme habite,
> Sous ce rapport humiliant
> Ce n'est qu'un atome insensible
> Dont l'étendue imperceptible
> Diffère à peine du néant;
> Et tu crois que mes mains prodigues en miracles
> Aux yeux seuls des humains déployant mes trésors
> Pour décorer leurs nuits du plus grand des spectacles,
> De tant d'astres divers animent les ressorts;
> Tu crois que mon pouvoir qui féconda l'argile
> Dont ton globe vit naître et l'homme et le reptile

> Dans le reste de l'Univers
> N'a prétendu créer que d'immenses déserts!
> De créatures animées,
> Sur d'autres modèles formées,
> J'ai tout peuplé, tout vit, pour punir ton orgueil.
> Que leurs rangs et leurs destinées
> Soient de tes lumières bornées
> Et le désespoir et l'écueil'.

Le téméraire philosophe se voit alors précipité et reprend ses esprits dans cette retraite charmante où il s'était d'abord rendu, et le développement final a pour objet la véritable appréciation des grandeurs humaines et sociales auxquelles le philosophe préfère les joies d'une amitié pure, le charme d'une étude débarrassée 'd'un fatras imposant', la fuite d'un luxe élégant et il conclut en demandant à Uranie (p.12):

> Faut-il vivre encore pour les autres,
> Ou ne plus vivre que pour moi?

La conception cosmique de La Fautrière n'est pas anthropocentrique, et il serait en bonne compagnie aujourd'hui. Il est vrai que la pluralité des mondes n'était pas alors un thème nouveau et que Fontenelle avait ouvert la voie. D'ailleurs le conseiller dans son lyrisme ne s'écarte pas d'une sage prudence, puisqu'il prend soin de dire, que les créatures animées des autres mondes sont formées sur d'autres modèles que l'espèce humaine. Quant au trait final, il fait penser à un Port-Royal adouci, moins austère et plus aimable que celui des grands ancêtres jansénistes.

De l'*Epitre newtonienne* dans laquelle l'assaut contre le nouveau système est à peine entrepris, passons à l'*Idée du vuide*, dont voici l'argument en prose: 'L'on entend par le Vuide une étendue ou un espace sans matière qui n'est ni esprit ni corps. Le but de ce petit ouvrage est de prouver que l'idée de l'étendue ou de l'espace pur ne nous est venue que de la décomposition purement intellectuelle de la matière; et qu'après avoir reconnu différents attributs dans l'essence de la matière, il a plu à l'imagination humaine de considérer celui de l'étendue comme une substance séparée, quoique l'étendue n'existe physiquement et ne se trouve que dans les corps'.

De cette ode en douze strophes, les deux dernières nous suffiront

> Mais quelle yvresse vous guide?
> Quoy de la Divinité
> Dans les abîmes du Vuide
> Vous noyez l'Immensité!
> Aux humains impénétrable
> Elle est incommensurable
> Avec le Tems et le Lieu
> Vous confondez sans lumière
> L'essence de la Matière
> Avec l'Essence de Dieu!
>
> Tombe, Substance incomplette,
> Disparois, fantôme obscur!
> La nature te rejette,
> Tu n'es point espace pur.
> Vuide, chimère frivole
> Que Descartes de l'Ecole
> Sçut heureusement bannir,
> Fuis et qu'au néant ton frère
> La Physique plus austère
> Daigne enfin te réunir.

Mais le sujet tenait à cœur au conseiller métaphysicien et l'*Examen du vuide*, auquel on arrive maintenant, est la pièce maîtresse de l'argumentation de notre franc-maçon janséniste. Il débute par un sonnet de dédicace au cardinal de Polignac auteur de l'Anti-Lucrèce qui 'sus à la raison montrer Dieu sans nuage' et par l'épigraphe latine que voici: 'Si Numen nescis, nihil est quod caetera dicis', si tu ignores la Divinité, tout le reste que tu apprends n'est rien.

Le point important est de savoir, se demande l'auteur, ce qu'est le vide ou espace pur des Newtoniens. Est-il un être physique ou imaginaire. Ne serait-ce pas la matière ou le néant sous le nom du vide?: 'L'idée de l'étendue selon trois dimensions est une idée sensuelle. Elle ne nous est point venue de si loin que l'on puisse méconnaître son origine; nos sens trouvent naturellement l'espace ou l'étendue dans la matière; ils ne trouvent d'ailleurs ni la matière sans l'étendue, ni l'étendue sans la matière; l'entendement peut séparer ce que la nature a uni et substancier à part l'étendue de même que tout attribut quelconque de la matière; mais cette prétendue substance, née d'une décomposition fictive de la matière n'aura jamais d'autre existence physique. Le Vide n'est donc qu'une substance imaginaire. Si ce raisonnement est juste, il faut bien se garder d'en faire présent à l'immensité divine' (p.5).

Pour La Fautrière l'idée du vide n'est que l'idée de l'étendue séparée de la matière par l'entendement, et physiquement inséparable d'elle. Il se refuse aussi à admettre qu'il y ait également des millions d'autres substances étendues différentes de celles que nous appelons matière, tandis qu'il admet des espèces de la matière différentes les unes des autres, mais non différentes de ce que l'on appelle génériquement matière. Mais sur sa route, notre philosophe rencontre le plus illustre des propagateurs de Newton, c'est-à-dire, Voltaire. Voltaire 'définit le vide d'après Newton comme le lieu des corps, l'espace étendu en longueur, largeur et profondeur. Il reconnaît donc l'étendue des solides pour un attribut essentiel ou du moins pour une propriété inséparable de la matière, et dès lors on ne peut plus lui croire permis d'en faire un attribut de Dieu: cependant, il se demande où est Dieu? Et il se répond, Dieu n'est pas dans un point mathématique; il est immense: qu'est-ce que son immensité, sinon l'espace immense' (p.14). Et un peu plus loin (p.15) il cite Voltaire: 'Je me démontre, dit-il, l'impossibilité du Plein et la nécessité du Vide [il consent de s'en convaincre] sans avoir une image du vide, car je n'ai d'image que ce qui est corporel [il devait ajouter ou extrait des corps] et l'espace n'est point corporel'.

Le point qui nous intéresse avant tout dans cette discussion philosophique, c'est la position respective des newtoniens et des anti-newtoniens. Emile Bréhier dans son *Histoire de la philosophie* vient ici à notre secours: 'Par son côté philosophique, écrit-il, la science de Newton nous laisse en somme dans une grande incertitude: son mécanisme peut nous orienter aussi bien vers la théologie que vers le matérialisme' (ii.318-319), et c'est pourquoi l'analyse finale du système newtonien par La Fautrière est claire et correcte lorsqu'il écrit: 'L'espace newtonien que l'on prétend être l'immensité divine ne peut se considérer que comme séparé de la matière et existant seulement dans l'entendement, ou comme uni à la matière et existant physiquement en elle. Dans le premier cas l'immensité divine n'est autre chose que l'espace imaginaire, dans le second elle est matérielle'. Et un peu plus loin, il pense mettre les newtoniens en contradiction avec Newton même: 'Qui le soupçonnerait?, écrit-il encore, M. Newton comme philosophe et métaphysicien condamne par une proposition contraire, celle de ses illustres disciples, lorsqu'il dit, Deus. .; non est duratio vel spatium' (p.19). Dieu n'est ni temps ni espace. Nous avons ainsi l'essentiel condensé de l'argumentation de La Fautrière.

Le dernier texte à examiner est la *Lettre de l'auteur de l'Examen du vide . . . à m. l'abbé Desfontaines*. Celui-ci avait en effet dans ses *Observations sur les écrits modernes* des 18 et 21 mars 1739 rendu compte des opuscules du conseiller. Sans entrer dans le détail du texte et pour ne pas prolonger davantage, limitons-nous à l'essentiel: 'Vous avez commencé l'examen de mon Examen par les deux Extrémités, le titre et l'approbation. Vous observés que c'est le prendre sur le ton le plus sérieux, puisqu'il ne s'agit pas de moins que de prouver que l'opinion Newtonienne sur le vuide est un athéisme déguisé' (p.4). 'Il s'agit véritablement ici de prouver que l'hypothèse des vacuistes newtoniens conduit au matérialisme?

Oui, Monsieur, je traite cette dispute aussi sérieusement que s'il s'agissait d'une croisade. Il me semble que c'est également défendre la religion, et je pense d'ailleurs que d'aussi grands philosophes sont plus difficiles à réduire que des Sarrasins' (p.4).

Voilà qui est net et sans bavures, et ne saurait surprendre sous la plume d'un janséniste, dont il n'est pas interdit d'admettre, que son jansénisme n'a pas été seulement politique, mais aussi religieux, et ce qui le confirme c'est le passage suivant où m. de La Fautrière donne son sentiment sur la raison humaine: 'La raison ajoutez-vous, est aussi de l'essence de Dieu. Pardonnés-moi, Monsieur, si je vous chicane sur cette expression. Je regarde la raison comme une propriété particulière et inséparable de l'homme. Dès que nous reconnaissons la post existence de l'âme humaine, au corps humain, il est naturel de croire, que tandis que l'âme humaine unie au corps commerce avec la matière par l'entremise des sens, sa faculté intellectuelle est bien moins lumineuse que lorsqu'elle est séparée du corps. Pour moi je regarde le corps d'un œil platonicien, et je ne vois en lui que le sépulcre de l'âme.... La raison qui est le partage de l'homme n'est nullement digne de Dieu qui doit voir, comme on le dit ordinairement les conclusions dans les principes et les effets dans les causes' (p.11).

La prise de position de La Fautrière est d'une netteté parfaite. Le dernier extrait qu'on vient de lire est dans la ligne de ce que Calvin appelle l'honneur de dieu. Dieu raisonnable, c'est le ramener à l'échelle humaine et celle-ci n'est pas la mesure de dieu. Mais l'échelle humaine peut-elle être aussi celle du grand architecte de l'univers? Pour le janséniste franc-maçon qu'est Davy de La Fautrière, l'admettre serait aller contre l'analyse et les extraits essentiels que l'on vient de donner. On pourra peut-être essayer de contester sa qualité de franc-maçon, bien que cela soit difficile après la démonstration du début de cet exposé. Ce qui est évident, en tout cas, en cette période des débuts de la franc-maçonnerie, c'est qu'il est sûr que les ateliers ont pris grand soin de travailler dans une atmosphère respectueuse de la religion en général et

LES IDEES RELIGIEUSES DE LA FAUTRIERE

qu'il s'y est trouvé, parmi les frères, des maçons très religieux, comme La Fautrière dont le jansénisme attesté n'a pas été pour lui un obstacle à son entrée dans la Fraternité, mais peut-être même au contraire, une raison supplémentaire de diriger ses pas vers elle.

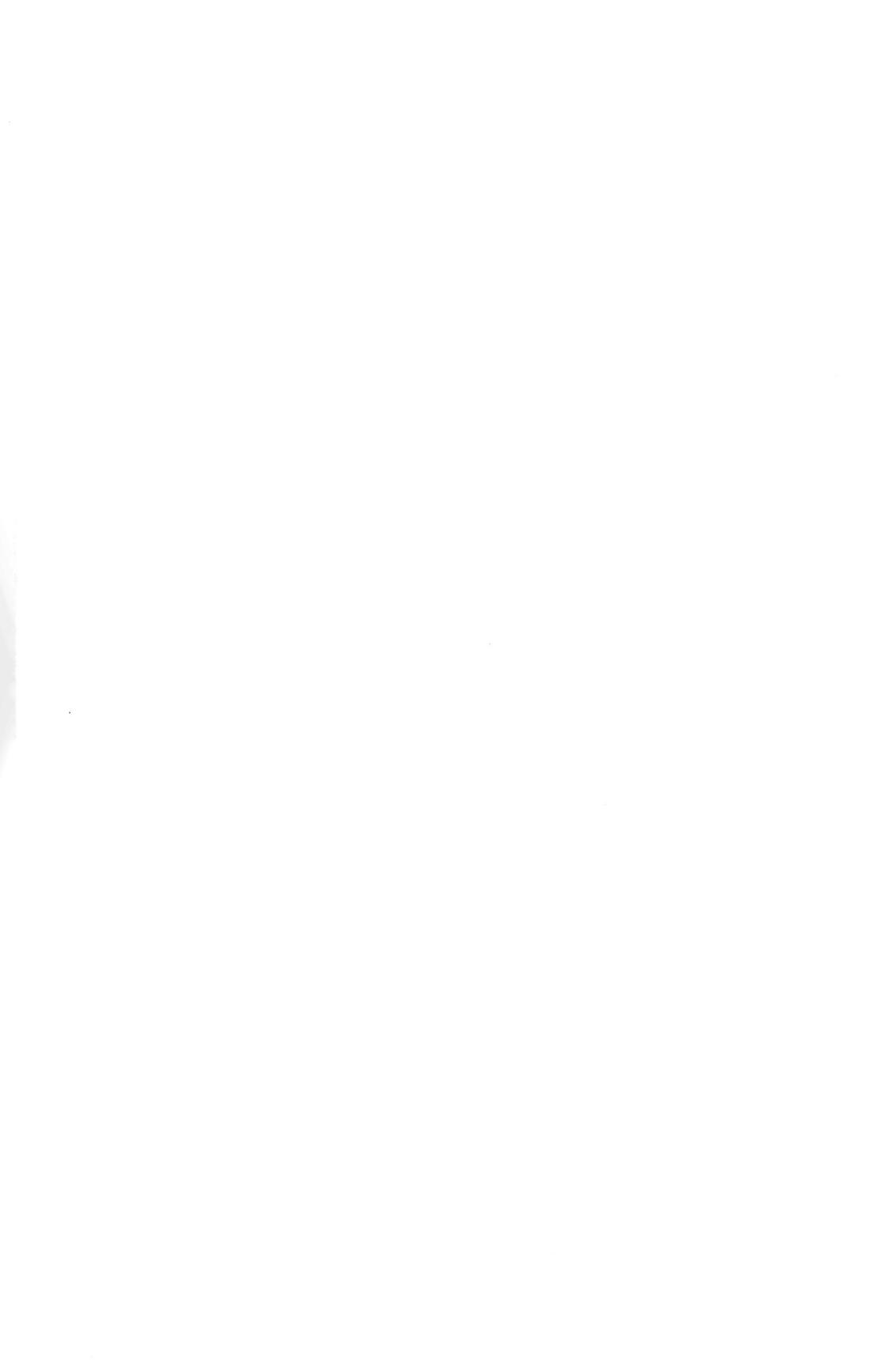